Lisa Jo'inson
Move⸱ - Spaces - Places

Culture and Social Practice

Lisa Johnson, born in 1988, is a postdoc researcher at the Institute of Ethnology at the University of Trier and a lecturer for Cultural Studies at Saarland University. She completed her doctorate in the field of cultural anthropology in 2020 as a member of the DFG-funded International Research Training Group "Diversity: Mediating Difference in Transcultural Spaces" at Trier University. Her research focuses on mobility and migration, border studies and transculturality, culture, music and sound, in Jamaica and North America.

Lisa Johnson

Moves - Spaces - Places

The Life Worlds of Jamaican Women in Montreal. An Ethnography

[transcript]

Diese Studie ist eine aktualisierte Fassung der Arbeit: Moves, Spaces and Places: Roots, Pathways and Trajectories of Jamaican Women in Montreal, die im Februar 2020 am Fachbereich IV – Soziologie/ Ethnologie der Universität Trier als Dissertationsschrift angenommen wurde.

Bibliographic information published by the Deutsche Nationalbibliothek
The Deutsche Nationalbibliothek lists this publication in the Deutsche Nationalbibliografie; detailed bibliographic data are available in the Internet at http:// dnb.d-nb.de

© 2021 transcript Verlag, Bielefeld

Cover layout: Maria Arndt, Bielefeld
Cover image: Pixabay
Copy-editing: Anna-Maria Duplang
Proofread: Anna-Maria Duplang

Print-ISBN 978-3-8376-5808-8
PDF-ISBN 978-3-8394-5808-2
https://doi.org/10.14361/9783839458082
ISSN of series: 2703-0024
eISSN of series: 2703-0032

Contents

Entry and Framework

Ethnography

For Amina & Cairo
You are loved. You are powerful. The future is yours.

Acknowledgments

"Knowledge is power. [...]. Study and examine all, but choose and follow the good. The knowledge you have acquired so far is no end in itself but a reminder for the further responsibilities that await you" (H.I.M. Emperor Haile Selassie I. qtd. in Selassie/ Tafari 2004: 33-34).

Writing this book was an exigent balancing act between scholarly intent, familial responsibility and spiritual growth. Ultimately, this study is a perpetual reminder to be content and thankful for the immense privilege of having gained a deeper knowledge and having spent time with people and places that –both in a professional and personal way– truly move me. In times of the current pandemic, ethnographic fieldwork as it was pursued here seems as if from another time; especially, with its close personal contact with fellow humans in far-away places and its immediacy of sensory and affective perceptions. Therefore, I am extremely grateful to have been able to finish this project in late February 2020. My sincere gratitude goes out to the inspiring women who agreed to be the interlocutors of this study. Thank you for sharing your time, your experiences and your personal viewpoints with academia and me.

I am forever indebted to the DFG-funded International Research Training Group "Diversity: Difference in Transcultural Spaces" for supporting my research project through a programmatic and scholarly frame as well as monetary funding. Thanks to the speakers, the faculty and my dear colleagues at the University of Trier, Saarland University, University of Luxembourg and Université de Montréal for the open-minded discussions as well as the dynamic interdisciplinary and transatlantic exchanges. My special thanks to the entire coordination team, above all Klemens Wedekind, and to my lector Anna Maria Duplang.

'Jungle academia' is a better place thanks to people who are truly willing to guide, mentor and lead young scholars in their formative years. I am very grateful for my great supervisors, Michael Schönhuth and Astrid Fellner, who were constant advisers, constructive criticists and encouragers throughout this entire process. Thank you both!

My deepest gratitude goes out to my family, especially to my grandparents, my mother and my wonderful husband. Without your continuous support, love and care, this project would have never become a reality. Thanks and blessings go out to my Jamaican family at 'yard' and abroad, the immediate and the extended ones!

Abstract

The following ethnography provides a deep insight into the life worlds of Jamaican women in Montreal. Historically, Jamaicans primarily migrated to Anglophone cities in Canada, the USA, or the UK. In the mid-1950s, the government of Quebec began recruiting care and domestic workers from the Caribbean through the so-called West Domestic Scheme. The impact of this labour migration –mostly performed by women from Jamaica– has received little attention in the scholarly literature to date. Thus, this study offers a first approach to understand motives, narratives, practices, and perspectives of second and third generation Jamaican migrant women in Montreal. Here, socio-cultural and bodily practices as well as processes of inclusion and exclusion play an important role to examine the diversity of their individual ways of life. Through a deep 'immersion' (Ingold 2007) into the daily lives of five female interlocutors, the ethnography provides a discernment of the construction of their 'beyond transnational' belongings and identities, and opens up a understanding of the women's sense of self. Moreover, the 'multi-sited' (Marcus 1995) study actively follows the interlocutors on their journeys 'home' and analyses strategic forms of migratory return and mobility. The temporary or final return to Jamaica emerges as a life-long, multi-layered process that reveals profound yearnings for childhood memories, traditions, places, culture and people. Here, the ethnography highlights the relevance of the recourse to and the passing on of intergenerational knowledge about Jamaica as a continuously oscillating narrative and physical practice. Utilizing social networks to family, kin and friends across cultural, geographical and national borders unfolds as an important key to endure a life that has a 'here' and a 'there' (Simmons 2010) at the same time. Hence, Jamaican women's mobility functions as a dynamic, pragmatic, indeterminate, and irreversible tool of migratory agency and belonging.

The study was developed within the framework of the DFG-funded International Research Training Group "Diversity: Mediating Difference in Transcultural Spaces" and resulted in a dissertation at the department of Ethnology at the University of Trier, Germany.

Entry and Framework

1   Introduction

"More Jamaican women migrating to Canada, Statistics reveal" is a headline in the Jamaican newspaper *The Gleaner* in January (2018) discussing the recent census results gathered in Canada from 2012 to 2016. The data indicates that almost 20,000 more Jamaican women than men migrated to Canada within that time span, demonstrating a recent disparity in migrants' gender distribution. The socio-economic phenomenon of Jamaican women contributing as labour workers to the Canadian economy is, however, not new. Initially, Jamaican men were among the first Caribbean people to enter the country during the colonial period to work in the mining industries. After World War II, men worked seasonally in the horticulture industry or as railroad labourers. However, women started to dominate Jamaican migration to Canada in the mid-1950s. Each year from 1955 onwards, women from Jamaica and Barbados between the ages of 18 and 35, received entry visas to work in Canadian households and nursing professions (Thomas 2012). During this period, over 2,000 women took the opportunity and entered the Canadian territories (Magocsi 1999). As immigration policies changed to a less discriminatory points system in the 1960s and the *Family Reunification Act* after 1970 allowed spouses and children to join family members who had migrated earlier (Kelley/Trebilcock 2010), Jamaican migration to Canada remained increasingly steady. Already in the 1980s, with the intensification of international relations as well as neoliberalist and globalizing processes, the focus of migration research expanded. Alongside an increasing interest in intersectional parameters of migrants, the positionality of women as social agents in the migratory process became relevant.

According to a report from the *International Migration Organization* (IOM) in 2018, an estimated number of 1.3 million Jamaican-born persons permanently reside abroad, amounting to at least 36.1 percent of the national population (Thomas-Hope et al. 2018). Additionally, the foreign-born second and third generations –who associate their ethnic origin and identity with Jamaica– bring the total number that comprises the diaspora to a size equivalent to that of the population of 2.9 million of Jamaica itself (Plaza/Henry 2006: xvii). Jamaican-Canadians make up one of the largest non-European ethnic groups in Canada and are the leading collective of West Indian migration in general. Census data of 2016 shows 309,485 Jamaicans with permanent residency or citizenship are living in Canada (Statistics Canada 2017). Since the conditions for Jamaican immigration and visa requirements were tightened in the UK in 2003, in the USA after 9/11 and recently during Donald Trump's presidency, Canada has become the country of choice for many immigrants (not only from the Caribbean). Most Jamaicans settle in Anglophone metropolitan areas such as Toronto, Ottawa and Hamilton. Currently, 11,775 Jamaicans reside in Quebec, of which the majority has settled in the metropolitan area of Montreal (Statistics Canada 2017). However, the available categories for 'ethnic origin' implemented in the Canadian census are prone to inaccuracy since individuals can make multiple choices among numerous different national and ethnic categories, such as Black, West Indian, Jamaican, Caribbean, African. This choice leads to inexactness about the genuine number of Jamaican-born residents residing in Montreal, especially as ethnic belonging or identity are not solely grounded in place of birth. Additionally, intra-provincial labour migration –for example people who enter Canada through Ontario and then work in Quebec– is not sufficiently documented.

Montreal is attractive for Jamaican women seeking economic opportunities in the domestic and care work sector, in spite of a French language barrier and a previously unknown place compared, e.g., to the Ontario region. As the second-largest city in Canada, Montreal already hosts a considerable number of Francophone Caribbean immigrants, specifically from Haiti. Still, Jamaicans shape, among other immigrants, parts of the city's socio-cultural life and contribute to the diversification of a so-called 'intercultural' setting in the province of Quebec. Jamaican popular culture is present in the Anglophone Canadian media. Caribbean carnival parades such as Montreal's *Carifiesta* or Toronto's *Caribana* are symbolic representations of a 'successful integration' of Afro-Caribbean people into Canadian society and a source of many articles both journalistic and academic (e.g. Henry/Plaza 2019) as are other aspects of popular culture such as Rastafari or Reggae music (e.g. Price 2015; Austin 2007; Walcott 2003). Besides, typical research projects on Jamaican migration to Canada often focus on negative impacts such as drug crime, gang violence and deportees (e.g. Barnes 2009; Golash-Boza 2014) or on tourism (e.g. Bennet 2017; Burman 2011). In addition, Toronto (e.g. Rose 2016; Simmons 2010; Toney 2010; Hepburn 2019) represents *the* Jamaican enclave in Canada and is therefore the research area of first choice for many scholarly inquiries. However, Montreal as a research area is underexposed, e.g., in comparison to Toronto, Vancouver or Hamilton. The book "Jamaicans in Canada: When Ackee meets Codfish" (Gopie 2012), which was released for the celebration of Jamaica's 50 years of independence (1962-2012), depicts the impact that Jamaican people have had in Canada over the centuries. The volume features profiles of 250 Jamaican-Canadians that "help this and other Canadian cities run, manage the health-care system, educate, pass and enforce and litigate the law, grow business ventures, volunteer, donate tens of millions of dollars to cultural and educational institutions, [...] drive the trains, sweep the streets and care for the infirm. [...] in every province and territory, Jamaicans have set down roots. [...]. This odyssey has been going on since before Canada was a country; since before the inhabitants of the former British colony were a free people" (Gopie 2012: 1).

The publication recognizes that there are not only socio-economically successful or popular migrants such as famous Olympic champion Donovan Bailey, but also many Jamaicans who work in middle-class jobs or the lower service sector, drawing a more differentiated picture about the Jamaican immigrant experience. This study will highlight that Jamaican migrant experiences in Quebec, especially those of women, deviate from those in Anglophone Canada and are rather invisible to the host society in Montreal. Hence, this study contributes to this desideratum of research. Concerning Jamaican women's individual interpretations of migration motives, practices and perspectives in Quebec, this study also aims at bridging a transatlantic gap between scholars in Europe and North America in this respective field, especially to those researchers who analyse migratory life worlds beyond the assumption of methodological nationalism towards an 'intertwined modernity' (Beck 1998).

My interest in the topic of Jamaican migration to Montreal developed during my five-year stay in Kingston (Jamaica). Respecting the fact that Canada, after the USA, plays an essential role in the emigration objective of many families and individuals in Jamaica, I quickly learnt that representatives of different social classes of Jamaican society –from worker to university graduate– are mobile in various ways (i.e. mentally, virtually, physically) and aim at migrating to North America. Highly qualified and professionally successful people often migrate by choice to metropolitan centres; female and male skilled workers from the working and middle class mainly migrate due to poverty, labour market opportunities or family reasons. For many Jamaicans this 'culture of migration' has been a ubiquitous modus operandi since the 1950s (Thomas-Hope 1988; 2002; 2010) with a majority hoping to find a better life away from the island. After admission to the transatlantic German-Canadian International Research Training Group "Diversity: Mediating Difference in Transcultural Spaces" at the University of Trier, I decided to take a closer look at the Canadian side of this phenomenon. Here, I deliberately chose Montreal as the research location because, as noted earlier, other cities seem to have been covered in the scholarly literature.

After my initial exploration phase in Montreal in July 2016, the focus of this study concentrated on a small number of Jamaican women. Five ethnographic portraits of women, who represent different migratory life pathways, unveil specific temporal and spatial experiences. Each migratory trajectory aims to highlight so-cio-cultural practices and narratives concerned with relocation experiences as well as an individual yearning for the homeland. In an anthropological manner, I en-tered into the lives of the interlocutors and followed them, as much as possible and feasible, on their local ventures as well as on their travels overseas. Therefore, fieldwork was situated in different migratory stages in various places in Montreal, Toronto and Jamaica, following concepts of 'multi-sited' research (Marcus 1995; Hannerz 1996). The reason to focus primarily on women is a result of the inductive approach to the field. Prioritizing women to narrate their individual stories and implementing a gendered approach, however, enriched the study tremendously. Of course, these individual portraits are not meant to generalize experiences of Jamaican women in Montreal, nor their social networks or travels. Therefore, this study acknowledges the specific historical and socio-cultural impact that female migration from Jamaica has had on the province of Quebec. The simultaneous en-countering of the 'Jamaican' and the 'Québécois' in the city of Montreal creates a dis-tinct socio-cultural field in which my research interest lies. Due to their temporal-spatial absence from the Jamaican homeland, interlocutors, seem to bond together through the identification of Jamaica as their (imagined) homeland and place of 'heart'. Concomitantly, they are part of a wider cosmopolitan culture in Montreal, which shapes their lives outside of typical migratory enclaves such as Toronto or New York City. A continuously growing number of Jamaican immigrants and an ongoing cultural diversification in Montreal requires taking a closer look at mi-gration as a "cultural process linked to global and transnational forces" (Simmons 2010: 2). Globalization and its outcomes changed relations and the social stratifi-cation of migratory people over time and shifted cultural values concerning mobil-ity, space, place and belonging. Critical aspects that affect not only transnational ties, but also the level of individual as well as group-based consciousness regarding identity and representation. Jamaican women form an intimate affiliation to the countries they live and lived in, tied together through a globally dispersed variety of social networks to different Jamaican diasporic localities. These networks also include relatively immobile people for whom connection improved through tech-nological advancements over time: Easy and cheap air transportation, real-time electronic communication, same-day money transfers, all at once evoking a com-pression of space and time in a globalized world. For women, the cost of migration is high. They often carry the burden of sending remittances that feed and sustain their families in Jamaica, while leaving behind their children in the foster care of relatives. Hence, the connection to home is an important constant in their daily lives, for example, through technological-virtual communication practices or vis-iting Jamaica regularly (if possible). As this ethnography will show, many women manage to be proficient agents in the securing of their own and familial needs, even in times of struggle, isolation or setbacks. Their life worlds have a 'here' and a 'there' (Simmons 2010: 169) of being and belonging to several diasporic places at the same time in different ways.

In Montreal, the observation and exploration of specific cultural practices became relevant. Daily practices of inclusion and exclusion mediate and articulate difference, identity and imaginaries in the context of historical transformations. Discourses about ethnic 'roots', memories and biographical accounts of the homeland and its people give insight into female perceptions of different contact zones and localities. The appropriation of certain spaces in Montreal, the stylization of the body or simply food-cooking practices are examples of ethnographic depictions that this study discerns. These socio-cultural practices inform about the inscription of diversity and difference in the minds and bodies of Jamaican women in Montreal. The ethnography emphasises, hereby, Jamaican women's feelings of isolation and homesickness as well as experiences with structural discrimination and racism that hinder comprehensive integration. Through the exploration of specific experiences, the ethnography also answers questions concerning the embodiment and mediation of 'othering' (Spivak 1985).

Although the core of this study focuses on diverse practices, narratives will be of specific relevance in analysing how female relatives –chiefly mothers and grandmothers– shape migratory practices and imaginaries through articulation. Intergenerational narratives, storytelling and handed down knowledge from ancestors play an important role in the choice of migration destinations, in the remembrance of Jamaica, and in the maintenance of certain cultural traditions and values. Accounts of women's life courses offer inside views into interpersonal family and kinship networks in relation to space, belonging, identity, and aspirations of return. Additionally, this study will discuss mobility after initial migration and return migration. According to the *International Migration Organization* (IOM), the voluntary return of Jamaican women (and men) is not yet systematically captured (Thomas-Hope et al. 2018: 36). In many cases, the move 'back home' is part of a series of returns of short duration and, for some, it becomes part of an ongoing cross-border residential and livelihood pattern (Thomas-Hope 2002). Here, diverse female strategies and decision-making processes concerning traveling or returning to 'their' homeland will become visible. The phenomenon of Jamaican returnee women is not only interesting because of their privilege of holding dual passports, but also because many returnees are economically powerful, which gives them options that extend beyond the boundaries of a socio-economically rather struggling island society. At the same time, these privileges do not safeguard them from unexpected disappointments.

Importantly, this study's returnees are not only ageing individuals as is typical in previous studies about Jamaican homeward migration (e.g. Horst 2013; Olwig 2012; Hepburn 2019), but also younger women who feel the urge to return to their ancestral homeland even though they have never physically departed from it.

Therefore, female returnees in this study highlight a complex interplay of cross-generational Jamaican belonging, responsibility and identity, which goes beyond living or being born abroad. Since these 'voluntary' home seekers and returnees are a minority group in the Jamaican context, their behaviours, expectations and difficulties differ widely from those of the local society; despite their self-assumed 'shared' ethno-cultural heritage. Hence, the analysis of the ethnographic portraits also examines the idea of the transformation of knowledge before, during, and after migratory movements as a dynamic process that constitutes meaningful interactions (Knoblauch 2005: 142 qtd. in Treiber 2013). Jamaican women's migratory trajectories are often pre-structured by various, individual, preliminary expectations and imaginaries, by familial and social histories and networks as well as new adaptation strategies gained from the travel processes, in which new forms of contextual and situational knowledge about places, people, and particular localities in Jamaica is gained. This can also lead to a revision of interlocutors' previous considerations about life in Montreal. Ultimately, a deep insight into the mediation and negotiation of cultural identity, belonging and displacement in a post-colonial world setting is given, in which new, conflictive boundaries and at times 'myths' about geographic spaces are discovered. Through flexibility, practicality and redefinitions of space, Jamaican women are hereby able to develop altered routes towards a desired future.

2 Historical Overview

Canada is a prime example of migration. From the first European settlers in the 16th and 17th centuries to the mass-immigration waves after the *Confederation* in 1867 (Troper 2018), Canada established as a multi-ethnic nation (Simmons 2010: 2). While immigration closed down during both Great Wars and the 1930s depression, a high level of immigration regained its strength after World War II. Since the late 1980s, most immigrants are coming from Africa, Asia, Latin America, and the Caribbean (Troper 2018). The earliest Jamaicans to arrive in Canada were small numbers of West Indian slaves imported into Nova Scotia and New France. The Maroons of Jamaica were the first large group to enter British North America in 1796. These runaway slaves, who occasionally raided plantations and revolted against the British colonial regime, e.g., by freeing other slaves or occupying the island's interior areas, soon created self-reliant communities (Zips 2011). Two wars with the Maroons, the second in 1795, made the British realize they could not win nor control these 'rebels' on the island. After several unsuccessful attempts to enslave the Maroons, the British governor signed a peace treaty with them and deported some into exile to Halifax (Labelle et al. 2019). However, due to their rebellious spirit and complaints about the Canadian climate, they soon voyaged onwards to Sierra Leone in 1800. Apart from the Maroons, no other early contacts between people from the West Indies and Canada were reported at that time. From 1800 until 1920 only a few Jamaicans, most of them men, came and worked as labourers in the Sydney and Cape Breton mines. This ended suddenly with the change of immigration laws set by the Canadian government (ibid.). The new policy refused to allow non-whites into the country (Sherlock/Bennett 1998). As a result, immigration from Jamaica and other Caribbean countries halted.

After World War II, Canada had a great need for cheap labourers, which resulted in the *National Act* of 1948 (Walker 2013). Many overseas workers from the British Commonwealth colonies, including Jamaicans, came to Canada to seek a better economic life. By 1960, Canada introduced its 'point system' under which each applicant was awarded points for their language, job and educational skills (Troper 2018). During this time, 21,500 immigrants from the Caribbean of which 33 percent were categorized under the 'ethnic origin' Black were granted a landed immigrant status (Labelle et al. 2019). The growth of immigration from 1945 to 1960 corresponded not only with post-war economic expansion but also with the *West Indian Domestic Scheme* (1955–60) which was established solely for the immigration of women from Jamaica and Barbados as domestic workers (ibid.). Women dominated Jamaican immigration to North America in the post-1965 era; twice as many young and single females than males left Jamaica for domestic service and factory work (Foner 1985; Brown 1997). Many Jamaican women established themselves in occupations such as nursing, caretaking, domestic help, and teaching. Jamaican dominance in these occupations in part evolved around pre-established networks that created so-called 'ethnic niches' (Foner 2005; Vickerman 1999, 2001). In addition, their presence corresponded with increasing numbers of North American women who began entering the workforce outside of the home in the 1970s. Therefore, the creation of jobs in childcare and domestic work flourished. Milton Vickerman (1999: 71) observes, "Once women had secured jobs as domestics, they would set about seeking other work in the same field so that in some cases a single individual would juggle two or three jobs at the same time". Women in such demanding occupations often left behind their partners, spouses, and children in Jamaica and had to rely on the help of their stay-behind family members (mostly aunts or grandmothers) who –in their absence– took on child-rearing responsibilities. In exchange, the remittance sending resulted as a socio-economic practice and created the first active "transnational households" (Soto 1987; Thomas-Hope 1988). This study will highlight these historically grown aspects of reciprocity and responsibility in border-crossing family connections as well as the importance of family constellations and expectations for the course of migration. For example, negotiations about return migration oftentimes involve several members of such a transnational household (see Olivier-Mensah/Scholl-Schneider 2016).

After the exclusion of the race-based discrimination from the Canadian *Immigration Act* in 1944, the number of Jamaicans migrating to Canada increased (Walker 2013). Since that period, Canada has sought more and more migrants from the Caribbean islands due to the gradual decrease of European immigration. In the following years, Canada began to depend predominantly on 'cheap labour' from the global South. For comprehensibility and completeness, it is relevant for this study to discuss specific historical contexts in Jamaica and in Canada's Francophone province Quebec. The following three sub-chapters help to understand how current situations came about and under what socio-cultural circumstances many Jamaican migrants live in Montreal today.

2.1   The Historical Context of Jamaica

Jamaica is the third-largest island of the Greater Antilles and with 2.9 million inhabitants; it is the third most populated Anglophone country in the Americas after the United States and Canada. Jamaica is a culturally diverse country with most of its residents being of African descent. The indigenous Taino (Arawak-speaking people) were eliminated by warfare and diseases brought through the transatlantic slave trade under Spanish conquest and British colonial rule. Over 300 years of slavery –from 1502 until 1807– established prevailing uneven, post-colonial power relations based on skin colour and social class (Bush 1981). The forced displacement of African people to Jamaica is the basis of a colonial history of exploitation, suppression, and uprooting. The historically difficult stand of Jamaican women in slave society ascribed, through the ideology of white supremacy, ethnocentric bias, colourism and inferiority into the minds of people (ibid.). Throughout the time of slavery and with the introduction of capitalism as well as class-based colourism, certain hierarchical power relations continue to control and influence access to economic, social as well as political resources (Bush 1981; Miles 1989). Since the island's independence from the United Kingdom in 1962, a noticeable number of Chinese, Indian and European immigrants have come to Jamaica while at the same time an extensive diaspora emerged around the globe. Jamaica's national theme "Out of Many, One People" highlights this issue of unity in difference and evokes a modern way to "recognize the different parts and histories of ourselves, to construct these points of identification, those positionalities we call in retrospect our 'cultural identities'" (Hall 1990: 234).

Jamaica has a long history as a migration hub. The present-day persistent growing emigration rates to North America are a result of the ongoing search for a better future and increased standard of living, which, due to a marginalized economy and poor career options, has not changed yet. The Jamaican government used to interpret the migratory transference of its people to North America as "brain gain" (Hunger 2002: 1). Acknowledging the fact that less and less people return to Jamaica before their retirement, this alleged gain turned out to be a fallacy. Especially in the health sector, but also in other sectors of the economy, Jamaica lacks young and well-trained staff as they often emigrate directly after their education. Jamaica has struggled for decades with low growth and high public debt. Over the last 30 years, real per capita GDP increased at an average of just one percent per year, making Jamaica one of the slowest growing so-called 'developing' countries in the world (The World Bank 2015). The unemployment rate in the country is nearly eight percent (Statistical Institute of Jamaica 2019), with youth unemployment being specifically high (20.2 percent). As Beine stated already in 2008, "as far as small states are concerned, three out of every four skilled Caribbean live outside their country of origin" (Beine et al. 2008: 4). Docquier and Marfouk (2005) claim that Jamaica is the third-highest source country of skilled emigrants with a rate of about 85 percent, exposing Jamaica as a factory of "social capital" (Bourdieu 1983). Furthermore, the *Canadian International Development Agency* (CIDA) provides billions of monetary assistance each year to the *Caribbean Community* (CARICOM) countries, including Jamaica (Government of Canada n. d.).

2.2   The Historical Context of Quebec

The province of Quebec is constituted by a distinct historical condition. Especially, national identity constructions, which are firmly related to heritage and French-language policies, are root causes of integration difficulties of immigrants (not only from Jamaica). In this context, people who identify as being authentic Québécois strive to make the province their 'own' nation, encapsulated and separated from the rest of Canada. Historically, the origin of this insular mentality founded in the beginning of the 15th century when the 'original' Canadian nation was formed in New France. Jacques Cartier and the French colonists brought along their language, cultural values, Catholicism, and social hierarchy (Allaire 2013). Many wars over land ownership and fur trade monopolies between the French and British settlers followed until British troops occupied New France and Montreal capitulated in 1760 (Couture 2018). After the establishment of British North America, New France was made a colony of the British Empire and was led by a military government. The main aim of the people of the former New France region was to conserve and protect their language and traditional cultural values from British influences. Because of the Indian rebellion under Pontiac, the British government changed its policy towards the French. In the *Quebec Act* of 1774, London guaranteed the French majority protection of their mother tongue and religious denomination. However, the former French-Catholic majority was now a minority (Couture 2018). In the year 1791, 30 years after their defeat, and due to a sharp increase of the British population, the Franco-Americans regained territory with the division of the province of Quebec. However, language disputes further prevailed in their newly established, albeit limited autonomy. Through the *Confederation* in 1867, Canada established as a nation in which Quebec became a province significantly deprived of its former size (ibid.).

Fast forward to the 1950s and the radical changes leading up to the *Quiet Revolution*, the emphasis on traditional cultural values and a French-nationalistic ascent were again relevant. In the course of the *Quiet Revolution*, several political groups, which began to break away from the narrow, provincial context, became pertinent. They acted as a regional arm of major political movements. The *Front de Libération du Québec* (FLQ) was responsible for more than two hundred bombings and robberies between 1963 and 1970, of which the victims were mostly English-speaking

Quebecers (Morton 2012: 505f.). The new upsurge of violence addressed amongst other things, the difficult working and living conditions of French speakers and their minority role in a society that they claimed to be their historical heritage. These aspects were connected to the idea of gaining freedom from the overarching power of Anglophone institutions. Consequently, this process was infused with complex and multi-layered upheavals from the historical past. The turmoil culminated in the so-called *October crisis* (ibid.). More fruitful were the enterprises of the *Parti Québécois* led by René Lévesque who believed in political dialogue. In 1974, the party managed to mandate that French was the sole official language. As a broader goal, they pursued independence. In 1976, they formed the provincial government and a year later, the use of English was pushed back through the release of a French language Charta. Nevertheless, the Quebecer party did not succeed in dissociating from Canada because in the referendum of 1980, nearly 60 percent of voters decided against independence (Morton 2012: 505f.). To date, Quebec has still not ratified the 1982 constitutional law, although Ottawa tried to negotiate acquiescence. In the *Meech Lake Accord* and the *Charlottetown Accord*, Quebec was recognized as a "distinctive society", but these constitutional revisions failed in 1989 and 1992 due to Anglo-Canadian resistance (Couture 2018). In 1994, again the *Parti Québécois* won the election and initiated a second independence referendum in 1995. With a paper-thin majority, Quebecers decided to remain in Canada (ibid.). The wish to conserve and protect Quebec's national identity, French language, and related cultural traditions exists until today with at times fanatical as well as romanticized proliferations. Quebec has historically tried to reject an adaptation of an urbanized and westernized lifestyle that societies across Canada celebrate.

Concerning immigration, the former laws that were constitutionalized (1867) as a shared jurisdiction changed in the time after the *Quiet Revolution*. Quebec created its own *Ministry of Immigration* (1968) to ensure the prevention of English language transformation and to promote the idea of an 'intercultural' society model that values Quebec's 'distinct identity' (Labelle/Salée 2001). During this period, French philosophers, Marxists and Black intellectuals visited or lived in Montreal and had a tremendous impact on socio-cultural, anti-colonial and political rethinking in the province. While the *Congress of Black Writers* in 1968 and the *Sir George Williams Affair* in 1969 played a huge part in the Black Power movement's engagement with racial politics (Austin 2013), the influential "Autobiographie précoce d'un "terroriste" Québécois" from Pierre Vallières (1968) claimed that French Quebecers' were the "Nègres Blancs de Amériques", which established a questionable viewpoint in the evolving debate about race. Even though Black politics, especially the Black left, helped greatly to define the socio-political momentum in Montreal's 1960s, the dominating viewpoint and understanding of who was influential in making history in Quebec are blurred in favour of a white perception (Austin 2013). Therefore, negative socio-economic as well as political implications for Black people in contemporary Montreal remain unsolved. Above all, Black people are continually being denied their historical existence in the province (Williams 1997: 39). Unfortunately, Quebec still holds onto a historically articulated 'othering' (cf. Spivak 1985) and a self-spun 'master narrative' (cf. Geertz 2003) of being a nation of French-speaking, white, European settlers.

2.3   The Historical Significance of Jamaican Women in Montreal

During the mid-1950s, female Caribbean immigrants were employed in Canada under a unique one-year program, after which they could apply for permanent residency. Beginning in 1955, the Canadian government admitted 100 Jamaican and Barbadian domestic workers annually. These young, educated female workers were, in contrast to their male counterparts, able to support and sponsor other relatives' immigration endeavours to Canada (Winks 1997). Large numbers of Jamaican households have one or more family members living abroad, and many people benefit from migratory networks established in Canada (and elsewhere). In 2001, 91 percent of the entire Caribbean-Canadian population lived in the major urban centres of Ontario and Quebec (NHS 2016). The largest population of Canadians of Caribbean origin are Jamaicans, followed by Haitians, people from Trinidad and Tobago and the Bahamas (Statistics Canada 2019). Due to their French language background, Haitians make up the largest Caribbean immigrant group in the province of Quebec. Over the past 40 years, female migration to Montreal has built strong relational ties between the women and the city. Quebec is still in a process of a political and economic opening of immigration, for example, with the recent introduction of an *Express Entry* visa (2015) for skilled nurses and healthcare labourers, intentionally attracting women from the Caribbean, Latin America, and Southeast Asia. However, ongoing difficulties with migrants' access to equal job opportunities and full access to societal life prevail (Grenier/Nadeau 2011). Since the 1990s, Quebec has had an immigration agreement with Canada, which gives the province the right to select immigrants according to their labour market needs and demographic growth. In 2019, Quebec altered the name of its *Ministry of Immigration, Diversity and Inclusion* to *Ministry of Immigration, Francisation an Integration* signing of the over 50 years-old inclusive vision of ex-Premier Jean-Jacques Bertrand. Categories of integration and inclusion varied greatly over the years, always depending on the governments in power. Recently, however, Quebec has been increasingly divided on the immigration issue. Premier Francois Legault's current majority government passed new and controversial laws, Bill 9 and Bill 21 (2019), which for example allowed the administration to cancel nearly 16,000 immigration applications (family members not included). Among other things, the Bill 21 for example sets a new framework for a "Quebec value test" that immigrants need to pass in order to become permanent residents who respect the 'laicity' of the state.

The markers of difference between cultural 'others' and 'native' Quebecers prevail. Immigrants in Montreal fare worse than in other parts of Canada because Quebec's immigration policies still put too much weight on the acquisition of French language skills. Problems with work-related language discrimination are omnipresent and hinder a positive and comprehensive integration of newcomers. Thus, Québécois conservative tendencies that are strongly language based stand in the way of a working 'intercultural' society model. Contemporary political debates surrounding the sovereignty status of the province as well as related, often nationalistic, political reforms account for a picture, which leaves Quebec's future state open and ambiguous. Discussions whether nationalist tendencies are rather ethnic, linguistic or territorial signify a continuing process of the province's search to define its socio-cultural identity as a people. This ongoing process has significant implications for policymakers in Jamaica as well as in Canada, who are looking to maximize the profit and minimize the cost of migration along with mandating suitable immigration policies. Currently, Quebec's government still holds on to a notion of culture that identifies ethnic groups as insular societies. However, for Quebec, the benefit of successful integration of young and skilled immigrants would be very high. The province is one of the most rapidly ageing populations in Canada (Grenier/Nadeau 2011: 20), and a sharp decline in birth rates is changing Quebec's demographic substance unwaveringly (Labelle 2015). Already in 2014, an article in the Jamaican newspaper *The Gleaner* (2014) reported a higher demand for nurses in the province reflecting one of the main reasons for the increase of Jamaican female immigration to Quebec. Well-educated Jamaican nurses are willing to fill the gap in geriatric and domestic care work, which is of great relevance for the provincial health sector. Since Quebec's ageing population needs more caretakers than ever before, Caribbean women are invited on attractive work programs. In addition to work opportunities, family reunification programs are other vital factors shaping an individual's decision to migrate to Quebec. The ongoing process of Jamaican immigration to Canada, and especially to Quebec, is a reflection of specific shifts in both international and national contexts and highlights the historical importance of emigration to the society of the island.

In Montreal, my anthropological encounters with women, who are personally or through a close relative, connected to this history of emigration and familial chain migration was significant. The Jamaican community is highly segregated and different groups account for a heterogenic picture of the local diaspora. There are older, established institutions that are trying to revitalize their former influential character as well as newer community-based projects. Many art and musical events help to keep Montreal on the map as a place of Afro-Caribbean creativity, especially with events like *Carifiesta*. Over the past 40 years, the first generation, early immigrants are slowly losing their impact because significant institutions and neighbourhoods have shifted, e.g., in terms of gentrification. Many of the second generation Jamaicans, who live in Montreal through familial chain migration, are also involved with the communal activities in the traditional institutions of their ancestors. Nevertheless, this generation is ageing and with the prospect of their upcoming pensions ahead, many are seeking new ways of accommodating themselves, either by moving to other Anglophone cities or by returning to their Jamaican homeland. The third generation immigrant children, who were born in Montreal, are creating their own social spaces, mainly outside of traditional institutions. With no exception to other 'urban youths', many live highly mobile lifestyles. At first sight, Montreal as a multi-ethnic and multi-linguistic city seems to be more individualized and less exclusionary than the rest of Quebec, the ethnographic results of this study, however, draw a picture of ongoing structural and systemic issues such as language-based discrimination in daily life activities. In addition, many interlocutors report racialization to be a significant aspect of their aspiration to leave the city and the province of Quebec altogether.

3 Research Questions and Outline

While ethnographic fieldwork commonly starts with the idea of 'being somewhere', it is less clear what and where this 'somewhere' is when we talk about the "field" (Hannerz 2003), especially in a cosmopolitan city such as Montreal. Tracing the importance of place and understanding spatial practices as well as unusual dwellings is insightful when studying the everyday lives and practices of immigrant women and their connections and experiences with particular sites of a large urban area. In her comparative research (in the 1950s/ 1960s) in London and New York City, Nancy Foner (2005: 174) states "place matters" when researching Caribbean women's lives. Therefore, the relevance of this study bases on the lack of qualitative data concerning Jamaican women's practices and strategies of 'being and belonging' in/ to Montreal. Even though an extensive scholarly discourse about transnational migration exists, which introduced as Duany states "productive" (2011: 17f.) working concepts, it is relevant to provide more empirical data to examine the effectiveness of these ideas.

In the context of female Jamaican migration to Montreal, a lack of ethnographic data concerning return migration, mobility and transcultural enactment makes this research even more relevant. Therefore, my leading question, which helped jump-start the entire study, asks, *"How is cultural diversity and difference in Montreal mediated and translated in the context of Jamaican women's migratory and cross-border activities?"* Diversity as a commonly used concept to describe contemporary, urban societies can here be best understood as a continuous process of mediation and translation in which socio-cultural interaction and power relations transform potential differences into socially effectual indicators (Lehmkuhl 2019). These indicators have socio-cultural relevance in the construction of specific physical and symbolic spaces that change over time. Hence, the relational structure between space, place, and diversity can be debated through the meanings that social actors attribute to them. Here, mediation and translation serve as fruitful categories of social action, e.g., practices that structure interactions in spaces of diversity (ibid.). Therefore, it is also valuable to analyse how immigrants overcome or deal with socio-cultural differences and misunderstandings (mediation) in the context of changing locations, immigrating and integrating.

While approaching the "field" in Montreal as an ethnographer, I experienced several stages of getting closer and delving deeper into the life worlds of the interlocutors of this study. Accordingly, the following research questions arose inductively as sub-inquiries that evolved over the course of fieldwork. The first sub-inquiry focuses on my initial approach to the field, to the city of Montreal as such, and asks about general settlement structures and historical accommodation strategies of Jamaicans in the metropolis. Moreover, the encounters with Jamaican men and women of different age groups and immigrant generations sharpened my focus to female experiences, practices and biographies of the second and third generation (see further chapters four and six). Concerning Jamaican women's immigrant experiences in the city it is relevant to inquire, *"Why is the city of Montreal an important historical contact zone for Jamaican women? How do Jamaican women enter Montreal and how do they settle and accommodate themselves in this diverse city?"*.

Mediating belonging and negotiating connection to a specific place over time requires constant translation work across and beyond real and imagined borders. The concepts of space and place, meaning the focus on specific interconnected localities in the case of Jamaican migration, must be explored not only through the lens of historical immigration waves or new technological possibilities of globalization, but also in the cultural context of social actors. In particular, the appropriation and creation of specific communal institutions is relevant while living in Montreal. Searching for Jamaican-inspired places in the city raises further questions about women's experiences and values (across generations) and, e.g., their reinterpretations of gender roles or social power relations. Specific diasporic places in a city can hereby offer evidence about migrants' relations to new, former and present dwellings. Interactions in Jamaican female public, semi-public, and private spaces tell as much about the experiences with the urban environment and the host society as with the ongoing, dynamic cross-connections to other prominent diasporic localities. Therefore, intersections between the place of origin, new dwelling-places, and continuous interconnections with other sites simultaneously shape an individual's progressive identity construction. Analysing physical-material experiences in particular places in Montreal provides the contextual knowledge necessary for understanding later-life return aspirations. Being locally connected through a social network is an important part of living in Montreal, which leads to the second sub-inquiry of this study: *"In what ways do Jamaican women appropriate specific physical social spaces in the city of Montreal?"*. As much as the interlocutors in this study are trying to create or re-establish "homes away from home" (Clifford 1997: 244) the processes of translating home into a new locality demands discussions with the former 'home'. In this dynamic, dialogic and overlapping process, both 'new' and 'old' notions of home change over time. Already in the 1940s, Cuban anthropologist Fernando Ortiz coined the term "transculturation" (2019 [1940]) as a transfer process that leads to cultural re-configurations. This transfer is ongoing and triggered through the intersection of various socio-cultural contributions. Therefore, actual social practices on the micro-level shed light on the constant negotiation, mediation, and translation of cultural identities. In literature, there is still less qualitative data concerned with women's interpretations of motives, practices, and perspectives in the migratory process compared to men's. Hence, the women's individual identity constructions and representation mechanisms became important components of this study's analysis.

Moreover, it is necessary to extend the spatial approach and look into women's bodily practices that imply meanings and constructions about socio-cultural interactions between female bodies and the city of Montreal. Understandings and representations of beauty ideals can answer questions about the negotiation and mediation of cultural identity and feelings of belonging to Jamaica. Bodily modification, stylization practices and female communion through 'bodywork' reconstruct not only a familiar 'home-space', but also counteract experiences with racism, discrimination and feelings of exclusion as well as 'othering'. Therefore, the third sub-inquiry of this study asks, *"How do Jamaican women's bodily practices in Montreal reconstruct feelings of socio-cultural belonging to Jamaica and to Montreal? How does the stylization of the body counteract experiences with racism and othering?"*.

Beyond the analysis of bodily practices, the concept of space is again relevant when discussing women's personal reasons of yearning for the Jamaican 'homeland'. In the historical overview of Jamaican migration to Canada, various immigration waves give rise to the assumption that mobile, cross-cultural activities are not a new phenomenon. Since the mobile lives of the study's interlocutors' are tied and embedded in several localities and diverse transnational spaces, it is even more relevant to show that the places in Montreal actively interconnect with sites and bonds elsewhere in the diaspora and Jamaica. Hence, the anthropological notion of the "field" as a clear-cut, distinct site of enclosed research is as Clifford states, disputable (1997: 54f.). Since the field is not a static, 'spatially bound place' (Appadurai 1991: 191f.), it is crucial to understand the ongoing presence and dynamic influence of narratives in daily interactions. These are, for example, discussions about memories of Jamaica, perpetually evoked through ongoing social connections to family left behind and sensual experiences such as food or music.

Hence, Jamaican culture is a fluid and changing concept that has become strongly affected by different, multi-sited external forces and exchanges throughout the centuries. Therefore it is relevant to understand how migration has become "deeply embedded in the psyche of Caribbean peoples" (Thomas-Hope 2002: 2.1.2) and hence how stages of migration (e.g. leaving, staying, returning) are narrated via intergenerational articulation. Women's intergenerational narratives nurture individual images, memories, and viewpoints about life in Jamaica as well as in Montreal. Hence, these imaginaries and expectations of the homeland often influence the aspiration and yearning to reconnect with the homeland. In this sense, imagined and "real-life" spaces are interrelated and intersected by the social actors who move through or with(-in) them. Narratives of the past, handed down by mothers and grandmothers as well as the women's own childhood memories of the Jamaican homeland are the bedrock of their identity constructions and aspirations of return. Therefore, reinterpretations and imaginations of Jamaica and Jamaican life are mental preconditions of planning and executing return migrations and often contrast with unexpected and different realities upon arrival in the homeland. This practice of 'being mentally mobile' leads to the fourth sub-inquiry of this study, which asks, *"How do intergenerational narratives affect Jamaican women's reconstructions of the homeland? Which images and memories are important in the process of aspiring return migration?"*. In this study, travel, mobility and migration through different geographical localities and life worlds demonstrate the field as an interconnected, ambiguous "location-work" (Gupta/Ferguson 1997: 105). According to Gupta and Ferguson,

> "Fieldwork reveals that a self-conscious shifting of social and geographical location can be an extraordinary valuable methodology for understanding social and cultural life, [...]. Fieldwork, in this light, may be understood as a form of motivated and stylized dislocation" (1997: 136f.).

Consequently, a decentred analysis that takes various movement strategies of migrants into account highlights processes of transcultural exchange and interconnection. Therefore, it was necessary to accompany Jamaican women on their travels between Canada and Jamaica to detect how mobility after initial migration works in practice. Being mentally mobile through memories and imaginaries of the past and present set certain aspirations and expectations free and strongly enhance the women's plans for actual physical mobility. Being virtually mobile through modern communication tools such as instant messengers, Skype, WhatsApp, and social media channels helps staying in daily contact with the island and support planning travels, seasonal trips and return migration to Jamaica. Information and support via social networks and connections to local Jamaican friends and family should not be underestimated as they precondition physical mobility to the island. Moreover, physical mobility to Jamaica raises questions about migratory patterns or routes. Whether women are wishing to travel to 'paradise Jamaica' seasonally, attempting to make the best of their retirement payments or fulfilling the desire of their ancestors to return home, aspiring and actual returnees offer an unprecedented spectrum through which Jamaican culture can be analysed. Throughout the study and in the title of this book, I use the term life worlds in the sense of an 'existential anthropology' as described by Michael Jackson (2012). Jackson shows that existentialism, far from being a philosophy of individual being, enables the ethnographer to explore issues of social existence and coexistence in new ways. For example, to theorize events as sites of a dynamic interplay between the finite possibilities of the situations in which people find themselves in as well as the capacities they yet possess for creating viable forms of social life. Here, the study also seeks to inquire about conflictive aspects and unforeseen difficulties encountered in the event of Jamaican women's 'homecomings'. Here, local 'frictions' seemingly pave the way for new possibilities, for example, new forms of later-life mobility. Hence, the fifth and last sub-inquiry asks, *"How does return migration work in practice? How does being mobile after initial migration affect the women's perspectives about Montreal and Jamaica? Are there any conflicting narratives, interests, or representation mechanisms that occur along their mobile trajectories?"*. In the light of current global developments, the focus on the dynamic, inherent meanings of diversity, mobility and cross-border activities as well as migratory experiences are valuable tools to understand migratory agency in a more complex way. Instead of looking into oppositions or binaries, present-day mobile people and societies require the 'exclusion of methodological nationalism' (Wimmer/Glick Schiller 2003) as well as the idea of culture being a container. If we can assume that most Jamaican women have multiple and complex social networks that encompass more than just one place and, as a result, overcome visible borders, we can comprehend these people as social agents who "challenge many long-held assumptions about membership, development, and equity" (Levitt 2004).

Since the past informs the present, historical encounters between Canada and Jamaica were preconditions to deepen the understanding about the contemporary situation. The 'special' position of Montreal in Quebec (in Canada) with regard to immigration and integration policies and resulting internal, nationalist tendencies was hereby of particular relevance. The discussion of the research questions leads now to chapter four that elaborates on methodology and on the 'multi-sited approach' (Marcus 1995) to the field as well as the 'triangulation of ethnographic data' (Denzin 1970) for the analysis of the interlocutors' life worlds in various localities. This triangulation is necessary to compare interviews, informal talks and observation methods with each other to contrast what people say with their social interactions. In addition, the chapter on methodology informs about my positionality in the 'field' and the importance of the anthropological encounters (Spülbeck 1997). Chapter five introduces theoretical key concepts that help saturate the empirical results. Therefore, the theoretical concepts are a reflection of the improvisatory, ethnographic process of data gathering (Cerwonka/Malkki 2007) and are tailored to the ethnographic results. Chapter six to chapter nine illustrate the research partners' individual life worlds, biographies, intergenerational narratives, local practices and experiences in Montreal. The empirical findings show how Jamaican women navigate the challenges of space appropriation, inclusion/exclusion and identity construction in the city. Here aspects of being and belonging, bodily practices, racial discrimination, yearning for home, memories, imaginaries and the role of women in Jamaican society are reflected.

After the analysis of the Montreal-based results, the study adopts a traveling perspective (chapter 10) that detects and interprets mobility after migration and the challenges of finding 'new' routes to approach the homeland. Returning to Jamaica will also highlight the deconstruction of personal imaginaries, and shows emotional aspects such as the feeling of rejection and confrontations with an 'unknown' local context or 'lost home'. Through these frictions (chapter 11), particular previously held expectations about people, places, and life in Jamaica are seen to shift. Finally, the examination of new ways of redefining relationships and re-adaptations to the local environment (chapter 12) highlight the flexibility of Jamaican women throughout their temporal, spatial and socio-cultural relocation processes. These are exemplified through various stages of mediation and negotiation of 'being and belonging' in/ to the homeland and in/ to North America and finally mould into individual processes of migratory oscillation. Chapter 13 concludes with the study's main outcomes and gives an outlook on possible future research in the area of Jamaican migration and mobility.

Over the course of this study, the reader will get to know five different women. Their biographies and family backgrounds stand representatively for typical Jamaican migratory trajectories in Montreal. For a better understanding of who these women are, a short biographical information of each person is given here. Their real names are withheld. I chose typical Jamaican names as pseudonyms that resemble their own or their relatives' individual age group. Of course, it is challenging to anonymize some interlocutors due to their position in the local community. However, the research partners authorized any information used in this text. The following women guide the reader through the ethnography:

- Elisha: In her late twenties, born in Montreal to Jamaican parents. Severe experiences of racism in school and university made her see Montreal as an oppressive place. After several unsuccessful attempts to get a job in her profession, she now works part-time in her sister's beauty salon; she longs to leave Montreal and live in Jamaica, where she dreams of belonging and living a better life.
- Debby: In her late thirties, born in Montreal to Jamaican parents, Elisha's big sister; runs a beauty salon in Montreal that she took over from her mother; does not intend to leave Montreal.
- Ms. Brown: In her sixties, migrated to Montreal as a teenager following her mother in chain migration; works as a geriatric nurse; was married two times, mother of three adult children; invested in a retirement house in Jamaica; wants to re-migrate immediately after receiving her pension.
- Carol: In her late sixties, she intentionally migrated to Montreal as a young woman in order to have a career; has a science degree from Jamaica; worked as a teacher; married in Montreal and is the mother of two adult children; is

retired and recently moved to Toronto; engages on regular biannual travels to Jamaica.

- Josephine: In her late sixties, returned to Jamaica five years ago; initially migrated to the UK; came to live in Montreal in her forties; worked as a domestic and untrained nurse throughout her life; contemplates about returning to Canada or traveling to visit friends and family in North America and the UK.

4   Methodology

"Regardless of how the first-hand experiences are used in the text, we can assume that the arrival itself is an important experience. Any ethnographer would probably agree that first encounters generate personal alienation and a sense of extreme relativism that forever marks off the 'field'. First experiences belong to an experiential space that cannot be done away with literary criticism" (Hervik 1994: 60).

During the fall of 2016 and the winter of 2019, I conducted fieldwork in Montreal and Jamaica in several periods and trips from one place to another. I first came to Montreal in the summer of 2016 to gain orientation knowledge in the city and to explore the local setting. However, I quickly realized that I had chosen the wrong part of town since I stayed in a designated Francophone area at the house of a dear colleague from the *Université de Montréal*. Before arriving in Montreal for the first time, I was unaware of the linguistic divide of the city that has effects on residential as well as on livelihood patterns. For my second trip to Montreal in the fall and winter months of 2016, I therefore chose a more central area close to Mount Royal, from which I could easily travel to the western neighbourhoods of the city that are predominantly Anglophone.

An essential part of my field research preparation and orientation knowledge acquisition was, what Hine calls, "virtual" ethnography (Hine 2000). As practical examples of cross-cultural exchange, various social media platforms, including Jamaican-Montreal-based Facebook groups were very useful in exploring the 'virtual' field. Here, those interested will find help with migration/ integration related questions, visa requirements/ procedures, or just practical information about grocery shops, Jamaican-owned businesses, and restaurants in Montreal. In addition, Jamaican musical events, radio stations, and upcoming Reggae/ Dancehall parties in town are shared on various social media platforms. Besides, users frequently add links to YouTube channels or video platforms with Jamaican news, music videos, comedy, or commercials. Information about the local Jamaican association in Montreal and its events are circulated and are part of a conversation among the chat participants. These technological spaces are anticipated and used daily. Further, the ethnographic study had a "virtual" lens in the sense of following the interlocutors online on social media platforms, as well as planning and navigating mobility trips via modern communication forms, for example, via WhatsApp or Skype. Virtual networking with friends and family in Jamaica and other localities was often a precondition or a companion throughout mobility phases.

One of the aspects that "saved" the project from failing was my ability to speak basic Patois needed for conversations, especially to introduce myself to people in a language variant they were familiar with. Concerning events, an informal language policy exists, whereby events of the Jamaican community are advertised in English or Jamaican Patois, depending on the medium, i.e., Anglophone radio, media channels or their social media platforms. To establish myself, I had to "talk the talk" and "walk the walk" (De Walt/De Walt 2002) and in a way prove myself to be knowledgeable about Jamaica in order to be accepted as a visitor and interviewer of the local scene. Attending the *Carifiesta* as well as the *Jamaica Day* concerts in Montreal was another great way of entering the field. However, not only outside activities, events and the staging of Jamaican culture, but also contacts conducted through social media created critical entry points into the local spaces of the Jamaican community in Montreal. Here, Jamaican spaces, meeting points, or Jamaican-run events, apart from the public festivals and concerts, are rather exclusive, meaning that there are not many white people present. Even though a solid basis of contacts and frequent access to the field emerged through my attendance of events or online contacts, many people were suspicious about my sudden appearance. It took some time, endurance, and positivity to convince people to take part in this study. Hence, there was no formal means of agreement for participation, rather an organic growing of relationships that entailed a personal presence on my part at important places, events or meeting points.

After gaining a first set of contacts, I used a snowball sampling method to reach out to more and more people over time. During this process, I realized that there was a wide range of individuals from the working class to upper-middle class, some with tertiary level education as well as domestic and farm workers and some professionals and creatives from various disciplines. The access to male spaces and male life worlds had its limitations for me, both as a woman and an outsider. Realizing that the access to male respondents was proving to be difficult, I decided to pursue a woman-centred research. Initially, this focus was not my intention; however, from the beginning of the research phase, I faced major difficulties in approaching men as a female researcher. Unexpectedly, it was extremely hard to get into contact with men in semi-public social spaces without experiencing flirting or being ensnared in the androcentric-dominated Jamaican music scene. Here, gender played a crucial role in the course of my fieldwork since being a female researcher determined my path and whereabouts in Montreal. In chapter six, I explain precisely how the field access worked and why I finally focussed on female life worlds and experiences.

In the summer of 2016, I had luckily already met two of my interlocutors Elisha and Ms. Brown, which made it easier to obtain more research participants in the second phase. Until December 2016, I carried out interviews in Montreal with 20 participants, of which 14 were narrative, in-depth interviews (Weis 1994) with Jamaican women to learn more about their personal lives and local experiences. Weis explains,

> "Interviewing can inform us about the nature of social life. [...]. We can learn also, through interviewing about people's interior experiences. [...] We can learn the meanings to them of their relationships, their families their work, and their selves. We can learn about all the experiences, from joy through grief, that together constitute the human condition" (1994: 1).

Most interviews were longer than two hours. The interviews also entailed biographical depictions (Schütze 1983) that reconstruct life histories, which together with the participant observation and daily life activities, were crucial components of this study. Participant observation consisted of densely observing (Spittler 2001) and accompanying the women as they went about their daily activities at work, at church, at the salon, at quiz and bingo nights, at fashion and musical events or simply in their leisure time in the sense of a "deep hanging out" (Ingold 2007). Over time, a liberation from the pressure to act or engage (Reichertz 1999: 57) and an openness for "serendipity" (Hazan/Hertzog 2016) to occur and to just be there allowed me to grasp a sense of my interlocutors' daily lives in the city of Montreal and also their individual connections to Jamaica. Using participant observation (Malinowski 1922; 1935) was hence a tentative approach of distance and closeness, retreating from or participating in daily activities whenever feasible or possible for the interlocutors. However, this does not mean that the emic (insider's) and etic (outsider's) views were mutually exclusive; instead they complemented each other by giving both subjective and objective interpretations to the "thick descriptions" (Geertz 2003). Here, journaling (with a fieldwork diary) and collecting of my own thoughts throughout the research were essential techniques to follow up with a theory that evolved from the research material gathered in the sense of "grounded theory" (Glaser/Strauss 1967; Glaser 1999). Additionally, informal conversations at the kitchen table (Schlehe 2008) informed and enriched this study tremendously. Especially, eating at Ms. Brown's house became an important routine, where many "rich points" (Agar 2008) occurred, as the communal consumption of traditional Jamaican meals opened a window to the underlying socio-cultural subtext of values, traditions, childhood memories and intergenerational narratives. Daily conversations and in-depth biographical interviews were hence the ideal way to discover more about an individual's experiences.

One of these interviews led me to Carol as another vital source of information. Hence, I travelled from Montreal to Toronto to meet with her for an interview. Two days later, I met Ms. Brown who also came from Montreal to the Toronto Pearson airport to fly to Jamaica and followed her on her travels. As fieldwork evolved, it became more and more relevant to follow four of the five interlocutors on their travels to Jamaica. I spent over six months in Jamaica in several fieldwork periods. Since none of my respondents lived a stationary life, it became necessary to conduct the ethnography in a way that respected their individual life circumstances. The study thus aimed at a "follow the people" concept (Marcus 1995: 90f.) and strived for a holistic picture that drew its information from as many different angles as possible. However, I tried not to interrupt the daily activities of the research partners through my presence. This undertaking was a challenge, especially while I was present in relatively exclusive female spaces in Montreal or during the travels to Jamaica, where I undoubtedly influenced the places and spaces I entered and the people with whom I interacted.

My previous fieldwork in Jamaica for my Master's thesis on Reggae music led me to stay on the island for almost five years, therefore, former research and work contacts in Jamaica greatly helped approaching and acquiring local interlocutors. Because of this fact, a critical self-reflection on my part, mainly concerning personal contact, was essential. In Jamaica, the fieldwork consisted of following my respondents on their return or holiday trips to the island. Here, I engaged whenever possible in their daily activities and conducted interviews whenever this seemed feasible. I also met with interlocutors who had already returned to Jamaica some years prior. As an additional method, life course analysis (Rubinstein 1990) gained more and more importance towards the end of my fieldwork. While being attentive to socio-culturally effective structural (external) influences, it seemed to be a crucial method of understanding women's decision-making processes and defining them as wholly embodied and complex beings with agency over their lives. The combination of life course and interview analysis provided important biographical clues that highlight not only age-related patterns in conjunction with historically grown socio-cultural structures in Jamaica, but moreover commonalities amongst all the women of this study. While different in age and social background, they share certain similar migratory experiences.

The methodology and my inductive approach are mirrored in the written elaboration of my ethnography, which passes through various spaces, places, levels, and encounters that reflect how I entered the field and how I was able to look behind individual curtains, while other parts remained hidden. For example, sitting in front of the beauty salon of Elisha's sister Debby offered a totally different view (inside vs. outside) of the place, not only as an important space of female gathering, but moreover as a significant Jamaican hotspot in the city of Montreal invisible to the host society. Simply observing from outside how many different clients, workers, delivery people, friends, family, musicians and local traders passed through the salon in the course of a regular working day revealed the salon to be a vital community institution. The reflection processes also included rather lonely days of journaling, which, especially in the harsh winter days in Montreal and Toronto, were a personal challenge for me. Spending parts of the winter in Canada made me realize how difficult it must be for people used to a tropical climate surrounded by the Caribbean Sea to live in an environment that resembles a freezer. As Ms. Brown said: "Every single bone cracks when you step inna [in] di [the] ice [snow], it cyan [cannot] be good".

The prevalent themes of Jamaican women that often extend over a lifetime will become visible in the ethnography and, in conjunction with my theoretical approaches, will create a more complex and deeper portrait of their life worlds in Montreal. Concerning the overall selection process, I narrowed down the focus to the women I had the strongest personal contact with and who I understand as cultural brokers and translators of this ethnography. The study acknowledges that autobiographical narration is a process of defining experiences that are selective, overlapping, and evaluating. The problems of biographical reconstruction are well known in the literature (e.g. Fischer/Goblirsch 2006; Gardener 2001) and methodologically only partially resolvable. Knowledge and related worlds of imagination are subject to a dynamic process that puts life experiences into perspective. Narratives reflect actions, considerations, and popularize certain forms and acts of knowing. Migration, therefore, is a formative, dynamic learning process (Treiber 2013), where temporal and spatial transformations of knowledge and imaginaries build the foundation of making individual, formerly perplexing or incomprehensible actions in the host and home societies, coherent.

5 Theoretical Concepts

Before the ethnographic chapters begin, this section introduces theoretical key concepts that are relevant for the study. For example, the mobility and migration of the female respondents in this study calls for an analytical framework, which considers being 'on the move' as a mental and physical practice. Being mobile after initial migration requires taking the notion of transnationalism further than its classical sense. Additionally, concepts of gender and identity will be relevant aspects in exploring female ways of belonging to Montreal and their mobility strategies. The analysis of return migration (real or aspired return) requires the discussion of the terms diaspora and homeland in the canon of migration research. Local space appropriation strategies of Jamaican women in Montreal will reveal not only the 'exclusivity' of female spaces against interferences and frictions from outside, but also the upkeep and preservation of Jamaican traditions and values.

In an anthropological sense, we examine culture as the diversity of human ways of life. Therefore, this study aims to provide rich insights into Jamaican women's views and actions and make their diverse understandings of mobility and migration comprehensible. In doing so, it is necessary to act in a culturally relativistic way, i.e., to analyse culture from within, from an "emic" point of view. Hammersley describes the goal of the documentation of certain cultural perspectives and practices as "[...] to 'get inside' the way each group of people sees the world" (Hammersley 1992). Consequently, there is no privileged position from which culture can be defined. Culture is, hence, not homogeneous, but heterogeneous and changeable. The hermeneutic approach of this study understands culture as a collective "fabric of meaning" spun by human beings, which is repeatedly subject to productions and transformations and new interpretations (Geertz 2003: 5). The analytical concept of culture is intended to "decipher the way in which social individuals [...] manage and implement the raw material of their social [...] existence in a specific historical context" (Kannakulam 2008: 17). Together with the historical context, globalizing factors such as, for example, dispersal, digitalized communication, and advanced interconnectedness need to be acknowledged when analysing individual life worlds. Therefore, social actions of the respondents cannot be understood from a fixed or permanent location. In a continually changing, digitally ever-more-informed world, anthropologists need to move with the same speed as their research partners. Hence, it is necessary to discard binary approaches in thinking about migratory agency and belonging, especially considering migration as an ongoing process of being mobile and of belonging beyond national borders. As Carter states,

> "It becomes ever more urgent to develop a framework of thinking that makes the migrant central, not ancillary, to historical process. We need to disarm the genealogical rhetoric of blood, property and frontiers and substitute it for a lateral account of social relations [...]. An authentically migrant perspective could rather root from an intuition that the opposition between here and there is itself a cultural construction, a consequence of thinking in terms of fixed entities and defining them oppositional. It might begin by regarding movement, not as an awkward interval between fixed points of departure and arrival, but as a mode of being in the world" (Carter 1992: 7f., 101).

Since the postmodernist declaration that all knowledge is in flux, the reconsideration of the term 'culture', especially concerning traveling (Clifford 1997: 101), has changed anthropology as a discipline. Nowadays, an acceptance for both ethnographic knowledge and writing evolving from journeying exists (Coleman/Hellermann 2013). The travels undertaken by the interlocutors are now coordinated and combined with the mobility, travel experiences, modes of thought, and actions of the ethnographer as anthropologists are 'on the move'. Therefore, it is important to acknowledge that the interpretations of events, observations, travels and conversations relate intrinsically to my own experiences and perspectives (cf. Clifford 1986). Further, they relate to my own positionality in the field as a researcher foreign to the Montreal/ Québécois urban cultural context. However, my familiarity with the Jamaican context opened many doors for my active participation (cf. Becker et al. 2005). As Louch already stated in the 1960s, "relations, therefore, cannot be thought anymore as totalized, fixed or absolute sites. Relations need to be considered in flux and movement, and our research becomes a study of travelers as well as by travelers" (Louch 1966: 160). Movement activities of people do not take linear ways, but rather relational paths of 'entanglement' and 'translation' between transnational locations, nations, and human beings developed out of historical encounters and displacement (Clifford 1997: 7f.). The demonstration of how dynamic, affective and communicative ties and social networks to friends and family motivate the interlocutors to be mobile and to stay connected is central in this study. Social networks hereby continually exist based on 'socially shared images or imaginaries' (Salazar 2011: 576f.) that women keep and nurture through their own and second-hand memories of the Jamaican homeland as well as opinions about and experiences in their actual place of residence.

Another objective of this study is to explain that the physical process of changing locations, circulating or relocating, is greatly influenced by different forms of knowledge, beliefs, and hopes of the people who undertake these movements. Moving around or moving abroad starts with an idea about the destination, aspirations and economic planning of turning intentions into reality. An important aspect of the mobility of the interlocutors is the fact that they all have dual citizenship. Therefore, they can travel freely between the Caribbean and North America. This freedom to travel "visa-free" removes the threat or the fear of international immigration control. With this privileged position, these women inherit a different 'mind-set' regarding the ability to travel and to live in different destinations through current and prospective mobility. Their distinct 'state of mind' places this study at the heart of debating transnationalism beyond nation-states and national borders (Basch et al. 1994). Seasonal trips to Jamaica are an example of their migratory mobility and a transnational mode of 'being and belonging' for many Jamaicans today. While current scholarly debates usually analyse second home or residential tourism as permanent or temporal spatial movements of rather wealthy persons, more and more qualitative research shows evidence that this formerly privileged, lifestyle-oriented migration is now accessible and is spreading to more significant parts of the worldwide population (see King/Lulle 2016).

5.1   Beyond Transnationalism

This ethnography highlights the agency of Jamaican women to engage in recurring trips to their home country, fusing migration with a newer, privileged mobile lifestyle that also includes tourism. I understand migratory agency with De Haas as "a function of aspiration and capabilities to migrate within the given set of opportunity structures" (2014: 4). Here, De Haas draws on Sen's notion of 'capability' as "freedom" of people "to lead the kind of lives they value" (Sen 1999: 3). He develops his argument further and states,

> "Because people have agency, their mobility is also a potential force for structural change, because it can play an important part in altering the social and economic conditions in both sending and receiving countries. [...]. However, it is important to emphasize that all migrants face structural constraints and that the degree to which they can exercise agency is fundamentally limited. This also limits the extent to which migrants can bring about structural change" (De Haas 2009: 2).

Utilising his theoretical approach, agency in this study recognizes that Jamaican women's opportunities for participation and action are affected by political, socio-economic and socio-cultural conditions, but not predetermined by them. This perspective considers structural conditions, but these conditions do not cage individuals in their particular cultural background. For example, in the case of Jamaican women's agency, economic reasons for partial relocation are less relevant. Even though they do not belong to the upper social class in Montreal, they often live far above the means and possibilities of the socio-economic standard in Jamaica and because of that, they are at times excluded or isolated from their society of origin (see chapter 11). Hence, moving between places also creates social mobility. Furthermore, it is relevant to keep in mind that this rather new form of voluntary mobility does not only include people but also knowledge about migration and places, material objects, capital and information flows (Janoschka 2009; McIntyre 2009). While this research mainly focuses on the individual experiences and strategies of female migrants as well as their aspirations and choices, it will also look at the socio-economic effects on the interlocutors' local and often immobile family relatives. In Jamaica, returnees or second homeowners are often perceived as beneficial to the local economy by government officials, while other parts of the local population may see them as outsiders or sometimes invaders who cause local resentment (Hall/Müller 2004; McWatters 2008). In addition, many potential returnees are not old, i.e., they do not move for retirement reasons. Many young and working-age individuals are in search of a better life in Jamaica or others are merely seasonal movers who are not migrants or re-migrants per se (Janoschka 2009; 2014). Additionally, all of the study's interlocutors live in different yet 'mutually entangled' life worlds that produce significant cultural narratives (O'Reilly/Benson 2009). Their perspectives address both structural as well as intercultural frictions that can occur when people's aspirations or symbolic appropriations are confronted with actual local realities. Moreover, the study also acknowledges the simultaneous 'entanglement' of different female life worlds, i.e., Jamaican, Caribbean, Québécois, and Canadian and the links and relations that are constructed, maintained or reconstituted in the context of returning to the Jamaican homeland. Therefore, the approach lies on the micro-level, individual experiences stand opposite macro structures, e.g., differing historical, political, and communal viewpoints, and need to be analysed considering numerous individual and familial factors. Cultural practices are the key to understanding markers of identity, representation, and aspects of socio-cultural memory and images. These closely linked factors explain aspects of 'being and belonging' (Basch et al. 1994), whereby belonging through interconnection and socio-cultural relationships is not necessarily place-based.

Contemporary theoretical considerations in migration research incorporate the idea that migration and mobility are combined, relational, and fluid social processes that reveal much about the instability of migratory trajectories. Processes of mobility interconnect with immobility (King 2012; Wieczoreck 2018) and return migration becomes a tenacious 'transnational' movement (Carling/Erdal 2014). Individuals who are mobile after initial migration have to modify their actions and ways of thinking about problems that occur along their migratory trajectories. How people make sense of their movements, about staying, going away and returning, will be illuminated in this study. Migration, mobility, and immobility are aspects of Jamaican female life trajectories that explore relational and structural frictions across time and space (see chapters 11 and 12). As Hillman and Van Naerssen state,

> "People on the move look for immediate solutions to their problems and needs, [...], the way people think about their situation also frames their migratory agency. Their agenda is itself a reaction to the answers that people have already given to the situation of crisis and uncertainty they find themselves in" (Hillman et al. 2018: 5).

Hence, it appears to be crucial to identify migratory movement and agency in a broader framework of not only local, but also global interconnectedness and social relations as well as the individual mind-set of a person. Accordingly, accounts of the emotional ability to deal with unforeseen challenges and changes as well as an individual's socio-cultural and gender-based experiences and demands will be covered in this study. To develop this argument empirically, I will address aspects of memory, imaginary, identity constructions, geographic movement, and mobility as essential components. Besides, structural conditions or societal macrostructures of course play a relevant role in framing and understanding the experiences and narratives of the interlocutors in Montreal and in Jamaica.

Traditionally, scientific studies about migration assumed an assimilation thesis, immigrants breaking ties with their homeland and integrating into new host societies. Specifically concerning the Caribbean islands, the focus on the notion of an actual "brain drain" (Hunger 2002) viewed migration as a linear, singular life event caused by the socio-economic crisis after the islands gained independence from the British colonial regime in the 1960s. Early literature about migration addressed neither ethnic nor kinship connections nor the return to a respective home country. Even though a large number of, e.g., European settlers on the North American continent returned to their home countries in the early 20th century, migration scholars had little interest in the immigrants who left their destination countries in that time period (Cohen 1995). Migration literature started to acknowledge that relocating permanently was not a once in a lifetime event, but rather a frequent movement of people, ideas, knowledge, skills, and practices, keeping connections alive in a globalized world and, hence, establishing so-called transnational lifestyles. The 1990s approaches on transnational migration (e.g. Appadurai 1996; Basch et al. 1994; Glick Schiller et al. 1992; Grasmuck/Pessar 1991; Gupta/Ferguson 1992, 1997; Hannerz 1996) evolved as alternative drafts to the theory of assimilation. The idea of uprooting was abandoned since migrants were retaining their homeland ties and continued to move between different localities, social systems, and spaces. Anthropological discourse about transnational migration was at first concerned with identity constructions, the cultural effects of migration and also return migration in the home and host society. Further, deterritorialized flows, mobile life pathways, and urban to rural migratory movements were of scholarly interest (e.g. Said 1982; Appadurai 1996; Gupta/Ferguson 1997; Olwig/Hastrup 1997; Paerregaard 1997; Abu-Lughod 1991; Sassen 2003; Sheller/Urry 2006). The term "deterritorialization" coined by Appadurai refers to people, ideas, and goods of the modern age (Appadurai 2000: 37). Through technical advancements more and more people are seen to be experiencing a "global interconnectedness" (Inda/Rosaldo 2002: 3). The result is an increased global exchange and fluid borders. Appadurai further illustrates the "global flow" by which culture moves across national frontiers (Appadurai 2000: 45f.). This global flow comes about through the penetration of various porous so-called "scapes". Culture now is not only based on, for example, national entities, but rather stems from a global stream, exchange and transfer of ethnoscapes, mediascapes, financescapes, ideoscapes, and technoscapes (ibid.). Anthropology has had to take into account a global development in which more and more people were able to participate in the (imagined) realities of others (ibid. 48, 53).

The pioneering research of the sociologists and anthropologists Nina Glick Schiller, Cristina Szanton Blanc and Linda Basch (Bach et al. 1994) built the foundation of the term transnationalism. Increasingly, questions of territorial and social spaces have become relevant, and the nation-state as a fixed category of reference was criticized (Beck 1998; Glick Schiller et al. 1995; Wimmer 2002). Because of these debates, transnationalism in this study is understood as a form of cultural and social belonging beyond national borders. Moreover, the idea of the deterritorialization of nation-states and ethnic groups loosened their formerly fixed character and insularity (Appadurai 1996; Glick Schiller et al. 1992). As a result, new representations of identities and new cultural self-images emerged, which enhanced external self-confidence (Hall 2000). Additionally, new concepts such as "transnationale soziale Räume"[1] (Pries 2001: 32) were coined to describe recently emerging cultural spaces. To understand Jamaican migration patterns, a transnational orientation is necessary to identify how migrants straddle life between the host country and the homeland. Furthermore, they are at the same time influenced by both places in different ways. Migratory narratives, practices and interactions, hence, structure the negotiation and mediation of difference in transcultural spaces (Lehmkuhl 2019: 11). Globalization and its possibilities have changed the relationships and the social structure of migratory people over time and have shifted cultural values regarding mobility, space, place, and belonging. Globalization has not only affected transnational ties but also the level of individual and group-based migratory consciousness regarding the immigrants' own identity constructions and representations. Here, cultural artefacts play a significant role in maintaining identity and in creating or re-creating an image

---

1   Translation: Transnational social spaces.

of oneself, of shared values, and of the so-called 'others' (Spivak 1985). Already in 1985, Spivak described 'othering' as a multi-layered process that contains several different variants of social differentiation, therefore, can be examined together with intersectional parameters of an individual (see the next sub-chapter).

The mobility framework introduced a less static point of view of the movement of people as being influenced by systematic purposes and forces and less by de-territorialization or inactiveness. Noting the significance "of the systematic move-ments of people for work and family life, for leisure and pleasure" (Sheller/Urry 2006: 208), migration as an integral part of Jamaican culture is a constant socio-economic practice. The desire to move or circulate in 'foreign' countries or to re-turn to one's place of origin because of economic welfare or old age are important aspects. Migration literature examining patterns of emigration and return show the emergence of a transnational return migration culture in the English-speaking Caribbean (cf. Chamberlain 1998; Thomas-Hope 2002; Olwig 2007). These stud-ies highlight how deeply migratory movement and agency have been rooted in Ja-maican culture and the 'mind-set' of its people since the early 19th century. Vital connections to relatives who reside in the USA, the UK or Canada and a deep inter-est in American media is commonplace; a keen orientation to a culture of immedi-ate gratification and consumerism supported by popular Jamaican Dancehall music and the related 'bling-bling'[2] lifestyle are shaping Jamaicans' widespread foreign-mindedness on a daily level. Potter views "international migration [...] contributing substantially to the population diversity that characterizes the small insular soci-eties of this oceanic region" (Potter et al. 2004: 48). Marshall claims that the present movement of Caribbean people strongly results from a historical construction of the Caribbean populations as main migration hubs (Marshall 1987: 16f.). This claim mirrors the actual historical course and points out that transnational migration is not a new phenomenon. The first migration waves originated in colonial times, amid violence and political conflicts. Jamaican immigrants from different genera-tions carry with them various world understandings and generational traumas.

In the context of globalization theories, the development of migratory move-ment and mobility after migration are most clearly illustrated by the interplay be-tween universalism and particularism, or more precisely, between the 'global' and the 'local'. According to Robertson, globalization has channelled the restoration and the production of categories such as "homeland", "community", and "local-ity" (Robertson 1998: 200). As a result, considerations of the local as the antagonist of the global no longer hold. Moreover, global cultural connections remain rele-vant via literature, art, and the media, or music, e.g., Reggae (Jung 2012), factors,

---

2   Note: 'bling-bling': used to describe shiny (expensive looking) jewellery and bright fashion-
      able clothes worn in order to attract attention to yourself, e.g., women with big hair and bling-
      bling jewellery (Oxford Dictionary 2015).

which are incredibly insightful when analysing the Jamaican local to global context. These bridging categories offer possibilities for continually strengthened cultural exchange between people and various localities.

The 'mobility turn' further connected anthropology's approach to migration with dynamism and fluidity (Brettell 2017). However, returning to Glick Schiller and Schmidt (2016), place and space remain important concepts through which national boundaries and the dynamic flow of migrants become visible. Transnational movement activities of people have changed our view of border crossings to a view beyond particular localities and points of identification that uproot individuals from certain values that associated them with certain cultures. Recently, however, place-making strategies and the analyses of locality (e.g. De Genova 2016) established the place as a meaningful category back onto the agenda of scholarly debates (e.g. Hinkson 2017). Places are produced through ongoing practices of everyday life related to migratory belonging and identity. Migratory movements back to the homeland –whether mental or physical ones– are processes that construct and re-inscribe 'place' as a significant aspect into migrants' lives. Therefore, place-making strategies can also hint at a critique of national discourses of immigration and integration.

5.2   Gender, Identity and Migration

Since the 1990s, the number of scholarly studies concerned with the female experience of migration has increased. Feminist scholars have discussed how women and men sense migratory movement and change in settlement differently (Oishi 2005; Pessar 1999; Pessar/Mahler 2003). While early feminist literature concentrated on gender hierarchies as shaping migration, post-colonial and anti-racist researchers nowadays focus on multi-layered approaches that combine individual categories such as gender, race, ethnicity, class, and citizenship (Brand 1984; Cohen 2000; Ong 1993; Stevenson 2007). Differences in age and social status also affect mobility opportunities and experiences in, e.g., the work field or socio-cultural institutions. While simultaneously being embedded in socio-cultural as well as economic and political contexts, women mediate between different local and transnational processes, networks, and ideologies.

A look at Foner's case study (1985) on Jamaican women in New York and London highlights how crucial it is to consider gender when examining migratory experiences. She has found that Jamaican women are often victims of sexism as well as of low social class and racial inequality and that their position is one exemplary of subordination and oppression. As people of colour, Jamaican women in Montreal also face racial discrimination in housing, employment, and education and as a result, are eager to distinguish themselves from other Black Canadians. As my study will show, hierarchical gender role ideals in Jamaican society regarding motherhood, childrearing, and caretaking often prevail and are relevant for the deconstruction and analysis of migratory trajectories.

In Jamaica, gender separation exists in socializing practices in public and private spaces. In general, there are differences between female and male-dominated spaces, e.g., when one spends one's leisure time. About 2.9 million people live in Jamaica, half of them women. The crime rate is in the upper third of the world comparison. The willingness to use violence is one of the highest in the Caribbean region. Economic stagnation, political divisions, high unemployment, and a climate of unrest often lead to riots. The gap between rich and poor is immense. Although violence in Jamaica is a known variable, gender violence against women is a rather silent topic. Sexism is part of everyday life in the macho-dominated culture of the island. In Jamaica's post-colonial setting, many men believe they have to prove or act out their masculinity according to traditional gender roles (Hope 2010). Statistics show that men are the main culprits of intimate partner violence (Williams 2018). In general, they exercise the most oppression against both women and men. Still, the source of gender violence and sexism cannot solely rest on the shoulders of men. The latest UN study on violence against women in Jamaica confirms that many women misinterpret partner violence as a declaration of love (Williams 2018). Financial obligations, childcare, and a need for social security are further reasons that abuse is often overlooked. Shame and fear of talk or further attacks inhibit women from demanding their rights or seeking help. Nevertheless, economic or family reasons alone are only part of a cultural standardization of violence. Root cause analysis inevitably points to Jamaica's colonial history (Lafont 2000). The adverse effects of colonialism and slavery led to certain mentalities that belittle abuse and violence in society. Indeed, absolute control and, above all, sexual exploitation of Afro-Caribbean women were cruel elements of maintaining the colonial power that led to the emergence of a brown middle class. In this context, colourism established in Jamaica which still exists until today: a class-skin-colour-relationship that attributes more privileges, social status, wealth, and opportunities to fair-skinned people. This colourism still prevails in, e.g., female beauty ideals today. Looking at Jamaica's economic structure and employment rates, the significant role of women in society, albeit their vulnerable social status, is striking. Often women are the ones who undertake the lion's share of financial tasks in everyday life. The "housewives" policy of the post-emancipation era created a gender-specific division of labour that nurtured the untenable construct that women are the weaker gender (Lafont 2000). The patriarchal nuclear family, which had nothing to do with the kinship reality of the chiefly West African slaves, represented the ideal in the British colonies. To this day, this ideal, introduced by capitalist colonial society, has led to immense pressure to fulfil specific gender roles (not only in Jamaica) for women and men alike. However, household forms such as mother-father-child units living together under one roof are not the norm in Jamaica. Parents do not have to live together, nor be married, and not all people living in a household are necessarily relatives. A Jamaican household is instead an accommodation shared for economic as well as socio-cultural reasons. Female income is an essential component of maintaining the home, and, commonly, women lead the family. Although Jamaican women outdo their men in education and economic power and occupy many high positions, legal gender equality is, however, not a norm in everyday life. Therefore, women's life trajectories are often more constrained and concealed by gender related expectations of marriage, reproduction, domestic responsibilities, kinship obligations, and so forth.

In contrast, through migration, women can gain a higher level of personal autonomy in their receiving countries despite the prevailing gender inequalities on the job market (Foner 1985). Contemporary studies also highlight that migration can be empowering for women and transform them into breadwinners (see Platonova/Gény 2017; Gaye/Jha 2011). Olwig (2012), in her research on transnational Caribbean families, also uses a gendered analytical lens. She describes how Caribbean women find new and socially higher positions in their home countries upon return. By narrating successful returns and taking ownership of their biographies, women can counteract conventional gender norms in their respective cultures (Olwig 2012: 833). According to the *United Nations* (UN) *Entity for Gender Equality and the Empowerment of Women*,

> "Gender is not only about women. It is important to emphasize that the concept of gender is not interchangeable with women. Gender refers to women, men [and other gender groups], and the often unequal relations between them. [...]" (UN Women Training Centre Glossary 2017, n.p.).

Gender is crucial to any debate on the causes and consequences of migration; it influences reasons for migrating, who migrates, and why and where, how people migrate, what networks they use to secure their movement intentions, and the opportunities that are available for them at the destination country in relation to their country of origin. Gender also shapes risks, vulnerabilities, and needs. The tasks, expectations, connections, and power dynamics associated with being a woman play a significant role throughout the migratory process and in turn can be affected by migration in numerous ways. Accordingly, it is relevant to understand how gender interacts with migration and to find answers that explain these interactions.

The term intersectionality coined by Crenshaw (1994) refers to a theoretical construct that outlines how individuals can face discrimination and marginalization depending on overlapping and dynamic identity categories such as gender, race, and class. In the multidimensional process of 'othering' (Spivak 1985), these different forms of social differentiation are again relevant. Addressing processes of 'othering', hence, is not an alternative to acknowledging intersectional parameters, but it is rather examining the consequences of their combination in experiences of degradation and reduction (Jensen 2011: 65). Addressing this threshold of a person's experiences in society, the sociological attempt to intersect individual attributes may lead to valuable answers regarding societal positionality. This metaphoric umbrella prevents the analysis of individual experiences from being unidirectional. The original idea of intersectionality, however, needs an extension, as other aspects are relevant in an individual's experience as well. For Jamaican women in Montreal not only the geographic location, but also language regulations, the acquisition of Canadian citizenship as well as retirement and age are essential components of shaping personal forms of identity constructions. Especially since many returnees are ageing individuals and people of colour with dual Jamaican-Canadian citizenship and Canadian pensions. Hence, multiple social identity markers at a microlevel intersect with numerous social power structures and inequalities on a macro level. With this approach, micro and macro analytical perspectives work together in a distinctly empirical way on spatial zones as multi-layered (concrete as well as symbolic) configurations in an intertwined temporality. The acknowledgement of an expanded intersectionality approach in combination with processes of 'othering' works well with differing forms of methodological as well as theoretical concepts and thus, enhances the analytical perspective of this study.

In addition, intersectionality enables a different view on cultural identity, which juxtaposes attempts to create homogenous cultural containers of one shared monolithic Jamaican or Afro-Caribbean culture. For example, women may face sexism in the workplace, which for women of colour can also be associated with institutionalized racism. If a woman faces this double discrimination and is, e.g., over 50 years old, she is potentially more vulnerable than others are when it comes to her job security due to ageism. Although intersectionality traditionally applies to women, the phenomenon of an overlapping minority status affects persons of any gender. Originally, Crenshaw coined the term to express how institutions and governments ignore discrimination of immigrant women of colour; and to criticize both the feminist and anti-racist movements of her time. While intersectionality might not be flawless, e.g., viewing its uses in the contemporary social sciences and current civil rights movements such as "Black Lives Matter", the core idea of the concept helps to ensure that the overlapping challenges faced by women of colour who might belong to diverse and multiply marginalized groups are not being overlooked. Importantly, reviews of Spivak's theorization of 'othering' (e.g. Gingrich 2004) in which 'others' seemingly become objects of colonial processes of 'interpellation' need to be taken into consideration for Crenshaw's intersectional theory. Here, (migratory) agency as the capacity to act within and against social structures (De Haas 2009: 2) is again important. Insofar 'intersectionality' in combination with 'othering' can help to understand to what extent these multidimensional experiences would influence individual processes of cultural identity formations in everyday life (Jensen 2011: 66). However, the intersections suggested above are not the only vectors that are of critical importance in forming and reforming a person's identity and subjectivity.

The term identity is defined at the social level as a continuous individual process of "Sich-selbst-als-gleich-erleben"[3] (Schönhuth 2005). Accordingly, this means taking on various social roles as well as group memberships or recognizing those roles. In the process of forming one's identity from within, the development of one's own interests and needs through either appropriation or delimitation is implemented. The demarcation of oneself against, e.g., peers, parents or the socio-cultural appropriation of certain patterns of behaviour altogether constitutes the creation of a sense of self and others. Importantly, the identity formation process is constant and ongoing with differing external socio-cultural situations influencing and highlighting different parts of an individual's identity (ibid.). Insofar, non-essentializing collective identification processes can vary at the transnational level (diasporic consciousness) or at the national level when thinking about one's affiliation to specific localities (dislocation; migration; homeland) (ibid.). Essentializing processes can cause the fixation of exclusionary categories ('we' and 'them') resulting in differences within a group context. Ethnicity or ethnic identity (as a form of collective identity) can play a crucial role here as individuals carry feelings of belonging to an ethnic group with shared traditions, language, or religion, e.g., many Jamaicans in Canada keep their culinary traditions, Christian values or their Jamaican language Patois through which social belonging can be mediated. While culture points to socially produced and constructed categories of meaning, ethnicity deals with socio-cultural inclusion or exclusion. Further, identity constructions can be "hybrid" and reveal historical experiences (post-colonial, migratory experiences). Throughout their life courses, female identities form alongside these and other aspects such as the (maternal) family, cultural values, work commitments, religion, education, and migratory experiences. Here, Stuart Hall's writings on cultural identity contrasts with Crenshaw's intersectional viewpoint. He deconstructs identity as victimhood and the make-up of the Black subject as an identity 'in difference',

> "[…], as well as the many points of similarity, there are also critical points of deep and significant difference which constitute 'what we really are'; or rather –since history has intervened– 'what we have become' […] We cannot speak for very long, with any exactness, about 'one experience, one identity', without acknowledging its other side –the ruptures and discontinuities which constitute, precisely, the

---

3   Translation: To experience oneself as similar (Schönhuth 2005: Kulturglossar, http://www.ku
     lturglossar.de/index.html [10.02.20]).

Caribbean's 'uniqueness'. Cultural identity, in this second sense, is a matter of 'becoming' as well as of 'being'" (Hall/DuGay 1996: 225).

Hall utilizes the works of and draws relations between, e.g., Said, Gandhi, Garvey, Rastafarianism, China, and Jamaica, intending to contribute to existing identity discourses the notion of an identity 'in difference'. In his reference to cinematic representations, Hall defines his viewpoint by seeing strength in uncovering traits of difference and diversity for the analysis of Caribbean cultures as "more superficial differences, [is the truth,] the essence, of 'Caribbeanness', of the black experience. It is this identity which a Caribbean or black diaspora must discover, excavate, bring to light and express [...]" (Hall 1996: 223). In terms of identity constructions, it is hence crucial to remember that heterogeneity and contradictions are components of individual identity constructions within a particular socio-cultural setting. Feelings and emotions often accompany the construction of a distinct identity in contrast to 'others'. These affective traits can be either negative, e.g., regarding antipathy or positive as, e.g., the feeling of being at home ("Heimatgefühl"). Hence, cultural identity is about producing differences or coherence between others. Here, construction is a process in which diverse individual realities develop under the cognitive, social, situational and cultural conditions of an individual (Reckwitz 2001). The prerequisite for this construction is communication because the exchange of information creates reality. What follows from this is no real objectivity, but at best an inter-subjectivity of perception and action. As reality is subjective, individuals depend on the constant confirmation of their designs of reality. The notion of cultural identity has frequently been negatively connoted and used in conflictive situations, e.g., in the defence against foreign influences or the suppression of other cultures. Huntington's famous "Clash of Civilizations" scenario (Huntington 1993: 1) points to these negative characteristics of emphasizing and 'essentializing' cultural identities. In the context of globalization debates, people's resistance to foreign influences is also described (Breidenbach/Zukrigl 1998: 49f.). However, through increasing opportunities for intercultural contacts, globalization can offer an opportunity to broaden one's horizon and thus, cultural identity. No longer is a firm reference to the demarcated attitude or distinction of 'others' alone relevant, but each individual's condition for cultural identity taken into consideration (ibid.).

According to Sen, every person is "different in different ways" (Sen 2007: 33f.). Through analysing migration experiences and the adaptations of foreign goods and ideas, the phenomenon of the extension of one's own cultural identity becomes visible. The existence of a single identity is, according to Sen, an illusion (ibid. 17f.). According to Sahlins, people use foreign material to "become more like themselves" (Sahlins 1988 qtd. in Breidenbach/Zukrigl 1998: 57). Thereby, many indicators show how the global can be transformed and integrated into the everyday life of the local (Breidenbach/Zukrigl 1998: 61), i.e., individuals and societies find new ways to transform and domesticate the influences they are theoretically threatened by to impose them on their identity (ibid. 57). This is a thesis that once again contradicts the homogenization approach. The worldwide expansion of mass consumption, media, and institutions, therefore, cannot cause a cultural melting, but the replacement of an "old" with a "new" cultural diversity (ibid. 77). For cultural identity, this means that it is not in an enclosed frame of reference, but it is frequently hybrid and permeated by the diverse cultural interdependencies of the global world (ibid.). Migrants are in a continual process of identity development since they are forced to cope with the culture(s) they live in without being assimilated (Hall 1999: 435). However, the nation-state as an identification point often remains a valuable tool in the process of self- differentiation or of experiencing differences in the migratory process, whereby Jamaican migrants often stay connected to their countries of origin through, e.g., remittance sending practices, landownership or homeland travels.

5.3 Diaspora and Homeland

Closely linked to cultural identity is the term diaspora, which illustrates the usually involuntary dispersal of a people from a centre (or homeland) to multiple areas. Further, diaspora signals the creation of communities and identities due to histories and consequences of dispersal. The term derives from an ancient Greek expression that dates back to the biblical story of the dispersal of the Israelites. In the past, classical diasporic studies were often concerned with, e.g., the Jewish dispersion. However, over time diaspora research became both a conceptual and analytical framework to explain diverse practices of global mobility and community formation. Since the second half of the 20th century, anthropology has grappled with the definition, constantly shifting the interpretation and critiques. The notion of diaspora continues to be characterized by classical theoretical concerns of dialectics between homeland and host country, the relationship of nation-state and diaspora as well as contemporary politics of control over global population movements. Mainly, considerations about exile, refugees, and immigrants, form important pillars of diaspora research. Several related essays and books are worth mentioning.

As early as 1994, Clifford examined the concept of diaspora as a "traveling" term that withstands any exclusivist paradigm used to denote the complexities of transnational identity formation, by tracing and reviewing the currency of diaspora theory and discourse through the popular invocations of the diaspora in Black British and anti-Zionist Jewish scholarship (Clifford 1994: 302-338). His exposition and analysis of the term are probably the most cited across all scientific disciplines and relevant for this study. The term diaspora is widely used to describe the Jamaican cultural experience of being highly mobile and globally dispersed. In his essay on Jamaican diasporic culture, Zips (2003) identifies the Eurocentric usage of the term and aims for a more emic and Afrocentric perspective in looking at individual and collective Jamaican diasporic experiences. Viewing the dynamism of the term diaspora, he recognizes its creative, unfinished, and manifold potential (Zips 2003: 22f.). The Jamaican diasporic experience is, therefore, not only a unilineal process informed by past encounters of domination, dispersion, and exile, but also a process-oriented tool that exposes Black diasporic endeavours as an invariably evolving global network with ever new angles and network formations (Zips 2003: 32f.). As examples, he uses Jamaican socio-cultural export hits such as Reggae music, the Civil Rights activist Marcus Garvey, and the transatlantic dispersal of the Maroon rebels in the 18th century. In his book, "The Black Atlantic" (1993) Gilroy also observed that diasporic movement is not a singular lifetime event out of Africa or out of Southern peripheries, but rather a relational web of entangled regions of Black diaspora. Okphewo contextualizes in the book "The African Diaspora" the particularity of this continuously evolving network:

> "Given the fluid movement of persons and of ideas from both sides of the Atlantic, [...], it becomes clear that diaspora represents a global space, a worldwide web, that accounts as much for the mother continent as for wherever in the world her offspring may have been driven by the unkind forces of history" (Okphewo et al. 2001: xiv).

With quickened global connections and fluid diasporic formations, more and more individuals recognize that their living conditions are changing. Especially in the urban centres of the world, a "thrown togetherness" (Massey 2005: 149ff.) of encounters and conflicts reflects a post-colonial perspective of migration that exists between the socio-economic and political demands of the global North and global South. Therefore, scholarly research about migration, integration, and diaspora always has to take into account the inherent colonial presences (Keown et al. 2009). One methodological solution to discern this inherent presence is the research 'with' migrants, instead of the research 'about' migration. With this study, I attempt to engage in a research with migrants as research partners and a situational approach that understands and addresses the local as a product and place of the global (see Bojadžijev/Römhild 2014). As the World Migration Report (IOM 2015) shows, migrants play a significant role in local social spaces as well as in the development of urban centres since their various support networks and international exchange of resources provide support in their residential communities. The role of returnees as sources of knowledge about migration and as intermediaries is again relevant here. In general, it is crucial to keep in mind that the majority of people are stationary since their attachment to a specific place is stronger than the opportunities that migration offers. However, in order to understand the dynamics behind certain moves, the analysis of this study focuses on practices, imaginaries, and narratives that inspire individuals to move elsewhere. With this, each individual's migratory story connects with structural aspects that go beyond the commonalities of socio-economic 'push and pull factors'. Homeland as an important category of diaspora research is primarily representative of a place or locality where one feels at home, feels connected to or where one wants to live; opposite to the concept of homeland is, for example, the term foreign land. Home is hard to explain and thus is more an affective affiliation and emotional connection than anything tangible. To feel at home in a specific place or country, one does not have to have been born there. Homeland, therefore, is not necessarily 'bordered' or defined by nationality. In contemporary anthropology, the homeland is understood as an often-loose concept of self-representation that individuals use to symbolize their intact social and emotional relationship to a socio-cultural space (Greverus 1979 qtd. in Schönhuth 2005). As the ethnography will highlight, homeland can also be perceived as a metaphor for romanticized longing as well as a yearning space for connection and nostalgia.

By combining aspects of gender, identity and diaspora, it is necessary to be aware of the fact that throughout colonialism, the independence-era and the contemporary post-colonial period, European and North American countries have always had a socio-cultural impact on Jamaica. Simultaneously, Jamaican immigration and globalization enhanced processes of what Carolyn Cooper identifies as a "colonization in reverse" (Cooper 1995: 175), which highlights Jamaica's transformational power by influencing the 'centres' of the global North with its migratory people, their stories, language, music, and culture. These influences are especially important in a transatlantic context, where diasporic Jamaican people immigrate to a cosmopolitan and diverse city such as Montreal that in itself is already a culturally hybrid, urban space in which various 'world understandings' meet each other. Concerning Jamaican women, it is especially interesting to look at Euro- and Afrocentric assumptions when confronted with spatial and bodily practices. Throughout the writing process for this study, which examines various forms of experiences of blackness, it was always critical and vital to ask "from whose perspective" (Oyěwùmí 1997: 544) is the story told.

Ethnography

6 The City: Localizing Perspectives

The first part of the ethnography explores the general living conditions of Jamaicans in Montreal, settlement structures, and historically grown local circumstances. Vast cities and modern urban spaces are essential hotspots of the globalizing world bringing forth constant innovation. The global city, as Sassen (1991: 154) states, is a strategic site with a broad socio-economic structure. Additionally, a high level of cosmopolitanism characterizes the global charm of the city. Academic research therefore often locates global cities in the northern hemisphere, reflecting a Euro-centric or 'western' view about city development in general. Here, the promotion and representation of cultural diversity provide a positive image; a label that northern global cities like to wear. Cultural diversity and cosmopolitanism are essential features of Montreal. The city's bilingual charm represents internationalization. An article in Montreal's English newspaper *The Gazette* (Barone 2015), in the light of the city's 375th birthday, illustrates study results concerning Montreal's distinct character. The attributes given in the article enhance the positive connotation of diversity and multiculturalism.

My initial assumptions before traveling to Montreal were similar, reading about the city and the endless opportunities to have a great time in a bustling, urban area influenced by its many immigrants and international students, filled with cultural attractions. However, the article also shows that numerous residents define Montreal's charm as conflicted with identity politics and language controversies, contesting the use of diversity as a marketing strategy or mere attraction for tourists and foreigners. In understanding the broader context of this study, it is necessary to look into historical and political changes in Montreal that narrate, according to David Austin, a "myth" of Canadian cities as innocent and welcoming places for all (Austin 2013).

6.1 Controversies

Another view of Montreal is that of a divided city, historically separating its inhabitants into different categories in terms of language and national identity, i.e.,

French-Quebecers, Anglophones, Allophones, immigrant and ethnic categories (Simon 2006). My personal experiences led me to view the city as a place in which local Québécois people are a factual majority, but feel like a somewhat oppressed minority. Living in the city for a while as neither an Anglo- nor Francophone native speaker made me realize how defensive Quebecers are about their language in daily life situations, e.g., at the grocery store or in a restaurant. For example, ordering in English in a French-speaking restaurant in a designated French area of town can cause unforeseen difficulties and misunderstandings with the service staff. The city ranks amongst the largest French-speaking metropoles in the world. As a contrasting example, Paris has no significant Jamaican population (less than a thousand people) as the capital of France. Even though Montreal promotes bilingualism in terms of language usage in public spaces, it is still predominantly French.

In 1977, the province of Quebec implemented a monolingual French language policy (Busque 2015). After the introduction of this Bill 101, a massive exodus of Anglophones to other parts of Canada and the USA followed suit. The longstanding history of language controversies and nationalist tendencies also fuelled by the *Parti Québécois* still prevails in daily life situations, in the media and public discussions as well as in the memories of some of the older interlocutors of this study. In the online accessible Encyclopaedia Canada, Busque informs,

> "Despite the implementation and success of Bill 101 policies related to the francization of immigrants (the majority of whom now learn French before English), according to the 2011 census, one in five immigrants does not understand French in Québec. Further, several hundred francophone and non-anglophone families send their children to anglophone private schools every year with the object of enrolling them in the anglophone public (school) system" (Busque 2015: n.p.).

The ongoing language debates are problematic for many Anglophones, specifically for the interlocutors of this study, who describe the French language regulations as restrictive and divisive conditions on the job market and in daily life activities. Even if Simon suggested as early as 2006 (Simon 2006) that those clear-cut divisions are no longer the case, the challenge of spatial and cultural division prevails. Due to historically and politically grown normative dynamics in Quebec, a postcolonial atmosphere of uncertainty and changeableness exists. All women of this study mentioned incidences of overt and covert acts of racial discrimination in daily encounters, in the streets, in stores or at their work places. The representation and promotion of Montreal as a diverse and tolerant metropolis is a rhetorical modus operandi to cover up many internal problems, especially concerning racialization. Issues of past and present socio-political discourses about heritage, belonging and whiteness as well as historical occurrences in the province of Quebec have shaped the reality of many immigrants today. Negative experiences of interlocutors in Montreal concerning ethnicity and racializing tendencies infused by a history of language politics, nationalism and othering were omnipresent throughout the study.

6.2   Settlement Practices and (In)visibility

Jamaicans in Montreal live in diverse residential areas largely unnoticed by the local population even though they have strong relational ties with the city. Here, a difference in entering public and private Jamaican spaces exists, specifically from a linguistic and gender perspective. Male and female spaces are differently accessible. At the beginning of the field research phase, male-dominated spaces were accessed first. These are the more public events, e.g., concerts, dances, bars and restaurants. Especially, Afro-Caribbean musical contributions are seen as an 'exotic' and suppositional enriching cultural contribution to the city. Jamaican cultural entrepreneurs, i.e., food sellers or artists or musical performers, represent a positive image of the integration of Jamaican immigrants in the public and the media. For example, several radio stations play Jamaican music daily. Reggae music is commonplace and part of the cultural landscape. Besides, Francophone radio stations, for example, Radio Canada (radio-canada.ca) and Le Monde Bouge (CHYZ FM 94.3) periodically feature reports about Jamaica and Jamaicans in Quebec. The city has quite a number of cultural events, concerts and festivals (especially during summer), with bars, restaurants and nightclubs across town all displaying a positive "multiculturalizing presence" (Davis/James 2012) of Jamaican popular culture in Montreal. In the Canadian integration system, the concepts 'multiculturalism' and 'interculturalism' are relevant to describe immigrant entry. Bouchard and Taylor describe multiculturalism as a concept that "favors bilingualism, the protection of multiple cultural identities, and a 'mosaic' vision of society" (2008: 214). In contrast, interculturalism is a concept that "emphasizes social cohesion and integration through communal values, as well as the respect of differences and diversity" (ibid. 19-20, 118, 120f.). In their report, both authors viewed multiculturalism as being insufficient for describing the situation in Quebec since the term cannot address the wish of the province to conserve its French language and distinct national character. Language, which is a category of belonging for many societies, is also anchored in government documents produced to integrate new immigrants (MICC 2011: 2). The two paradigms were originally created to assist cultural groups in retaining and fostering their identity and in promoting positive encounters between cultural others. Since 1971, both concepts have been part of Canada's, and specifically Quebec's, dealing with immigrants. Cultural pluralism is the backbone of interculturalism, whereby cultural exchange between homogenous groups is postulated. The criticisms of both terms are similar. Walcott (2011: 24) argues, for example, that the only consensus about multiculturalism in Canada is that there is no consensus on its actual meaning. Above all, both terms are highly ethnocentric and imply that culture is fixed, creating island-like cultural groups that are demarcated. Galabuzi (2011: 64) illustrates that both concepts are essentializing culture, ethnicity, and race, which makes people's agency meaningless. James (2011: 195) comments on multiculturalism as a way of assimilating new immigrants or cultural minorities into the dominant English-speaking culture in Canada, which secures the state's national identity plan. The same can be observed for interculturalism and the French language policy in Quebec. Tremblay (2011: 56f.) sums up the critical debate by making clear that the distinction between both terms is solely political. Hence, multiculturalism and interculturalism can be seen as Canada's and Quebec's ways of defining ethno-cultural diversity and accommodation of culture. There is little consensus amongst scholars and government officials when it comes to either concepts (Chiasson 2012: 13).

For this study, it is necessary to acknowledge the existence of both terms as politically active concepts in the immigration and integration process; however, neither of the terms is useful to describe the existence of cultural diversity in general or to analyse the ways of life and customs of Jamaican people in past and contemporary cultures in Quebec. Aside of Jamaicans, a large number of various Afro-Caribbean immigrant groups reside in Montreal. Especially, Haitian migrants live in mainly ethnically dominated neighbourhoods in French-speaking parts of the city. Immigrant communities, which are transformed into demarcated domains, confirm the local opinion that people of colour mainly reside in marginalized, poorer suburbs. Jamaicans, in contrast, live among other Anglophones across the city; less recognized and in a way unnoticed by the Franco-Quebecer people of Montreal's society.

> "In the Montreal area, Haitians are among the most dispersed of the immigrant groups who tend to live in neighbourhoods dominated by francophones, whereas Jamaicans live in the most segregated concentrations, mainly in the city of Montreal itself" (Preston/ Wong 2002: 33).

This segregation reflects, on the one hand, the differing numbers of residents coming from Haiti (est. 129,010 in 2016) and Jamaica (est. 11,775 in 2016) (NHS 2016); on the other hand, the ability of Jamaicans to blend 'inconspicuously' into the physical landscape of Montreal. However, to argue that Jamaican immigrants are non-existent in the locals' minds because of the significant number of other immigrants is a wrong conclusion. The distinguishing feature of Jamaican immigrants in the city derives from their local settlement practices and space appropriation strategies that make community in a geographical sense less meaningful. In Montreal, their presence goes beyond spatially fixed terrains, and Jamaican spaces are segregated and scattered across town. Hence, there is no significant Jamaican residential concentration as in other cities such as Toronto, Vancouver, or New York City.

As a historically relevant urban contact zone for Jamaicans in Montreal the Little Burgundy neighbourhood needs to be discussed, which was an important entry point for the Afro-Caribbean community and the immigrant generations of the 1960s and 1970s. Little Burgundy became famous for its talented Jazz musicians Oscar Peterson and Oliver Jones (both born of Caribbean immigrants) from the bebop and post-bop era. Nowadays the once important neighbourhood has lost its former significance. The area bordered by Atwater Avenue, Saint-Antoine Street West, Guy Street, and the Lachine Canal was for decades –after the construction of the canal and the railway lines– a mostly Afro-Caribbean populated neighbourhood. Yet, current census data shows that they are no longer the majority population of the district (NHS 2016). Little Burgundy is evolving; the railway lines have lost their relevance, and so have the enterprises close to the Lachine Canal that formerly provided jobs and incomes close to where people resided. The dismantling of the historically relevant Negro Community Centre (NCC) building in 2014 is exemplary of this change. Gentrification in the form of townhouses has contributed as well (see De Verteuil 2004; Rose 2010). While the area still has a distinct, working-class atmosphere, the newer, more expensive housing meant the displacement of many traditional dwellers. However, the echoes of a past inextricably associated with the contributions of African and Caribbean people can still be found in certain areas of Little Burgundy.

Other known residential areas are, for example, Côte-Saint-Paul, Cartierville and LaSalle, Verdun's Crawford Park and the Norgate Project in Saint-Laurent. Côte-des-Neiges is another historically popular neighbourhood. As in Little Burgundy, gentrification changed the face of the neighbourhood over time. Services deteriorated, and proprietor agreements ensured that many buildings were sold or rented only to white people. Even though approximately one-third of Montreal's English-speaking Afro-Caribbean communities still live in the Côte-des-Neiges area, the middle class, and with it many Jamaicans have moved to the English-speaking areas such as Notre-Dame-de-Grâce (NDG), LaSalle, the West Island and the South Shore (Statistics Canada 2017). Without the need for concentration in an 'own' district, Jamaican immigrants maintain several cultural entities scattered across town. The invisibleness that causes Jamaican spaces in Montreal to be hidden or in a way 'particular', shows that a diasporic community can exist without the cliché of being bordered by a physical sector. The settlement practices of the majority of Jamaicans are oriented along the French-English language divide in Montreal. However, inclusion and exclusion to the community are hardly negotiated through the notion of geographic space, as residing in Montreal is much more connected to social networks. Strong social networks among women are the key to understanding important dwellings and places in the city of Montreal. In addition, close friends and family open a gateway to enter the city as an immigrant or newcomer. Since Quebec has a strict immigration policy, family reunification programs or interprovincial entries are the easiest migratory routes to Montreal, besides the existing, mostly female-centred, (health) care work programs. The dynamic interaction within this 'somewhat-invisible' Jamaican community requires the ability to be flexible and adaptable in accordance with a process of "inconspicuous assimilation". Because of this challenge, communal ties and people's social networks, instead of physical proximity, are fundamental factors to be able to manoeuvre oneself successfully through the city.

6.3   Montreal and Jamaica: Overlaps and Juxtapositions

During fieldwork in Montreal, I realized that my previous research in Jamaica certainly influenced my 'being' in the city as well as my anthropological encounters (Spülbeck 1997). Therefore, my subconscious mind-set, as well as subjectivism and perceptions of the interlocutors, need to be taken into account. During the initial research period, I realized, for example, that my assumption about a Kingston to Montreal, city-to-city connection was short sighted. Jamaican immigrants in Montreal hail from various parishes, mostly from the more rural areas of Jamaica, e.g., Manchester, Saint Elizabeth, Saint James or Clarendon. The reason for this "rural" immigration lies in historically grown economic demands for farm and seasonal workers in the province of Quebec. Here it seems as if fewer people from the 'urban' areas migrated directly to Montreal, especially in the early years of migration. This circumstance explains to an extent the strong 'traditional character' of Jamaican-run institutions in Montreal, especially in terms of their program and events. Leaving Jamaica for Canada certainly includes some organizational processing, e.g., in the capital city Kingston operated via visa services in the Canadian embassy or other administrative institutions, the reason or motive for emigration is, however, not necessarily connected to a previous life in Jamaica's urban centre. It has much more to do with the demands of Quebec's labour market, especially for the past 1960s and 1970s generations with resulting opportunities for a later family reunion. Hence, migration and integration are not unilineal processes. Migratory movements are affected by economic structures, historical developments as well as Jamaican socialization practices that embedded particular memories and layers of identity in the following generations (see chapter nine). Insofar, a noticeable difference in the encounters with first and second generation immigrant women concerning their migratory experiences and the children of immigrant families, third generation females who were born in Montreal, can be detected. For example, many of the children of the second generation chose to leave Montreal to go to English-speaking parts of Canada, the USA or the UK after they finished business training or university, despite having learned French as their first language in school. As research partners' family networks demonstrate, this is not an isolated case. Many young people leave the city of Montreal. Between 1981 and 2017, Quebec lost 229,700 people below the age of 45 to interprovincial migration, according to a new report published by the Montreal Economic Institute (MEI 2018). The younger Jamaican generation is seemingly more likely to leave Montreal after growing up. Due to labour shortages and, in the Jamaican case, because of discrimination in the labour market and experiences with racism, there is a significant exodus of the younger generation. As per law, people who do not identify themselves as white Francophone or white Anglophone are aggregated or categorized as so-called "visible minorities". For example, the visible minority status in the Canadian census explains whose languages are not recognized. Likewise, "Black" as its own category for ethnic origin raises considerable criticism by both post-colonial and feminist intellectuals (e.g. Ahmed 2007; Bhabha 1994; Gunew 2004). These scholars dispute that, without the need to acknowledge any socio-cultural differences, diversity becomes a bodily categorization that enhances linguistic and racialized divisions.

Moreover, I underestimated the time I would need for grinding into everyday processes, especially regarding field access. Accessing Montreal via the more publicly inclusive male spaces led to some initial hurdles. Overall, it was difficult to approach men without facing compromising situations. It was complicated to meet or, further, talk to men –aside from discussions surrounding their careers– or to build up trustworthy professional relationships in general. Men were willing to talk about work or hobby-related topics, but it was impossible to discuss private aspects of their lives openly. Even though I had some male gatekeepers, sufficient information about their individual lives and migration stories were hard to obtain. Possibly, fieldwork time was too short to gather further gatekeepers or more context knowledge of why it was so difficult to approach men as a female researcher from Europe. In contrast, on previous research stays in Jamaica, I had never faced any such issues that kept the fieldwork from progressing; even after a long reflection period, I am still unable to explain this juxtaposition. However, the Montreal-experience with male willingness to communicate often ended in flirtatious and inconvenient situations, in which I at times felt extremely uneasy or even vulnerable (see Johansson 2015). In the further process, I therefore decided to dismiss male research participants from the study as I was unable to delve deeper into necessary conversations and because sexist talk and macho postures of some men annoyed and limited me to an intolerable extent. However, male spaces supported my general access to the field and helped with, e.g., gaining orientation knowledge and in finding specific places that led to other sources and respondents.

Another aspect that I underestimated prior to the fieldwork was my assumption that Jamaican people in Montreal are more 'up-to-date' about local changes, events and occurrences in Jamaica, e.g., new musical events or infrastructural changes, which I initially used to build up conversations. However, I quickly had to realize that only a few people were informed about current happenings on the island since they had been disconnected from social life in Jamaica for a good amount of time. Here it is worth mentioning that men were overall better informed than women were. Regarding these preconditions, the analysis of specific, meaningful female Jamaican spaces shows where Montreal is "composed differently", where Jamaican and Québécois life worlds, as well as localities, overlap or juxtapose each other (Lehmkuhl et al. 2015: 14f.). In the following chapter, the term social space is introduced to determine the existence of a distinct Jamaican experience under such a geographical circumstance. Looking into the similarities and differences associated with a relational or spatial approach makes boundaries more visible. As Simon states, in Montreal "travel means translation" (Simon 2006: 4); therefore many interlocutors avoid going into the streets without a specific purpose, e.g., shopping, working or meeting someone. Simply going for a walk in the sense of strolling is inconceivable, especially for women of the older generation. Jamaican female spaces are here of specific relevance and important options of spending recreational and leisure time without outside interferences. Tracing the importance of space, place and homemaking helped me to understand the everyday sphere of Jamaican women's lives. Therefore, fieldwork was established and conducted in different meaningful places. For example, the homes of my research partners were important meeting spots for informal discussions, while other semi-public spaces together completed the mosaic of the women's life worlds in Montreal.

7 Womanhood: Female Spaces

This chapter provides illustrative depictions of daily routines and activities of Jamaican women in empirically relevant social spaces in Montreal. Matching the actual course of the fieldwork, the written ethnography delves deeper into the life worlds of the interlocutors by passing through various places, narratives, and practices. These stages unveil individual experiences and challenges within the metropolis. Social space as a core concept highlighted by Bourdieu will serve as an entry point into this discussion. "What exists is a social space, a space of differences, in which classes exist in some sense in a state of virtuality, not as something liable but as something to be done" (Bourdieu 1998: 12). Bourdieu explains how social actors occupy certain positions in social spaces through the distribution of economic and cultural capital (ibid. 15), which he identifies as the central organizing component of any social space. Space is a construct, modified and structured through principles. Social actors take their positions within spaces by using their (own) capital resources and strengths. Through combining different capital of various actors, social space becomes a processual representation of lifestyles, cultural practices, choices, preferences, and economic abilities. Because of this, according to Bourdieu, individuals form groups based on their "realized" commonalities that constitute clusters or "sub-spaces" within a broader social space (Bourdieu 1998).

Bourdieu's illustration of social space as a shared manifestation of a closely linked set of like-minded people is a useful approach for this study. However, in contrast to Bourdieu's considerations, geographical proximity of social actors is not the main component of communal interaction and relation in this study. Hence, physical distance or closeness are not the main components to determine self-positioning or identification within a group. The key spaces of Jamaican women in Montreal are, while being scattered across town, rather constructed via social networks of various social actors spanning across and beyond the urban environment of the city. The interpretation of practices related to the everyday geographies and symbolic spaces of the interlocutors in the city highlight this differentiation between interior and exterior, as well as the self-positioning of women, which is embedded in extensive spatial and virtual socio-cultural networks. Unlike Bourdieu's observation in Paris, these social spaces are constructed by cultural practices and structures that go beyond spatial closeness itself, reaching out to other areas in North America, the Caribbean, and the world. In conformity with Faist's statement, "transnational social spaces are combinations of ties, [...] that reach across the borders of multiple states. These spaces denote dynamic social processes, not static notions of ties and positions" (2000: 191). In Faist's typologies of transnational spaces, he identifies 'community' as a socially cohesive, committed group of people that continue to exchange or care for each other over time, e.g., via transnational kinship networks (ibid.). Here, the strong point of his analysis lies in the concept of "border-crossing expansion of social space" (ibid. 201) that goes beyond the nation-state of the host country. Drawing on Faist, Jamaican women have agency by not only building new social links and maintain existing ties in both the host and home society, but also by further switching or dispatching links to life worlds and expanding their social space to other localities. Space, therefore, is not a basic fact; it is much more, as Clifford clarifies an ongoing composition "[...] practiced by people's active occupation, their movements through and around it" (Clifford 1997: 54).

7.1   The Pop-Up Shop

I met 29-year-old Elisha at a regular event of the Reggae music scene on Plateau Mont- Royal, where I experienced her as an enthusiastic dancer and music lover. Even though she was born and raised in Montreal[1], Elisha feels an intense connection to Jamaica and talks incessantly about her dream of living there. She explains her engagement in the creative art and music scene with a form of spiritual consciousness: "When you live in Montreal, no matter if you are born here, you realize how Black you be. I was always an outsider because of my complexion" and further "music and art keep me alive; it gives me the energy to survive in this cold place". Elisha describes her school days as a severe period of facing xenophobia and racism through her environment, "I did not know I was different until they told me I was", she emphasizes. Therefore, Elisha's relevant relationships revolve around a small network of the local African and Caribbean diaspora. Hailing from different families and ethnic backgrounds, most of her female friends are also children of immigrants born in Montreal and similar in age group as well as educational background. Accompanying her to fashion shows and exhibitions as well as meeting her at her friends' musical events I was shown, how distinctively this network embraces their ethnic homeland ties. These attachments are not only a feature of Jamaican

---

1   Her grandmother came from Jamaica back in the 1960s as a domestic worker, followed by Elisha's mother a few years later. Elisha grew up in a well-off home, bilingual, fully immersed into the local environment and studied at Concordia University.

culture and Rastafarianism, but also of a Pan-African consciousness that is geo-graphically linked to specifically meaningful locations in Africa, e.g., Ethiopia or Egypt. In general, this network consists of women, while men were mostly present as partners or as friends at musical events. Together with her social network, Elisha is organizing fashion, health, yoga, and art exhibitions and events as well as meet-ings that serve to empower the young and Black (and female) generation around town. Their aim is to build communal ties against the experiences of daily racial-ization and exclusion, which they share, regardless of their familial ethnic origins.

Concerning the more traditional Jamaican community-based institutions that exist in Montreal, Elisha has no means of engaging with their events as she ex-plains: "They are handed down and old-school, you know bingo nights and eight-ies dances. They do not speak to us as a younger generation; they stay on their grounds amongst themselves. [...] We, we want people here to see us and change something!". One way of engaging with the younger network is visiting their pop-up shops. The shops that wander across town to different locations in periodic intervals bring together the same set of people recurrently, highlighting their cre-ative talent and their appropriation strategies in the establishment of their own spaces for communication and cultural exchange. African, Jamaican, and Egyp-tian symbols and icons together with other fashionable designs handmade from African fabric, for example, inspire Elisha's jewellery and clothing. "I am always happy to share my art with others. It is so important that people learn more about Africa or Black culture in general. Then people will have less prejudice. Sometimes it is hard to get white people to come inside the stores, but it's better in summer when we can build up outside", clarifies Elisha. Another "sister", also a woman of Jamaican heritage, makes Rastafari-inspired female clothing and sells natural cos-metics. Another acquaintance of Elisha creates and manufactures Black 'Barbie' dolls for children. These spaces are not private, but invite outsiders to visit and take part in the socio-cultural happenings by buying clothes, jewellery, or by shar-ing thoughts and having a conversation. In doing so, these spaces also revitalize vacant or abandoned places through the displaying of Afro-Caribbean pop-up cul-ture and at the same time serve as creative, income strategies against unemploy-ment. Most of Elisha's female friends, including herself, face a hard time gaining sufficient employment, although well educated. Similar to Clifford's (1994: 312f.) findings on Maghrebi diasporic consciousness, here women from different African and Caribbean backgrounds unite at shared pop-up shops. These coalitions do not only ground in shared racial and economic marginalization, but also stem from a shared history of colonial and post-colonial exploitation. The positive connotation of 'Africa' or 'African symbols' thus strengthens shared diasporic consciousness and solidarity within the network.

Temporariness is another essential factor in maintaining cultural as well as commercial activity. The women practice a rotational system of responsibility as

Elisha explains: "This week it is my turn to take care of our pop-up so that I can keep a share of all things sold, next week it is somebody else's and so forth". The temporal and spatial flexibility of pop-ups seemingly creates networks of participation, sharing and discourse. During the fieldwork in Montreal and beyond, Elisha's friends' network had numerous temporary stores across the city, which assisted them in maintaining a livelihood, and a socio-cultural space that fostered community and sisterhood. While pop-ups are not a unique phenomenon to Montreal, it is valuable to acknowledge conflicting ideologies that lie in these temporary spaces. Through flexibility and resourcefulness, Afro-Caribbean (mostly female) artists such as Elisha found a way of sustaining themselves in the urban environment of the city.

After Elisha finished her Master's degree, she made every effort to find a job in Montreal, two years long, without success. Assured at job interviews, she never had a real chance or access to an upscale opportunity because of her skin colour, affected her to view life in Montreal as negative, robotic, materialistic, and stressful; a place negatively connoted, intolerant, and filled with racial discrimination. Jamaica, in contrast, personifies anything positive: great music, fashion and food, great weather, inspired by her childhood memories and glorified as a romantic, stress-free living space. Hirsch and Miller describe the essentializing of the homeland as a practice of "spiritual familiarity" that generates a longing for return (Hirsch/Miller 2011: 112f.). For Elisha the work at the pop-up shop is an escape from the city as such, a safe environment, in which she explores her positivity about Afro-Jamaican culture and blackness in general. Besides, she can indulge in her passion for alternative art and shares communion with other Afro-Caribbean women, which creates a feeling of togetherness and stability.

Moreover, the pop-ups travel from time to time with their exhibitors to other cities, e.g., to Brooklyn (New York City) where Elisha and her arts network connect to other like-minded women who run similar pop-up shops. They exhibit together on Afrocentric or Afro-Caribbean musical events and engage in a border-crossing social network of conscious, Black women who all 'struggle' to make a living in North American centres. The creation of these pop-up spaces produces 'difference' within the city of Montreal by highlighting Afro-Caribbean culture and by giving diverse women of colour a voice and visibility in the city. A space in which heterogeneity, discourse and various self-understandings help shaping individual identity constructions and belonging of the younger generation within the setting of Montreal. As Hall states "more superficial differences, is the truth, the essence, of 'Caribbeanness', of the black experience. It is this identity which a Caribbean or black diaspora must discover, excavate, bring to light and express [...]" (Hall 1996: 223). These young people chose to not exclude themselves, but invite outsiders to buy, to share and to ask questions about Afrocentric products and events. These spaces differentiate less between the notions of 'othering', but instead try to create a dialog in the historically and politically troublesome grown relation of post-colonial Montreal with Black diversity.

7.2 The Salon

Though Elisha actively engages in her art network, her sister Debby's salon lastly gave her a substantial income opportunity that pays her monthly bills. Debby's beauty salon is another important locality for Jamaican and Afro-Caribbean women to participate socially, economically, and culturally. The beauty salon is a site of collective bonding and a social space of constructing professional as well as personal relationships by and for women. The small space, which is located in her sister's private home, consists of a manicure and pedicure station, a hair salon and a make-up store that also sells hair products. Debby's salon is an important community institution in Montreal, but before I realized how meaningful this place was, I firstly was astonished by the ways in which clients negotiate their styles and wants, although I assumed prices were fixed as they were listed on a poster that hangs in the entrance area. Negotiations between Debby and her clients are essential components of women's interactions at the salon. Mediation between personal preferences and potential monetary investment as well as the stylist's professional expertise, creativity, and advertising potential (meaning that clients advertise for the hairstylist by wearing her creations) intermingle. For example, women use different mimics, gestures, expressions, questions, and often jokes (or sarcasm) to com municate their preferences. Even though many of these discussions seem to show indecisiveness or lack of knowledge, i.e., the need for consultation with Debby or Elisha, customer narratives signify negotiations of identity. Because of this, different debates can occur between commonly accepted hair practices, e.g., the installation of the so-called 'good hair' and Afrocentric hairstyles such as dreadlocks or afros. The choice of hairstyle gives hints about who the person is or wants to be, for that matter. At times, the extensive counselling sessions also decide about Debby's ability to accommodate her clients adequately. Through their clever and ironic questioning techniques, proficient patrons know how to negotiate the 'real' final price of a hairstyle. One client, for example, smiled at me and said, "If you don't bargain, it's your own fault!". Debby, who took over the hair salon and clientele from their mother, is one of the popular beauticians in town. Accurate and passionate as she is, she caters to her clients by ever informing herself about the newest styles, whether hair, nails or lashes and the newest gossip about celebrities and about 'what is going on' around town. To observe Debby negotiating client demands, e.g., about material resources (how much hair, which type of hair, which additional styling products), price and aesthetic visions, offered a way of understanding women's local discourses surrounding race, class and gender.

Many of her clients prefer artificial looks, i.e., long pointed nails, fake lashes, and colourful weave-ins (a technique of sewing in hair extensions), while others want to have a "natural look" with hair colours and textures matching their individual type. Furthermore, she also caters to clients who do not wear any artificial hair at all and come to take care of their 'real' hair, e.g., interlocking locks. From the beginning of fieldwork, I was spending hours at Debby's salon and involved in helping whenever a hand was needed. It felt more 'natural' to Debby to incorporate me in small-scale activities as, e.g., unwrapping hair, sorting in newly arrived products or making coffee, than to have me sitting around and "stare at people" in an already over-crowded shop. In general, people do not like to be stared at, which is prevalent in Euro-Canadian culture. In Jamaica, however, I experienced staring as a quite common practice, whether people try to figure out where someone is from or if they know the person. Maintaining eye contact is therefore not a taboo. This was definitely different in Debby's salon as I was a total (and white) foreigner. Debby was keen to keep the distraction as low as possible. During the time at the salon, she engaged me in activities, so I would not attract unnecessary inspection. If someone asked about me, which happened a few times, she usually referred to me as "some extended family member visiting from the USA". When final arrangements regarding the preferred styles are made, conversations turn around to topics such as living conditions in the city, fashion, events, food, men, children and homeland ties to Jamaica from a female perspective. No one sits facing their mirror, all chairs point sideways or towards the centre of the room, which makes it easier to engage in conversations. After a two-hour nail-procedure or a daylong hair braiding session, one hears quite a lot, from the latest gossip to personal stories. Even though the initial 'negotiation ceremonies' give reason to believe otherwise, Jamaican women stay with their hair and nail stylists as they do with their tailors or favourite pastors. In Jamaica, women wait for hours or go far distances to see their valued beautician. However, disappointment in a 'style' can lead to not returning. Consequently, the salon tries to keep patrons coming back with a high level of service, excellent work and of course music, the newest gossip, talk of fashion and men. Maintaining an active client base is a complicated affair as the business structure is highly informal and works through recommendations. Here, Debby's salon benefits from a "supply and demand" structure in Montreal where fewer locations are available compared to English-speaking metropoles such as Toronto or New York City.

At the beauty salon, Elisha encounters all different types and generations of immigrant women who come from various social classes and origins and have differing migratory experiences. Unlike her Afrocentric arts network, but indicative of the majority of Jamaican women, here various ideals of beauty –highly influenced by the looks of fashion models in the media or stars like US-singers Beyoncé or Rihanna– are at work. "Nobody here wants to hear something about 'back to the roots' that is stale and the men wouldn't find it great either." Elisha says sighing. To get one's hair done 'properly' (meaning, i.e., weaving, braiding or straightening it) is a commonality amongst both Jamaican and Afro-Caribbean women. While some do it every week, others only do it on special occasions. The salon in Montreal is a simple continuation of this tradition in a new locality.

Every hour inside the salon has its distinct feel and a different crowd. When the shop first opens in the morning, retired women in their golden years make up the crowd. The salon offers a socio-cultural space, where females can encounter understanding, sympathy, and like-minded people. The salon facilitates female bonding without interference. Debby generally likes to speak about her childhood memories with her clients, about her mother having the little, unregistered hair salon in their old apartment in Little Burgundy nearly 40 years ago. The older women who used to go to Debby's mother back in the days then rekindle into memories about the "good old days" in Little Burgundy. Times when the neighbourhood had "soul" (mostly by referring to music and working culture), "the community was less criminal", and "less divided between rich and poor", Anglophone and Francophone or different cultural groups. The elders especially are concerned with the fact that fewer and fewer spaces are available to gather and socialize. The low economic development in the Little Burgundy district and the lack of community services is a big challenge, primarily for older women who, as one of these regular patrons' states, "have to go far for a bag of rice". The devaluation of the community is an outcome of many violent incidents that happened in the past years and the fact that Black youths cannot find jobs inside or outside of the area. For Debby and Elisha's mother, who now is retired, doing hair was one of the ways to survive without relying on an employer. "She could build up a clientele, we could live [...] and I followed in her footsteps", she says, skilfully sewing curled strands of hair on a woman's head by using a long half-moon shaped needle.

During the day, many people pass through the shop to either have a short conversation with Debby, make appointments, deliver food from Jamaican restaurants for clients or drop off flyers and tickets for events and parties, which are also sold in the salon. Over time, I understood that Debby not only lived in the same house above her salon, but also engaged several Jamaican people, besides her employees (delivery people from restaurants, music personnel and Uber taxi drivers) into her daily work routine. When the afternoon arrives, many workers come from their shifts to have a little "after work" chat or have their nails done while talking over coffee. "You got to have that feel for your people, you have to meet them at their respective phase and place", explains Debby. Doing hair is far more than merely negotiating styles, mediating prices or sharing gossip; it is instead a location-based or rather a 'hair-based' community work. Through her beauty work, advice and 'open-ear' Debby has created a sanctuary space in the city and an anchor point for many Afro-Caribbean women. "Montreal is a small place when it comes to getting your hair done", one client explains. "Sometimes on my way from work, I stop by here to get the latest news", she continues. The statement indicates that the salon is also a significant site for the sharing of local information. In a city where activities can be limited for immigrant populations and senior citizens in particular, with most activities commonly being offered in French (therefore inaccessible to Anglophones) or solely being offered at too expensive prices for less affluent residents, Debby's salon presents an exception. The beauty salon is an example of the maintenance of cultural practices in a new locality that is within itself, inside the shop –in the composition of the furniture, of music played, of hairstyles created, of nails designed or of conversations spoken– a social space equal to other hair salons in Jamaica. Women looking for a great style and treatment or the fellowship come to Debby. As a result, the beauty salon offers an open and inclusive socio-cultural space, where women can encounter understanding, sympathy, and like-minded people.

Elisha's daily work at the salon and the continuous listening to the clients' discourses also continue to influence her perception about Montreal and Jamaica. "They constantly complain about Montreal and talk about Jamaica here and Jamaica there, but none of them would go back home", she assures me. On a Tuesday afternoon, Elisha asks the 40-something woman whose hair she is working on, about going back to Jamaica and triggers an immediate discussion in the salon: "Go back where, girl? Yuh cyan go back with nutten!"[2] The woman, who is one of her patrons, receives great agreement in the salon. "If you go who will do my hair?" the woman asks sharply, turning the indistinct chatter into a burst of collective laughter. Debby looks at Elisha with a mimic of wide-open eyes, bites her lips and shakes her head barely noticeably in an effort to set Elisha to stop this undesirable topic from going any further. Here, Elisha faces considerable opposition against her wish of living permanently in Jamaica as most of the regular customers tell her that she is 'foolish' in thinking she as a foreign-born 'pickney'[3] could go back and navigate herself on the island without facing problems. While Elisha is firmly holding on to her dream of going back to Jamaica, the "negativity", as she calls the comments of her customers, at times affects her. Elisha's social network of art friends, peers from school days and the university is, in comparison to her sister's, that of a younger, diverse generation, hence, more extensive in terms of, e.g., origin, occupation or education level. In contrast to her sister Debby, Elisha not only stayed within the "zone" and therefore has individual, yet varying images and aspirations that go beyond the common perspectives of the women she encounters at the salon. Africa or Jamaica as idealized and valued places amongst her peer group, i.e., concerning identity concepts, reveals the younger generations' grappling with identity politics and cultural symbolism. However, 'back to the roots' seems to serve in many

---

2   Translation: You cannot go back to Jamaica without any economic stability!
3   Translation: Jamaican Patois for child/ children.

instances more as an idealized identity umbrella or image and less as an actual materialization.

Later that day, during a break, Debby scolds her younger sister in the small salon kitchen: "You know how far this lady comes each time to get her hair done, stop chat foolishness in mi shop!"[4] Debby created a social space that nurtures her not only economically, but also socially and culturally. She is resourceful, successful and gets recognition for what she does from other Afro-Caribbean people, men and women alike. Her daily life and work experiences combined with the history of her mother's hair salon strengthen her belonging and feelings of attachment to Montreal and her "people" as she calls her clients and employees. With her salon, she built a community institution that nurtures people socio-economically, and that ranks her in a high social position within the wider community. Even though the sisters come from the same family background, their present-day economic and socio-cultural realities shape ambiguous perspectives of 'being and belonging' to Montreal and the Jamaican homeland. As Stuart Hall describes: "Cultural identity, [...], is a matter of 'becoming' as well as of 'being'. It belongs to the future as much as to the past. It is not something that already exists, [...]" (Hall 1990: 225).

7.3   At Home

When Ms. Brown opens the door, she surprises me with her appearance: Dressed in home wear, without any make-up, without one of her wigs and barefoot, she looks completely different from our first meeting. When I take off my shoes in front of her doorstep, she rushes back inside her two-and-a-half room flat where everything is prepared for my visit. "Nothing fancy", she points out while inviting me into her living room, which I later identified as the largest and most representative room, furnished extensively with heavy dark wooden furniture, a plastic-wrapped, checkered sofa, bulky golden silk curtains, colourful Caribbean décor and pictures of her children and family members. The oval dining table with its four small, upholstered chairs standing along the outside wall, which is adorned by a large, coloured 'sacred heart illustration' of Jesus Christ. Being at Ms. Brown's I always felt as if I had transitioned into another world and time. The moment I entered through the front door, I felt as if I was in a "little Jamaica" in Montreal.

Initially, I met Ms. Brown at a Sunday church service in Notre-Dame-de-Grâce, where I ended up going with an insisting friend. Christian religion or church service is an integral part of Jamaican society and everyday life, particularly among women. The Guinness Book (of World Records) declared that Jamaica

---

4   Translation: Do you know from how far this woman comes each time to get her hair done, stop talk about these crazy issues in my salon!

has the highest number of Christian churches per square mile with more than a hundred different denominations, e.g., Seventh Day Adventist, Pentecostal or Church of God. Hence, taking part in the Anglican Church service was highly informative for me. The attendance was small (maybe 60 attendees) for the 11 a.m. service, and Ms. Brown was among other well-dressed Afro-Caribbean women of her own age group. The congregation was a mix of diverse people many hailing from Jamaica, Bahamas, English Guyana, or Trinidad and Tobago. Additionally, a smaller number of elderly and middle-aged white people were present. The entire service was held in English and was joyful worship of call and response with an enthusiastic minister; singing and clapping, which resembled church services I had previously attended in Jamaica. During our following meetings, it became clear that participation in the local worship community played a significant role for members of the West Indian community. Especially for older women who, like Ms. Brown, have many friends and activities based in church. For example, many recreational activities, such as day trips and women's gatherings, but also community-based events are organized or at least discussed through the friends' network at church. A strong faith played a significant role in Ms. Brown's up-bringing. Especially the Christian nurturing of her grandmother and mother were sources of support and endurance throughout her entire life. Her childhood socialization in Christian values, e.g., attending church service every Sunday, studying the Bible, participating in the youth choir and youth meetings helped to instil important religious morals that are substantial for her life today. Church and education were the cornerstones of her upbringing in Jamaica's countryside. Ms. Brown's grandmother not only made sure that she attended church services, but also that she excelled as a student in school. Even though material assets were small and lunch money and textbooks were a rarity, the commitment her grandmother made for Ms. Brown's schooling served as a powerful motive for her to become a voluntary worker and a geriatric nurse. "My grandmother taught me one important thing that I still live by today 'reap what you sow my child, reap what you sow'", Ms. Brown remembers.

The nursing profession is historically and at present in high demand in the province of Quebec; and besides the domestic work sector, it has been the easiest way for female workers from the Caribbean to obtain permanent residency since the 1960s. The *Canadian Nurses Association* (CNA 2009) predicts that, if healthcare demands continue to rise, the country will need 60,000 nurses to fill its labour shortage by 2022[5]. One of the main reasons cited for this shortage is an ageing population that is increasingly in need of health services. As one of Ms. Brown's

---

5   Note: Although this study was written before the worldwide outbreak of Covid-19, this labour shortage in the healthcare sector became an increasing and persistent problem during the pandemic.

work colleagues puts it: "These people here, they rather take care of their dogs and cats [...], none of them want to take care of their elders, they just put them in old folks' homes, so we do the work [...]. We fill the gap!". The moral dimension beyond this brief, but essential statement shows a strong component of Jamaican culture –the morally accepted, hence, "proper way" of dealing with family– that transcends into their local lives in Montreal. In Jamaica, taking care of elderly parents or in-laws is still mostly done in the private sphere of the home. "Once a man, twice a child" Jamaicans say and caring for the elders in the family is a common practice, which many believe will be highly rewarded through blessings from God or 'good karma'. Caring commitments, according to Reynolds (Reynolds/Zontini 2006: 8f.), cross the boundaries of blood, marriage, culture, residence, and country and are significant components of successful migration stories of geographically dispersed families. Even though Ms. Brown worked in her profession throughout her entire life and often stresses her gratitude for having a secure job that pays well (especially compared to often 'semi-legal', private domestic care), she hardly speaks about work in general. The discrimination she suffered at work during her life is a vulnerable spot in her biography. Therefore, Ms. Brown prefers to remain silent about specific events and often gives only meaningful hints that suggest racism as the main problem. Alternatively, she makes use of Jamaican proverbs such as, "If yuh cyan get turkey, satisfy with John Crow"[6] or makes a gesture as if she were locking her mouth with a zipper to stop the topic from being discussed.

After two marriages and raising three children –her two sons migrated to the USA, and her daughter lives with Ms. Brown's paternal sister in London– Ms. Brown managed to return to Jamaica in 1993 through one of her church projects. Even though her children are independent and moved to different countries, she is in close contact with them via digital communication (mainly WhatsApp or Skype). She has been living alone since her second husband died and her social network primarily consists of her female friends and colleagues in Montreal. Additionally, she is in constant contact with extended family in North America, the UK and in Jamaica. Despite great distances or phases of not seeing them, the care and preservation of transnational kin ties represent not only an emotional connectedness to family and friends but also a socio-cultural insurance policy that facilitates return migration in the event of, e.g., old age or sickness (Levitt 2001; Burman 2002).

While waiting for Ms. Brown in her living room, I notice an older, slightly yellowed photograph, which shows a typical two-story Jamaican residential home in a lush green garden. Before I had a chance to ask about the picture of the house, she continues to utter her despair over the closure of her beloved church. "It is really

---

6   Translation: If you cannot get turkey to eat, satisfy with vulture (John crow is a vulture bird indigenous to Jamaica). Meaning: Make the best of a bad situation, and be content with what you have.

time now you know [...], no after dem have the nerves to lock down our nice church, no what a shame, what a shame"[7]. Eating at Ms. Brown's apartment became a crucial part of our regular meetings. In her apartment, she was able to unwind and for example, show me private photos of her children and family. One time she even took her old wedding gown out of the wardrobe while reminiscing about her second marriage. Ms. Brown's second husband, who was the love of her life, passed away shortly after her daughter was born and left her with his life insurance from which she could live and raise the children. After his death, she never married again and drew substantially on her female networks to help raise the children and engage in community activities. Not being able to grow old with him also adds to her reasons of leaving the city. Ms. Brown further preferred to meet at her apartment since she felt more comfortable talking about her life in her private space without the interference of others. By serving food, she could not only engage in being a great host to her guest, which is a common experience for anyone visiting Jamaican households, she was also glad to talk to someone "outside of the box" as she called it. "Since you say, you nah eat no meat [...]" she chuckles, while talking from her kitchen, "mi cook some food fi yuh still"[8]. I mutter something like 'thank you' while I cannot take my eyes off the photograph of the house. I try to ask again, while she puts a fully loaded plate of Jamaican food and a glass of reddish fruit punch in front of me. "Eat! Enough questions for now", she commands.

Practically, Ms. Brown never went out to the city to spend her leisure time, e.g., in a coffee shop. The only exception was when she would go to the salon to get her hair done occasionally or purchase something, which rarely happens since Ms. Brown does not want to spend a lot of money. Every move inside the city has a purpose, e.g., going to church, meeting friends somewhere specific, going to work or buying groceries, specifically in winter when "it is so horrible outside" as she once said. After meeting Ms. Brown in church, I was invited to her bingo and quiz nights, where I spent long hours of leisure time with older people, learning about the 1970s in Montreal, but also about hard work, achievement, endurance and social networks based on the religious community. At the beginning of November, we had another get-together at the women's club, a Jamaican Canadian community project founded in the late 1990s by a friend of Ms. Brown's mother. This friend, an over 90-year-old woman, decided to retire as its head and dissolve the organization in 2016 after she was unable to find a successor. The organization, which had received multiple awards, encouraged the full participation of women from "visible minorities" into everyday Canadian society. Despite the closure, the women still meet and organize events on an irregular basis. Since most of Ms. Brown's 'girlfriends' are

---

7   Translation: The time to leave and go back to Jamaica has come, especially after they decided to close our church, what a shame.

8   Translation: Even though you said that you do not eat meat, I prepared a meal for you.

in their late fifties to early seventies and retired[9], soon to be retired or have left Montreal, she is now more than ever concerned with plans of leaving the city for good. She reignited her decision in October when rumours became public, and her beloved church closed in the following year (2017). These incidents, together with the dissolving of the women's club, ultimately forced her to plan a trip to Jamaica to find out if she would be able to return there in the near future. Another necessary closure took place at the beginning of 2016 when the long-term chairperson of the local Jamaican Canadian association retired after over 30 years of community service and a younger director took over.

One afternoon, Ms. Brown explained how she came to Montreal. She was one of the so-called "barrel children"[10], knowing her mother mostly from presents and occasional phone calls from overseas while she remained in Jamaica with her maternal grandmother. In the 1970s, after her mother had finally made enough money to send for her and her sister, Ms. Brown had to obey, even though she never wanted to leave her grandmother and the little farm that she recalls as paradise. The unwanted migration to a foreign land and to a mother who had become a stranger to her was a significant break in Ms. Brown's life course and an essential point in our conversations because she talked about it often. In Montreal, her mother had a small one-room apartment in Little Burgundy, surrounded by Jamaicans and other immigrants from Africa and the Caribbean. Without any previous knowledge, she had to learn French in school[11] and was engaged in the household as well as work responsibilities to help her mother as best as she could. By that time, her mother worked as a domestic, nanny, and housekeeper in three different Canadian families. The women's club back then was an active association, which helped especially single women with children through a "food-clothes-shelter" and organizing of communal events. Despite Ms. Brown's desire to leave the hard-working hours and a feeling of unfamiliarity with the environment, she describes the early 1970s as a glorious time in Montreal. The Black Power movement from the United States had found a second home in the city, propelled by the *Sir George William protests* at Concordia University in 1969, while at the same time a dazzling Jazz music scene evolved. Beats crossed with other forms of Afro- Caribbean music, and Jamaican sounds enveloped the city. In the mid-1970s, her younger sister turned eighteen and immediately returned to Jamaica since, according to Ms. Brown, "She could

---

9   Note: Typical retirement age of registered nurses in Canada is at 65 years.

10   Note: Barrel children is a term that describes children who stay behind with close family members, mostly grandparents or aunts/ uncles until they get the call from their parents to migrate after a certain amount of time. Over the years, they often receive material presents and goods (food, clothing) sent in barrels by their parents from North American metropoles. These barrels often replaced 'direct' care (see further Crawford-Brown 1999).

11   Note: In Jamaica, English and Spanish are taught in school.

not deal with the cold". At that time, she started to be an active member of the local Jamaican association (founded in 1962) and other church and community projects, while working several different jobs to survive and starting her professional training as a geriatric nurse. Simmons and Plaza (2006) suggest that in the metropolitan areas especially the second and third generation form socio-cultural communities based on their shared identification with certain music, traditions or religious belief systems from the Caribbean region.

Hence, the female bonds formed in church are not just loose ties. These women are not just acquaintances; they are long-term companions who worked, prayed, and lived together. Church serves as a social space where they met, where they became friends and benefitted from the community outreach back in the days when they had a small income. Particularly church networks and the social connections into the local community institutions and her later engagements in local projects with other Jamaican and Caribbean women gave her, as she describes, a feeling of belonging and home in Montreal. Additionally, the simultaneous care for her family and the remittance sending to Jamaica kept her personally closely and simultaneously tied to the island, not only in terms of an emotional, imaginative connection, but also in terms of financial and social obligations and belonging (cf. Levitt 2004). King and Christou argue in their transnational framework that migrants keep a combination of "economic, affective, and symbolic ties usually based on principles of reciprocity and solidarity" (King/Christou 2014: 5). The communicative connections to her family and her remittance sending practices kept her homeland linkages alive and nurtured her desire to return home, while at the same time, being engaged and fully settled in her local life in Montreal gave her a sense of belonging. Here the idea of 'being and belonging' (Glick Schiller/Fouron 2001) in various localities at the same time is again relevant.

Moreover, the local involvement in Montreal embedded her into a diasporic community with various Afro-Caribbean people. Besides her job, Ms. Brown never had much or even avoided intimate contact with people from Quebec. Hence, she conserved her Jamaican cultural values and belief systems over the years. The current changes in Montreal, especially in terms of critical spaces for the older, more traditional Jamaican community reveal a phase of transition with past generations retiring or dying out and new generations taking over or mediating their own socio-cultural spaces and belonging. Since the 1990s, a large number of Anglophone elders in Montreal faced the out-migration of young Anglophones to other parts of Canada or North America. Many ageing individuals such as Ms. Brown wish to return to their homelands, where they built or bought properties, after receiving their Canadian pensions. Since the late 1980s, Ms. Brown had been sending remittances to support her family back home and to rebuild the house that she inherited from her grandmother. This form of "cultural remittances", a term coined by Reynolds (2008), is a means of developing ownership structures in Jamaica. The practice of accumulating social capital in the homeland strengthens not only ethnic identity while residing in another country, but also shows the importance of moral obligation and ongoing commitment to family and kin and to leave paths open for temporary or permanent future returns (Plaza 2008: 5).

7.4   Montreal or Toronto?

Carol, a university graduate in science, filled with enthusiasm and hope for her new life abroad, arrived in Canada from Jamaica in 1966. Immigration was an option for her. "There was no personal force in my homeland", she explains, and if she had chosen to remain, she probably would have had a high position, living a very comfortable life as she puts it. After almost 40 years of living in Canada, she still reflects on her place in her so-called "adopted country". At first, she lived in Mississauga for several years, but another job offer brought her to Montreal in the late 1980s, before she decided to move back to Toronto's suburbs in 2015. In Toronto, Carol and I met in early December 2016. "I was determined to accept any fair challenges that came my way, and to make a positive contribution to society. [...] I started working as a teacher, continued my education, and settled down to raising my son. I felt at ease with my choices. Some years later, a professional friend visiting from Jamaica expressed that although she thought life for me was good in Canada, she could not live here as a 'second-class citizen'. I denied that I lived as a second-class citizen, but every so often I think about her remarks".

As Carol continues talking about her experiences in Montreal, she primarily reflects on overt and covert acts of racial discrimination. The act of racialization is a way of 'othering' through giving racial meaning to a previously racially unclassified relationship, social practice, or group in terms of exclusion, marginalization or discrimination (Omi/Winant 2014: 105-106). Omi and Winant argue that despite the problematic nature of the process of racialization "it should be apparent that there is a crucial and non-reducible visual dimension to the definition and understanding of racial categories" (ibid. 111). As one example, the first apartment she had rented in Westmount had to be sublet to a local Canadian and white friend. After she filed an official complaint about the situation, she received a letter of apology from the owner who, after five years, finally offered her the flat. Another time she faced a problem with her son's schoolteacher who was failing him in English. After she offered to review his English assignments, being a teacher herself, her son's marks immediately changed from 'F's' to 'B's'. As a college instructor, she recalls several incidents of Black students telling her of discriminatory acts in and outside the classroom, especially bullying and receiving lower grades although fulfilling the same requirements as other white students. "These things happen. I never gave up my professional career because of discrimination, but I often felt that since I was not part of the 'old boy' network, being an outsider, a Black immigrant woman, I am at a disadvantage and doubly denied certain opportunities. Some people think that being female and Black, I have twice the opportunities. [...] I disagree with this", she states. While living in Montreal, Carol frequently faced hurdles due to career and work-related racism. The existence of institutional racism and the experience of the devaluation of her economic achievements by members of the host society were prevalent. "I remember I lived in Montreal and just purchased a new car; I was constantly stopped by the police asking me 'who owns this car' like I cannot afford a car by myself. Several incidences like that happened, to friends and to me. Racial profiling by the police is real in Montreal. [...] They think all Black people, especially Jamaicans, are criminals", Carol explains. Because Jamaicans were connected to many violent gang- and drug-related acts that were happening in the 1990s in Montreal, for example in Little Burgundy, Carol understands that most Quebecers stigmatized Jamaicans, men and women alike, as criminals afterward. "Earlier when I came to Montreal, it was just language. People thought all English-speaking Black people are Jamaicans and all French-speaking Black people are Haitians, that is no longer so. Racial profiling according to certain features and what the police think of as the 'standard image' of a Black person prevails. A lot of us have good jobs and can afford to buy a new car, [...]" Carol clarifies.

A newly published report (2018) by Concordia University highlights that problems of racial profiling and systemic racism prevail until today and enhance feelings of distrust due to traumatizing experiences with governmental institutions, especially for immigrant people of colour. While the report mainly focuses on youths and their experiences with racial profiling by the police in public spaces, the overall outcome of the study concludes that the longstanding problem provides little hope of abating. One of the main criticisms in the report is the constant law enforcement policies and programs that perpetually target racial minorities (Livingstone 2018: 10f.). A recent article in Montreal's English newspaper *Gazette* (2019) informs that efforts began by a local commission founded months after the release of the Concordia study to tackle administrative departments such as the police who disproportionately arrest and ticket racial minorities in the city of Montreal. However, as the executive director of the *Côte-des-Neiges Black Community Association* states in the newspaper article, "The intention of people of colour is to ensure that we are recognized for the systemic discrimination, profiling and excessive use of force against us [...]". As I am unable to delve deeper into the discussion of police-based racial profiling in my study, please find, in addition to the report from Concordia, other relevant studies about the context of racial profiling and police-related violence against racial minorities in Canadian cities as follows (e.g. Wortley/Marshall 2005; Tator et al. 2006; Wortley/Owosu-Bempah 2011; Chan/Chunn 2014[12]).

---

12   Note: This list is based on a selection process and does not claim to be comprehensive.

Racial profiling and the feeling of exclusion were reasons why Carol finally chose to move back to Toronto, where she feels fewer tensions and more at home. Although Carol learned to speak French fluently and tried to integrate as much as possible in Montreal, from her point of view, Toronto offers more opportunities for outside and recreational activities.

Unlike Elisha or Ms. Brown, Carol feels at ease living in Canada and does not plan to make a (final) return back to Jamaica, even after receiving her pension. Instead, she frequently goes on holiday trips to her country of birth through which she reconnects with family and also socialized her children in Jamaican cultural values. "It was important for me that they learned about Caribbean upbringing and culture when they were younger and that they see how I grew up [...]". Hence, many women such as Carol or Ms. Brown retain contacts with a home society, whose members they hope, value their sacrifices and achievements. When it comes to child rearing practices, school education and future-oriented life and career plans, women –respectfully mothers, grandmothers, sisters, and aunts– hold much of the decision-making powers over the future generation. Many initiate the migration of their children to North America, e.g., for studying, from early on to improve their living conditions in the future. Knowledge about migration as well as learning about cultural values and traditions rests on women's shoulders and the narratives they share with their children. Hence, their economic success, social networks, and kinship relations highly determine and are responsible for the coming generation. Still, there is no binary opposition between home and host country. The shared experiences of racialized differentiation also connect Elisha, Debby, and other women from the local Afro-Caribbean and Jamaican diaspora. Thus, permanent residency in Montreal as such is a dissuading factor for many Black women. Fittingly, Grenier and Nadeau state:

> "A main reason why the employment rate gap between immigrants and Canadian born individuals is larger in Montreal than in Toronto is language (...); immigrants in Montreal are significantly less likely to know French than their Toronto counterparts to know English and their knowledge of French is less rewarded than their Toronto counterparts' knowledge of English. Another possible reason is labour market discrimination. However, this discrimination would be French language related as opposed to being ethnicity/place of birth related" (2011: 19).

Even though this research explicitly focuses on the French-English language binary, there is an acknowledgment of discrimination in the labour market. However, from the standpoint of this study's interlocutors', the language issue is not solely the main restriction anymore. For example, Elisha who speaks both languages fluently explained what happened to her a few times when she was invited to job interviews. Although she pre-confirmed the appointments via friendly phone calls, the moment she stepped into most of the offices, the situation changed. In one of our meetings she explains one of the racial experiences she had: "I went into the meeting room, and they were all surprised by my appearance, telling me that I sounded so 'different' via the telephone and that they thought my last name indicated another 'heritage', asking me a couple of times 'Vous êtes de quel pays?'[13] [repeats three times]. They could not believe I was born in Montreal, in Quebec, like themselves". For Elisha, those conditions ended her attempt to find a job that was in line with her education and led her to create a life surrounded by people with the same experiences. Similar to Elisha, Ms. Brown, Carol and many other Afro-Caribbean women in Montreal, maintain themselves in spaces where tensions and traumatic experiences with oppression and systemic racism are less intense. "When we were living in Montreal we didn't really go out on the road as much as we do it now. In Montreal, you rather stay amongst your peers, your friends and homes or only go to certain places where you know people... [...]. Here in Toronto it's more 'normal' to be Black, at least that's my opinion", so Carol. Although she sees Toronto as her home, she draws heavily on her regular holiday trips to Jamaica, her socialization and her understanding as being Jamaican, e.g., using musical icons of her country of birth, especially when combating exclusion. "The most important thing is to speak up against racist people, like Bob Marley said, 'get up stand up, stand up for your rights', I always used Jamaican music as a tool in my classes", she remembers. Even though she does not speak of herself as Canadian, she has a strong sense of belonging to a broader Canadian society to which she contributed a lifelong process of work, education and Black liberal thinking. Carol's reflections show how far Canada still has to go to turn a politically propagated 'multicultural' or 'intercultural' society into a harmonious reality. In addition, her reflections on life in Montreal also show that 'being and belonging' in/ to the city is a process of simultaneous entanglement of various, locally and globally connected spaces, people and practices that counteract exclusionary tendencies of Quebec's 'distinct' society. The longer discrimination and racism continue to be a constant in people's daily lives, the more positive images, narratives, and memories of Jamaica seem to be sustained or recreated from inter- and intra-generational narration.

Many years have gone by since Carol came to Montreal; now that she is retired from her workplace and the children are grown up, she has time to reflect on life in Quebec. Her recent decision to move back to Toronto was a process that she put much thought into, but ultimately, she knew that she would feel more at ease in Toronto. Carol, who grew up quite similarly to Ms. Brown, namely in a rural town in Jamaica's countryside, with a grandmother and a grandfather, a strong faith in Christian values and "proper manners" as she says, always had a pragmatic attitude in dealing with racist behaviour. Though feelings of insecurity and vulnerability occurred, especially in her early years in Canada, she combated and dealt

---

13   Translation: Where are you from?

with workplace-related racism in her strict and determined way. "You can't let them see you sweat", she states her life theme. However, the reasons why the women and their 'foremothers' initially left Jamaica loses value or relevance in the light of prevailing experiences. Frustration with the environment fortifies their identification with the Jamaican homeland as well as an opposition to the main society, which ultimately prompted Carol to leave the city despite her ideals and though stands. Above all, the wish to return to Jamaica (seasonally or permanently) strengthens over time. Here, the mind takes journeys back to a glorified homeland with nostalgic memories and tales that often envision Jamaica as a harmonious paradise.

This chapter aimed to show that Jamaican female spaces in Montreal are not only socio-cultural sites of building a diasporic community and fellowship, but also social spaces of resistance and resourcefulness to the restrictions and failures of Quebec's integration policy. Ongoing power struggles associated with economic marginalization, nationalist tendencies as well as racialization are the major difficulties that so-called "visible minorities" from different generations, and ethnic backgrounds are confronted with. Further, and more importantly, the spatial undertaking of women creating alternative representations and their own spaces in a diverse city was prevalent. The pop-up shop, the salon, the church and their homes are different kinds of "safe spaces" created to offer an escape from the 'main' society and to reduce the pressure from outside. Claiming these spaces is an act of agency against multi-layered processes of 'othering' (Spivak 1985) and a way of building up a resistance against social differentiation and racialization. While not being located in a typical ethnic enclave but scattered across the city, Jamaican female spaces found a distinct way to foster and build community inconspicuously. These spaces are not enclosed entities merely existing as alone standing 'hotspots', rather they create a dialog with each other as well as with other localities and outsiders, and show the life worlds and experiences of Jamaican women in- and outside of these spaces.

8 Laws of Attraction: Bodily Practices

"Women negotiate a sense of self through beauty work and in relation to beauty standards, but they do so as socially located women positioning themselves in relation to socially located beauty standards" (Craig 2006: 166).

How does the practice of getting dressed or the style of one's hair matter when we speak about socio-cultural belonging, identity constructions and Jamaican female immigrant perspectives in a city like Montreal? When I first entered Debby's salon as one of the numerous social spaces of Jamaican women in the city, it did not seem different from a regular salon in Jamaica. Women get together and share stories about their daily lives while "prettying up" for an event or just having their hair done regularly. I may call this 'operational blindness' to the Jamaican context or merely the course of my fieldwork that at first led me to look into spaces and related aspects. The practice of attending to one's body, however, mattered much more than I had initially suspected. To re-fashion oneself and to style one's hair, nails, and other body parts, mirrors adaptations to, and demands from, the society on the one hand, and representations of self or expressions of self-empowerment, on the other hand. As Joanne Entwistle states, "dress in everyday life is always more than a shell, it is an intimate aspect of the experience and presentation of the self" (2000: 10), and she further notes that there is a "the complex dynamic relationship between the body, dress and culture" (ibid. 11).

As introduced in the previous chapter, the main reason why the females in this study –although being different in age, immigrant generation, occupation or education level– only meet at specific social spaces (besides meeting at home) and dislike to engage in other activities in the city results from their experience of daily racism. Everyday systemic racialization of women that not only correlates with skin colour, but also with economic disadvantages, e.g., in the work field. Gendered racism entails appearance, bodily features, and sexism. To uncover Jamaican perceptions about femininity, one has to look into a set of cultural attributes (Moi 1992) that highlight sexuality norms for women in general and in particular 'femininity' as being a racialized subject within 'western' cultures. Femininity is a process in which women become gendered and become specific types of women transforming their bodies into socio-culturally effective feminine roles. Experiences with everyday racism in Montreal, e.g., in the work field or in the streets, take part in this process in terms of rethinking oneself and one's outward appearance. Identity reconstructions then can become part of these internal processes (see Hall 1990), which are expressed in conversations as well as through actual bodily practices of altering, adapting, combining, rejecting or creating something new. Gilroy depicts relations between race and gender as follows:

> "[...] gender is the modality in which race is lived. An amplified and exaggerated masculinity has become the boastful centrepiece of a culture of compensation that self-consciously salves the misery of the disempowered and subordinated. This masculinity and its relational feminine counterpart become special symbols of the difference that race makes. They are lived and naturalized in the distinct patterns of family life on which the reproduction of racial identities supposedly relies. These gender identities come to exemplify the immutable cultural differences that apparently arise from absolute ethnic difference" (1993: 85).

Parameters such as race and gender intersect (Crenshaw 1994); especially when it comes to looking at perceived differences between masculinity and femininity and how both socially constructed categories interact within particular societies and cultural contexts. The assumption that there is one clear-cut Jamaican female identity concerning beauty ideals, the body and femininity neglects the existing variety of identities and bodily practices. Each person negotiates her blackness and constructs her identity within a specific 'intercultural' setting in Montreal surrounded by distinct societal norms and rules.

8.1   Complexities of Complexion

While waiting for Elisha at the end of her work shift, my eyes travel across the full display of the shop counter. On top, mountains of plastic packages with hair of all sorts and textures: curly, smooth, wavy, short, long, medium, red, blue, blonde, brown, and black (to name a few). Inside the glass case next to the many bottles of nail polish, I notice a label on a face cream that promises a "bright and glowing" complexion. Before Elisha became what she calls "conscious and self-empowered", she regularly used such bleaching products to lighten her skin. After work, she produces some old photographs of herself from the bottom of one of the counter compartments. The photograph shows a 20-something girl in skin-tight clothing, with a long, blonde bob and blue eye shadow, her skin numerous shades lighter than it is now. When I questioned her about when she started to bleach her skin, she revealed that she never made a conscious decision to do so. Growing up, many females around her practiced it, some of her friends in school, her mom, and her aunt, and so she did it too. For eight years, she used lotions on her face and body to become a "browning", as Jamaicans call a lighter-skinned Black person. "I could navigate myself much easier in school or outside activities. It was less a struggle than it is now, but I was someone else", recalls Elisha. Having a lighter complexion made her feel more beautiful for some time, however, the chemicals found in bleaching creams left her with rashes, discoloration and extremely dry skin. "Bleaching [...], it damaged my body and soul. Now that I know better, I want to encourage other women to wear their natural self and be themselves. That's what my art is for, too!" As Elisha speaks about her time as a bleacher, her sister Debby cuts into our conversation and clarifies, "the cream makes your skin look clear and smooth, these products are not so harsh anymore nowadays, [...] you don't even have to use that much, just a little tip, you know". Here, beauty performances are not only about a preference for whiteness, but also about female bodies in general and in particular about preferences for blackness.

Overall, women in Jamaica have a historically difficult stand concerning gender norms that restricted their behavioural and corporeal characteristics in relation to a predominantly male, hegemonic society. Similar, to the image of the 1950s and 1960s 'housewife' in Germany, females in Jamaica, often in connection with Christian values, have to be virtuous women. This virtuosity strongly connects with motherhood even though recent feminist movements have tried to counteract Jamaica's prevailing cis-gender, and also heteronormative society, the socialization of children is still oriented along clear-cut gender, colour, and class lines. While Elisha decided to stop bleaching and started wearing her real hair as locks, her sister Debby has a different perspective of what is beautiful. After all, Debby maintains her life by making other women 'more' beautiful. The debate happening between the sisters on this issue plays out among many Jamaican women who are grappling with what beauty means and what sacrifices are worth making for it. This debate is also tied to race issues in Montreal. Debby says, "It's not just here, you know it's all over America and Jamaica, too. We're women, and we're Black, we're not brown, so it's upon us how people see us", she explains. "Beautifying the skin" as Debby calls it and different stylization possibilities for hair and nails enable her to produce whatever style is needed for any occasion. "Like when you go to work, you want to look appropriate, you want to fit in, you know, [...] when you go to a dance, you want to stand out, you want to look good and sexy [...] sometimes you just want something new, it depends, you have to feel it [...]", Debby explains. Debby's statement highlights another important aspect, which shows that difference should not only be thought of as a binary opposition between opposing cultures or ideals (Canada vs. Jamaica), but also as difference that exists within the Jamaican socio-cultural context itself (natural vs. unnatural). A desire for a lighter complexion is not a new phenomenon in Jamaica. It is deeply rooted in the history of slavery and colonialism that dictated and indoctrinated imperialistic thoughts and assimilation to Eurocentric ideals and values. In his Jamaican-based research, Hutton deconstructs the prevailing Eurocentric and post-colonial 'white' aesthetic constructions of the Black body.

> "Masking is a far more sophisticated technological and scientific beauty business today compared to the balmy days of slavery when women of African descent working in the great house first started using the solution they used to clean the slaveholders' floor to bleach their faces" (Hutton 2016: 30).

The social stratification in present-day Jamaica is still oriented along different skin shades from light to dark, from top to bottom. Lighter skin remains a marker of privilege and access. A small number of light-skinned or white families own a major share of national wealth in Jamaica with a significant part held by Chinese and Middle Eastern individuals while the majority of the Afro-Jamaican population manage small and medium-sized enterprises and few are part of the upper social class. The majority of impoverished people in the inner-city communities are of African descent. Therefore, colourism plays an essential role in defining social affiliation. A common Jamaican saying for this phenomenon states, "If you are Black you stand back, if you are brown you stick around, if you are white you are right". Therefore, as Austin-Broos analyses, social class is mediated "through the idiom of colour shade and can reflect biologized notions of race" (Austin-Broos 1994: 218). Hence, many Jamaican women (and men) chemically change the colour of their skin, at the risk of skin cancer or severe organ damage through chemical ingredients. While the practice is a subject in Jamaican newspapers or on radio shows, bleaching is hardly criticized as a validation-seeking practice by a societal system, which historically rejected blackness in favour of assimilating or adapting to colonial and post-colonial values that marginalize Black people. In present-day Jamaica, this ongoing problem has quite recently attracted the attention of international media such as *Marie Claire Magazine* or the *Washington Post*. Jamaican Jody Cooper, the subject of a *Marie Claire* article, responded to the question of why she bleached as follows: "When you black in Jamaica, nobody sees you" (Kebede 2017: n.p.). Here, she is referring to a perceived absence of worth and devaluation of Black skin in her experience of daily colourism and classism.

Under the British colonial regime, the ill-treatment and negation of self were standard practices in the abuse strategies and enslavement of Black people and bodies. Attire and clothing were markers of social status and differentiation between e.g., master and slave (Buckridge 2004). Historically, 'brown' Jamaicans were the product of relationships between Black Jamaicans and white colonialists, and often received greater access to land and resources. As a beauty concept, skin bleaching and its less chemically infused siblings, e.g., the 'lightening' products in Debby's store of brands such as *Nivea*, *Garnier* or *Bio Claire* are commonly used amongst many Jamaican women to achieve their desired looks. Products for skin bleaching are over the counter cosmetics. They hide behind positive connoted synonyms, such as "glow", "clear" or "brighten". The belief that brown-skinned women are more beautiful and more attractive to men and have it easier in life are commonplace in Jamaica and across the Caribbean and African diaspora (Brown-Glaude 2013: 57). This ongoing colourism transcends into chances of upward social mobility and gives insights into a preference of lifestyles and clothing that reflect closeness to European or North American culture. While 'Africa' and 'African symbols' have gained international acceptance and likeability, specifically through the positive connotation and distribution of the Rastafari philosophy in Jamaican popular music such as Reggae, it is still a rather slowly growing shift in the mental landscape of the local society. With that in mind, it is hardly surprising that different ideals and models of beauty emerge in the Jamaican diaspora as responses or counter-activities to white beauty ideals. As migrants are forced to cope with the culture they live in without being merely assimilated, they are in a continual process of identity development (Hall 1999: 435). Daily stylization practices and the production of Black beauty ideals are recreated in certain power and hierarchical structures under the given circumstances and societal contexts. Famous Kenyan actor Lupita Nyong'o, who became a media phenomenon as a 'natural' Black beauty icon after her Oscar-winning star debut in the movie "12 Years a Slave", reflects on her own experiences in a 2014 article in *Glamour* magazine. Here she states,

> "European standards of beauty are something that plague the entire world – the idea that darker skin is not beautiful, that light skin is the key to success and love. [...]. When I was in second grade, one of my teachers said, 'Where are you going to find a husband? How are you going to find someone darker than you do?' [...]. I remember seeing a commercial where a woman goes for an interview and does not get the job. Then she puts cream on her face to lighten her skin and she gets the job! This is the message: that dark skin is unacceptable" (Bennetts 2014: n.p.).

Since post-colonial differentiations among colour lines prevail in Caribbean and African societies such as Jamaica and Kenya, and since beauty industries and media houses worldwide keep on publishing Eurocentric and iconic ideals of white beauty, it is hardly surprising that Montreal offers no exception. Here, a statement from one of the salon's regular clients emphasizes these circumstances and the invisibility of Black women in Montreal. "We, Black women, are not part of society, understood? Living in Montreal, I cannot even get my shade [referring to her makeup foundation]. I rely on Debby because she buys the shades we need when she goes to New York. [...] Our skin colour doesn't exist in Quebec [...]", explains the woman one day over a prolonged discussion about beauty, skin colour, and access to society in Montreal. Therefore, it is necessary to acknowledge the dialogical relationship within the community and the identifications of values that exist in the various crossings of Black and white beauty ideals. As Hall states, "cultural identities are the points of identification, the unstable points of identification or suture, which are made, within the discourses of history and culture. Not an essence but a positioning" (Hall 1990: 226). While Afrocentric discourses about skin bleaching often identify a "self-hate narrative", Charles (2010) argues in his Jamaican-based psychological study, that the decision to fade one's skin tone is not a rejection of blackness in general, nor is it a result of low self-worth. While some women who bleach their skin may lack confidence, his research has shown that bleachers and non-bleachers alike have the same level of self-esteem (ibid.). With lighter-skinned women viewed as more attractive and beautiful, the self-hate narrative is not the dominant one.

My preliminary expectations of what to encounter in Debby's beauty salon were different from the actual situation. Even though Debby offers 'over the counter' skin bleaching products and chemical hair straightening techniques as well as weaves and wigs, she also offers –in contrast to regular beauty salons in Jamaica– natural hairstyling such as cornrows, dreadlocks or afros. Even if Debby's salon (and her self-understanding) resembles more Eurocentric beauty ideals, the salon also opens up a space of discourse and a discussion of beauty as a racialized subject. In his concluding remarks, Hutton states,

> "[...] the ideational and practical ontological desecration of the black body continues in rhetoric, hairdo, skin do and other dos and is often articulated as expressions of freedom and universalism [...]. [...] the meanings and messages used to advertise certain "hair care/skin care" products aimed at obscuring/masking/altering Africa in the black body [...] are rooted, as ever, in the same racist aesthetic complex of slavery and colonialism" (2016: 30-31).

Elisha's current experiences in Montreal hail mainly from her involvement and friendships in the art and music scene. Here, younger and Canadian-born Afro-Caribbean people negotiate their place, meaning and belonging in the city. While their socio-economic place-making strategies were already discussed, it is crucial to examine individual styles of dress and hair to understand inherent identity constructions. This younger generation claims to be more self-empowered and self-confident, which is exemplified in, for example, communal efforts in "Black Lives Matter" demonstrations that were recurrently taking place during my time in Montreal. Besides, their mind-set as being "Canadian-born" makes them significantly stronger when it comes to fighting for their rights and for a Black diversity experience that should be, in their words "a major part of the mental landscape in Quebec". Even though the feeling of vulnerability, e.g., concerning police control, is strong and upsets Elisha a lot, their commitment to justice is part of their self-understanding. Amongst other things, they use their get-together for the sharing of critical thoughts and for the reading of Black liberation literature, for example, Walter Rodney or Frantz Fanon. In addition, some of Elisha's friends claim to be Rastafari. While artistic and musical presentations together with Afrocentric representations and ethnic symbols are commonplace, Afrocentric clothing and politicized hairstyles such as dreadlocks or 'natural' hairstyles such as afros are the norm.

Here attire, hair, and clothing symbolize an idealized closeness and identification with Africa and blackness. This group of third generation children of Afro-Caribbean immigrants consciously construct individual lifestyles and adapt identities of an idealized homeland that are closer to their self-understanding as empowered Black youth that counteracts (also politically) the mainstream society in Montreal and its inherent restrictions. As Giddens states "A lifestyle can be defined as a more or less integrated set of practices which an individual embraces, not only because such practices fulfil utilitarian needs, but they give material form to a particular narrative of self-identity" (1991: 83). The adaptation, production, and wearing of Afrocentric clothing and symbols, head-wraps, natural cosmetics made from African shea butter and jewellery made from wood, gold or shells represent one form of challenging the everyday beauty aesthetics and status quo of a Euro-centric, white society as they are not worn without facing counter-reactions. Therefore, identity politics here strongly align along the differentiation of 'real' and 'fake', whereby fake hair, nails or lashes, and too much make-up are undesirable and 'natural' hairstyles and symbols as well as specific clothing, elevate feminine beauty positively. As Bakare-Yusuf notes on the choice to grow dreadlocks by Rastafari people in Jamaica,

> "These motifs not only posed a challenge to the white capitalist and Christian ideology pervasive on the island, but they also drew attention to the permanent state of warfare (...). Rastafarian fashion, in particular the wearing of dreadlocks, performed a critique of the dominant regime, asserting an alternative cultural, ethical and aesthetic sensibility in its stead" (2006: 3).

For this chapter, it was crucial to apply an approach that is critical of the idea of white beauty as being iconic. Reproducing a white-Black binary means misconceiving the broader picture of the mixing and crossing of Black beauty styles, techniques, and traditions. There is nothing like the creation or mimicry of the "white women" in Debby's beauty shop. What is re-created here are beauty practices based on a Black Jamaican diasporic experience and therefore, varying beauty images exist depending on the occasion and the individual. In the case of Montreal, categories of race, class, gender and also age contest white beauty as much as Black beauty. Race, class and gender combine what constitutes "Jamaica's discourse of heritable identity" (Austin-Broos 1994: 218). No single style is assigned or limited to embody sameness or difference concerning a Black or white beauty ideal. Different stylization possibilities open up new opportunities for subjectivity and autonomy concerning assumed "essentialized" identities in cultural or bodily practices.

8.2   Dancehall Fashion

While I was researching in Montreal, Dancehall parties were one of the first entry points of my fieldwork and relevant for gaining orientation knowledge in the city. At Dancehall parties, few limitations exist, especially when it comes to extravagant clothing, jewellery, sexiness and style. Dancehall offers women the opportunity to negotiate every-day boundaries of the hegemonic (and patriarchal) society and give them control over their bodies and fears. "When I go out to a party, I dress accordingly to how I feel [...] you got to have that confidence and show it off when you go out if you don't do it nobody will do it for you", explains Debby while putting on her makeup. It is nearly 10 p.m. and throughout the next two and a half hours, everyone is getting ready for the party, drinking wine, smoking menthol cigarettes, listening to music and chatting about the upcoming night. Two of Debby's girls came over to "hold a vibes" before going out. For me, being able to participate in their "night-out", observing and taking part in their discussions (merely asking annoying questions) were useful components in analysing and understanding various imaginations about femininity (and masculinity).

Dancehall[1] being Jamaica's most popular musical genre encompasses numerous meanings regarding identity, culture, social class, masculinity, and femininity. A broad range of scholarly research exists (e.g. Cooper 1993, 1995, 2000, 2004; Hope 2006, 2010; Stanley-Niaah 2010; Stolzoff 2002; Lesser 2008), especially concerning cultural studies, i.e., linguistics, visuals, sounds or lyrical texts. In Jamaica, Dancehall is a historically and contemporary male-dominated industry, similar to Reggae. Dancehall is a 'battlefield' of hegemonic representations of male activities and pronouncements of dominant male voices and identity constructions. Lesser, for example, traced in her historical study on photography a total absence of women's agency in Jamaican records (LPs) and Dancehall images (Lesser 2008). Nowadays, women or better, female bodies, are highly visible, and usually the centres of (sexual) male attraction. As a genre, Dancehall is known to be homophobic and leaves no room for representations other than heteronormative sexual orientations. The Jamaican genre's digital rhythms inspire female bodies to "wine" or to "bubble", as

---

1   Note: During the late 1970s, Dancehall began to evolve as a musical genre in Jamaica. Initially, to describe the more upbeat sound of Reggae, Dancehall invented its own particular codes and styles with the arrival of digital keyboards and drum machines. Back then, Dancehall entirely evolved around sound systems and male, mobile DJ crews, who ran marathon sessions and street dances.

the dynamic rotation of the waist is called in Jamaica and the lyrics of "gyal tunes"[2] echo this connection. Since the 1980s, music videos with acrobatic dancers, so-called Dancehall queens, in extravagant clothing, coloured wigs, high-heeled boots, fishnet tops, latex clothes, massive jewellery, and "batty riders"[3] are widely known. These women do not only run Kingston's street parties, but also the halls of di-aspora nightclubs with their splits, headstands and other 'flexible' performances. While Dancehall minimized female voices for a long time, numerous female artists challenged the male gaze in the early 1990s and counteracted the chauvinist sex-ual politics of the genre by proving they could be as provocative and 'slack'[4] as their male counterparts could. Until today, female artists have been challenging a globally influential and often frustratingly misogynist music genre to reckon with long-held taboos and prejudices as well as to expand its traditionally limited view on femininity. Scholarly research (Stanley-Niaah 2004; Bakare-Yusuf 2006) on the role of Dancehall and aspects of gender, class, and identity, highlight that fashion and adornment as well as bodily practices played a marginalized role until after the millennium in comparison to the content of songs, sounds, and visuals.

While at the beginning of my study, aspects such as social spaces were more striking, the analysis of the empirical material highlighted the importance of women's bodily practices related to Dancehall events. The fashioning and styling of bodies give insight into female 'embodied and situated' phenomena (DeMello 2014), which reflect socio-cultural and historical changes. Additionally, fashion allows Dancehall-followers like Debby to challenge their social realities. The body here works as a "canvas of representation" (Hall 1993), so the outside world can see them as they are or as they want to be seen. Here, representations not only counteract structural and daily racism in Montreal, but also the constraints of pa-triarchy and an ideal Christian logic of femininity that still prevails in the context of contemporary Jamaican life. Cooper analyses the existence of a specific female role model in Jamaican society in which the image of motherhood is made central to a woman's worth and value; the woman is the guardian of the race –a Puritan moral institution (Cooper 2000: 381f.). In the context of a longstanding ambivalent discourse on racism and sexism, and taking into account the structural, physical and psychological violence of slavery and oppression, the continued importance of this ideal and of the patriarchal nuclear family is noteworthy. Paul Gilroy argues fittingly that race was associated with the reign of Black masculinity, the "integrity of the race is thus made interchangeable with the integrity of black masculinity,

---

2   Note: Songs that describe how a woman should dance or move her body to attract male at-
     tention.
3   Note: A very short hot pant.
4   Note: Slackness refers to a Jamaican term used to describe 'vulgar' behaviour and sexist lyrics
     in live performances or recordings.

which must be regenerated at all costs" (Gilroy 1993: 194). However, women are not just victims of systemic oppression, but find productive ways to express socio-cultural representations and constructions through their agency and bodies. The practice of dressing up and getting ready for a Dancehall event, therefore, says as much about beauty ideals and Jamaican taste for a 'bling-bling' lifestyle as it does about everyday experiences in the city of Montreal. The fact that Debby and her friends do not understand their bodily practices as a rebellion to hegemonic structures is of little relevance here. Debby explicitly states that she is dressing up for herself and that Dancehall parties allow her to express herself freely. However, it is less about whether Debby and her female friends deliberately reflect or verbally express their actions, but rather about the visibility and recognition of their female agency through their attire, accessories and styling techniques. What I encountered with Debby and her friends cannot be seen as an intentional activism similar to her sister Elisha's conscious counter-activities in the Afrocentric arts network. Hence, Debby's expressive bodily actions seem to be less conscious or outspoken self-interpretations. Instead, the analysis and participatory observation opened up additional, possible interpretations of these women's bodily practices.

While Dancehall music and culture have now become mainstream, the energy, creativity, and reproduction continue to be drawn from the socio-cultural existences of the marginalized urban poor. According to Cooper, the female body became the site of the "ongoing struggle over high culture and low, respectability and riot, propriety and vulgarity" (Cooper 2000: 350). Cooper states further that Dancehall is the "social space in which the smell of female power is exuded in the extravagant display of flashy jewellery, expensive clothes, [and] elaborate hairstyles" (1993: 155). Therefore, every Dancehall event is an opportunity to display and perform the most extravagant, sexy and sometimes grotesque, clothing and style. While Debby is standing in front of the full-length mirror, her friend is squeezing her upper body into a skin-tight bodysuit, trying to close the zipper. The bodysuit is a dark-blue, transparent mesh embroidered with rhinestones, lace, and flower applications. Her waist is cinched into a tight zipper corset, turning her figure into an hourglass shape. The fake diamond chain around her neck sparkles together with the rhinestone earrings and bangles. Her eye shadow in dark-blue matches the colour of the bodysuit while her long, glued-on lashes make the look complete. "The clothes we wear are made to emphasize your body. You can go out and dance in really anything. Everyone wants to just feel the best about themselves and fashion can do that for you", Debby explains while running her long, pointed fingernails through her silky-straight, black wig of the night that reaches down to her buttocks. "If you have something that bothers you, once you touch inna di dance, the stress just lifts off your head", says Debby's friend who is wearing a tiger-print negligee type dress with black transparent stockings and a heavy golden chain. Her red, short-bob wig hangs over one of Debby's chairs. While she applies vanilla-scented glitter lotion on her arms she states, "But your fashion has to be on top!". The other two agree with serious looks on their faces. Debby's outfit of the night and her friends' outfits show off their curves, every part of the wardrobe is made to highlight the most crucial female body parts such as breasts and buttocks. "You ready?" Debby asks me, while she helps her friend into a tight black corset leather outfit that does not cover more of her than a swimsuit.

Reflecting now on the evening and the entire "getting-ready-ceremony" with Debby and her friends, I realize how bold these women are to continue living this part of Jamaican culture in a city like Montreal and actually entering the streets in outfits like these. While it is nothing sensational to be dressed like this in the Jamaican Dancehall scene, in Canada as well as in other European and North American countries, this way of styling and dressing seems rather provocative or uncommon. Even though a dance club is a rather 'free zone' when it comes to "dressing up", one seldom sees women who get ready for the club in this specific way. Moreover, in the above-mentioned countries the personal space is different from in Jamaica. There is a significant distance or unspoken rule of approaching or even touching someone. In Jamaica, people who you interact with will touch you more often, e.g., put a hand on one's shoulder or stand closer to you in conversations without the intention of intervening into one's personal space. Distance and closeness simply function differently in different social spaces. In addition, the way of dancing is very different and connected with much closer body contact. However, physical contact and social closeness do not have to match. In addition, while common beauty ideals promote an attractive and sexy look for women, there is an invisible line of too attractive and too sexy that exists from a Eurocentric perspective, even for dance- and nightclubs. Notably, when it comes to bodily features and nudity, there is a borderline of what a woman can wear both when she is rather skinny or rather voluminous in body size. At Dancehall parties, this borderline softens and sexiness seems non-negotiable. It is a given circumstance, and the extravagant outfits become a source of confidence, not an obstacle. When Debby slips into her rhinestone covered stiletto high heels, she says, "you just have to look inna yuh-self and know say you a come first, you got to have that feel, because if you don't have it, nobody will have it for you"[5]. For Debby, her outfit is a way to show off her personality and her confidence. In understanding the importance of dressing up for an event, Debby's personal background is again relevant. Since she has a reputation to lose when it comes to beauty and her business, she has to represent her "best self" when going out. Debby explains that she sees herself as the best ad-

---

5   Translation/ meaning: At a Dancehall event, you have to realize that it is mainly about your own power of representation, you have to be confident, because if you're not confident, people can make you feel inferior about yourself.

vertising platform for her business and an ambassador of the newest trends and styles.

At the party, the friends find their spot in a corner close to the small club stage where everybody can see them. "This is our place, even if we come late everybody knows", Debby explains as a waiter brings a big bucket filled with ice, cups, Campari, Baileys and soda to the bistro table. Upon my questioning look, Debby's friend quickly adds, "They know what we drink". The party starts about 30 minutes later, with Debby and her friends showing off their dancing skills and love for the music. Interestingly, when men approach the corner to ask them for a dance or to compliment them on their looks, their smiles fade and they put on what I would call a "cool attitude". "We no jus dance with any man, you know, we sample dem out [...] dem haffi represent some style"[6], Debby screams into my ear while her friend inspects the next candidate. At the end of the party night, the friends only danced with certain men, obviously none of the other contenders was "good enough". Debby and her friends truly exercise power (cf. Cooper 1993) by choosing dance partners while at the same time visibly attracting a lot of male attention (through their styling and dancing skills). In that sense, their movements, sexy fashion and what they believe to be male desires remain nothing more than "eye candy" for most men. After the dance, they leave satisfied with numerous compliments for their appearance and moves, but without any men. Of course, "sex sells"; however, in a patriarchal society, dressing in a very sexy manner can also represent a playful way of asserting female power and breaking the rules. Moreover, these practices show Jamaican interpretations of female sexuality and appearance, images that counteract the hegemonic and patriarchal norms and values of a Eurocentric ideal. The music genres expressiveness concerning overt sexist behaviour and dominance over the female body can be visually and in its lyrical content quite overwhelming to outsiders. However, as any form of popular culture, Dancehall is a musical representation and an arena for socio-cultural negotiation (Cooper 2004; Hope 2006). Jamaican studies on Dancehall show that the representation of gender roles and female bodies can be interpreted quite contrary to the assumptions of 'oppression or dominance' of Eurocentric observers (Cooper 1995; Hope 2010). Provocative clothing and bodily modification highlight the "erotic play" and representation mechanisms in Dancehall. The female "vulgarity" at Dancehall events embodies traces of historical events, folklore rhymes and anticolonial resistance (Cooper 1995: x) and disrupts the everyday patriarchal gender norms by exercising 'performance power' (Cooper 1993) and by producing (at least in the encapsulated moment of the Dancehall) their very own 'non-ordinary' gender and fashion rules.

---

6   Translation: We're not just dancing with any man that comes along, we choose them [...] they have to represent a certain attitude/ attractiveness.

This chapter showed how the female body becomes part of a socio-cultural construction of gender and identity, through internal as well as external influences, and highlights in what ways beauty, hair, weight as well as fashion symbolize categories of difference, representation, inclusion, exclusion, and Jamaican female self-understandings. Women who are engaged in Dancehall culture, therefore, reveal femininity as an embodied construction that tackles the Eurocentric and patriarchal separation between the mother and the whore, everyday life and staging, natural and unnatural, conform and non-conform. Ultimately, bodily practices here means taking control over their image and how they want to be seen by others. The eroticized disclosure of voluminous, Black female bodies in revealing apparel disrupts the male "-schisms" between the sexy and the maternal body (cf. Cooper 1993). What at first seems like sexual vulgarity or availability becomes agency through which women such as Debby claim their positionality opposed to external and internal, normative pressures. Beyond bodily aesthetics, a non-Eurocentric or non-white opposition to embodiment and corporeal expression is at work here. Instead of having self-controlling attitudes towards the body, Dancehall fashion highlights women's alternative interpretations to common socio-cultural standards. Through Dancehall, Jamaican women like Debby push their love for pomp and splendour to the limit and celebrate the admiration for a full-figured, sexy female body (cf. Bakare-Yusuf 2006). Therefore, Dancehall fashion also ruptures social class in a socio-cultural environment such as Montreal; an environment that usually excludes women of colour as "visible minorities" and gives them limited access to society.

8.3 Of Wigs and Weight

While standing in front of her mirror, Ms. Brown unwraps her headband to get ready for her weekly bingo night. "I'm trying out my new hair, I got it the other day at the salon, makes me look ten years younger [chuckles], you will see". While she continues to praise her new look, Ms. Brown gently unwraps a wig from a plastic foil, carefully placing it on the dresser in front of her. "I was born in a time when my mother pushed down the pressing comb in our hair ['our' is here referring to herself and her sister], we had no choice than to sit tight, we didn't know anything about perms or relaxers, but about pain I tell you it hurt, it hurt. Now, I just wear these three styles [pointing at several wigs on the dresser], my hair stopped being fluffy, you know, so I buy fluffy", she laughs. Looking at the different styles, I point to the only straight, short, black-haired wig that sits on top of a small stand to the side of the commode and ask why this one is unwrapped. "This one? Oh, don't mind this one, this one is for work, trust me, you wouldn't know me at work", Ms. Brown declares and turns again towards her new wig with a shrug of her shoulders that ends this matter. In her occupation as a geriatric nurse, Ms. Brown learned how to dress for the 'standard image' or "appropriate look" as she refers to it. In her workplace, it was always essential for her not to stand out, which means that she has been wearing that same short, sleek, unobtrusive wig for the last 30-odd years, a wig that has passed as her hair with none of her white bosses or co-workers and primarily white patients ever calling it into question. Even though work is a sensitive topic, which Ms. Brown likes to avoid in our conversations, the "work-wig" says a lot about her relationship with work and the way she deals with work-related racialization. Experiences involved, for example, confrontations with racist patients who hindered her caretaking, who spat on her and vilified her. Other experiences with work hierarchies and structural racism made her learn to do her work silently, while never trying to be smarter or able to handle things better than her superiors or colleagues. The statement "you wouldn't know me at work" emphasizes this attempt to be inconspicuous at work and highlights a differentiation between her self-understanding and the role that she plays at her job. The wig becomes part of her uniform, which minimizes the debate about her bodily features and expresses her experience of mirroring a white 'standard image'. Through the wig, she mimics what a woman of her age and skin colour should appropriately look like at work from a Eurocentric, white point of view (cf. Bhabha 1994), an image that negates femininity for Ms. Brown. This styling practice, which she performs every weekday before leaving for work, includes her internal preparation and daily transformation of going to a workplace where she is somebody else. Work, in general, consumes a large amount of her daily life. Still, she allows other recreational activities such as going to church, going to the salon or going to bingo nights to have much greater importance in her life. The possibility of dressing up and wearing styles interchangeably as she gets ready anew for each occasion celebrates these crucial activities. Although she has a 'nice colleague' from Trinidad and a general love for her job despite recurrent adverse events, work is merely a means to an end. The prospect of her future pension and the financial support of her family has always been her main goal and focus.

Carol, who also grew up with the idea of 'good' and 'bad' hair, straightened her own and her daughter's hair throughout her life. Until today from time to time, her adult daughter goes to her house to let her do her hair. For Carol, this is normal and appropriate, and she has never really put this practice into question. In her sense, it was one way of avoiding any negative implications for her daughter in school and herself in her teaching occupation. Conform to her upbringing and 'properness', hairstyle and beauty are practical tools to fit into society, whether this society is Jamaican or Canadian. "To play by the rules, but not to duck" was always Carol's mantra. She explains, "Canada is now a diverse mixture of people, colours, cultures, and ethnicities from all over the globe. This diversity has created misconceptions in Canadians that often led to efforts to dominate and exploit people because of their differences in culture, colour, or ethnicity". On racial discrimination in Montreal she furthers, "[...] racism persists, the perpetrators continue, and the victims have to deal with its negative effects, especially in educational, economic, and career opportunities. [...] Overcoming certain challenges means to adapt by being confident, determined, strong, efficient, and proud", Carol contextualizes in one of our interviews. Throughout her years as a teacher, she dedicated lots of her work to workshops and seminars that dealt with the topic of racism and helped to build up students' confidence through advising how to deal with racist behaviour. Even though Carol persisted with her hair straightening routine and her understanding of 'proper appearance', it was never so much about the outside appearance of a person as it was much more about their inner attitude and self-confidence. "The situation is no matter how long you are here, and even if you are born Canadian like my children, you will always be different, a foreigner. It's just this thought in white peoples head that they have to ask you where you're 'originally' from. [...]. I put much thought into how to teach my children and students how they can react to such an incidence, and we have not yet talked about real discrimination. [...]", Carol puts forth. The processes of 'othering' (Spivak 1985), is in Carol's view a virtually never-ending situation for Black people in Canada, which resembles all my interlocutors' experiences in their daily life activities. Othering refers to "the process of attaching moral codes of inferiority to difference", which emerges as a critical discursive tool for understanding discrimination and exclusion used against individuals or groups based on their belonging to a marginalized population (Krumer-Nevo/Sidi 2012: 299-300). This status of marginalization is perceived differently by the interlocutors with a complex multitude of emotional as well as bodily coping mechanisms in handling exclusionary and racist tendencies. The negative experience of racism in daily life activities, together with discrimination in the work place, causes a high level of emotional frustration. This frustration transcends into socio-cultural, spatial and especially bodily practices that maintain positive imaginaries, remembrance, and narratives of being 'proud' Jamaicans.

In Ms. Brown's case, pride also plays an important role in bodily practices and discourses about traditional food consumption and culture. Discussing beauty with a woman like Ms. Brown is rather body-centred and less engaged with bleaching creams or a wide variety of hairstyling techniques. A good-looking woman cannot be "maga" (meagre) as Ms. Brown puts it. Throughout the fieldwork, she continuously argued with me about weight or my vegetarian diet. While Ms. Brown liked to make fun of me for not eating meat, eating food together was a way of discussing different ideals of beauty and especially Eurocentric images of an ideal, thin female body. Within Ms. Brown's home, similar to other Jamaican households, food is not something that should be controlled or limited when reflecting on female bodily attributes. Thinking about North American or European white perceptions, discourses, and images, e.g., in popular culture about the stereotyped ideal female body, automatically leads to a skinny, well-toned, longhaired, and sun-tanned model. Even though many 'body positivity campaigns' and advertisements have been trying to change beauty stereotypes in recent years, the overarching image of thinness remains the ideal one, whereby thinness often and supposedly equals health. The restriction of food intake, dieting, or calorie counting was, however, not part of the performance of beauty and femininity in the case of the interlocutors. By paying attention to what takes place in the home, eating food is uncovered as highly ethnic. Here, health plays a significant role again.

In Jamaica, full-figured, 'thick' women are considered beautiful and healthy. Telling someone 'you gained weight' is a compliment, and when somebody loses a significant amount of weight people wonder what kind of stress caused this deficit to occur. Food here is very much about well-being and eating right and enough food is a strategy for not getting sick. While being "thick" and having a large bottom is a feature of attractiveness for Jamaican females, having a large figure also indicates fertility and successful reproduction (Sobo 1996). According to Igenoza, food availability and the sharing of food play a central role in Black cultures. She argues further: "Slimness is not something that is valued, and mothers are continually asking their daughters and the younger women around them if they are eating properly" (Igenoza 2017: 114). When going to Ms. Brown's house, eating food was a given and a part of our interaction and socializing practice. Without food, there would have probably been no conversations. When it comes to health matters, Ms. Brown's doctor recently confronted her with the idea of slimming down for health reasons. While she knows the general warnings about the dangers of obesity and sicknesses related to overeating, she is less concerned with changing her dietary habits. As Sobo argues, "Notions of food and health influence the symbolic communications made through our bodies, which influence the ways we shape and experience our bodily features" (Sobo 1996: 323). Even though Ms. Brown accepts the recommendations of her doctor that she should control her fat and sugar intake due to her heart and her inherited risk for diabetes, she still holds on to her understanding of healthy cooking. This understanding involves cooking with certain spices such as, e.g., thyme, garlic, pimento, and ginger that are beneficial to overall health and therefore lower, in her view, the risk of sickness. Her Jamaican food culture and her self-understanding are closely interconnected. Hence, medical recommendations will hardly be able to change her perception of health and attractive bodily features. In her resolute and caring way, she will not get tired of offering 'good food' to all guests who visit her house. While we sit over another breakfast plate, she accounts her once in a lifetime attempt to lose weight at a popular local institute. "Listen, if nobody there can tell me how much points mi haffi count fi ackee and saltfish[7]or brown stew chicken [falls into Patois], what sense does it mek?"[8] While Ms. Brown internalized certain Eurocentric notions concerning her bodily practices (especially with regard to her hair), her traditionally practiced Jamaican 'food culture' as well as the related belief systems of health and wellbeing have im-munized her to accept a thin body as beautiful. Although she attempts to balance varying cultural understandings about food intake and health, her experience at the dietary institution uncovers a continual absence or ignorance of those insti-tutions concerning varying ethnic food cultures. The Eurocentric 'standard image' of dieting with specific food products leads to the exclusion of people who already account as ethnic minorities. Furthermore, besides socio-cultural values, food in childhood days was never available in abundance. Therefore, many older Jamaicans like Ms. Brown find it valuable and great comfort in eating as much as they like. However, there is less awareness of the fact that food quality differs significantly between North America, where high-quality food is costly and not affordable for her, and Jamaica, where local and organically grown food, as well as free-range meat, is a given circumstance, especially in the rural areas.

---

7   Note: Ackee and saltfish, Jamaica's national dish containing the Ackee fruit and dried, salted codfish.

8   Translation: It doesn't make sense to count points if there is no information on specific foods/ dishes.

9   Grandma's Tale: Mind-Trips and Memories

The Jamaican women in this study have biographies that often involve several (migratory) moves throughout their own life or in their familial history. This chapter, therefore, addresses retrospective accounts given by the women on the circumstances of leaving Jamaica that led to their current aspirations to return. Besides their negative experiences in Montreal, imaginaries, ideas and wishes prefigure actual physical movements and changes of location. Childhood or vacation memories, reports from others, music videos, and social media together contribute as varying pull factors to a mental journey into 'paradise' Jamaica. These inward, mental travels will then follow the actual movements and experiences of (return) mobility. Here, unexpected boundaries await women on their journeys back to their 'roots' that will ultimately decide their future plans.

With this part of the empirical findings, I aim to unfold that being Jamaican is not only related to an engagement in an ethnic community or social network, but also established through modes of living and socialization with certain cultural values as well as their conservation. Transmitted knowledge through intergenerational narration and own memories play an important role in understanding current movement aspirations. Ms. Brown, for example, influenced by her past childhood memories and longstanding remittance sending practices as well as family connections to her homeland, wishes to return as soon as possible. Furthermore, the current changes in her social environment in Montreal and her future pension are reasons that strengthen her intention to leave. Emotional sentiments to Jamaica as a place of 'heart' are also inspiring Elisha's plans, in which return becomes a process of 'seeking roots'. Thus, cross-border mobility or migration in its various forms is not solely a phenomenon of first-generation immigrants who want to go back "home", but also of later generations. Narratives of family, romantic imaginaries from past travels and a healthy optimism of going back for good inspire all returns. Actual movement between Jamaica and Canada, but also traveling to different destinations in North America or the UK, e.g., for spending leisure time or visiting relatives and friends, is part of their lives and self-understanding.

The following ethnographic depictions highlight how, within this framework and its emphasis on social fields of differential power, the interlocutors explore their disparities, inequalities, racialized representations and national 'myth-scapes' that facilitate and legitimate differential mobility and fixity. Investigations about 'home' or 'homeland' here reveal a notion of mobility as previously shown in studies on transcultural belonging (e.g. Basch et al. 1994, Glick Schiller/Fouron 2001; Glick Schiller 2005; Levitt/Glick Schiller 2004; Levitt 2004; Faist 2000, 2011; Thomas-Hope 1988, 2002, 2010). The homeland is here understood as a concept of self-representation that the interlocutors use to symbolize their intact social and emotional relationship to a socio-cultural space (cf. Greverus 1979 qtd. in Schönhuth 2005). Home comes to be located in a routine set of practices, in a repetition of habitual social interactions, in styles of dress and address, in memories and myths, in stories carried around in one's head (Berger/Luckmann 1984). As Berger states, people are more at home today in "words, jokes, opinions, gestures, actions, even the way one wears a hat" (ibid. 64). Some interlocutors of this study perceive 'home' also as a metaphor for romanticized longing as well as a yearning space for connection and nostalgia. To conduct multi-sited anthropological research then means to analyse the 'moving' homes of various kinds, i.e., behavioural and ideational homes that individuals construct and enact. Here a routine set of practices and narrations that do not merely tell of 'home' but represent it, serve as cognitive homes themselves (Wulff 1998 qtd. in Rapport 2014: 209). As Gaston Bachelard claims, "the human imagination always builds 'walls' of impalpable shadows, comforting itself with the illusion of protection, and so carries 'the notion of home' into any 'really inhabited space', whether cognitive or physical" (Bachelard 1994: 5).

As with emigration, return migration has been a constant facet of Jamaican social and economic life (cf. Thomas-Hope 2002). Returnees helped influence the formation of labour unions in the late 1930s and represented Afrocentric conscious-ness with figures such as Marcus Garvey (Chevannes 1996). Contract farm work-ers and other seasonal travellers to North America in the 19th and 20th centuries played a significant role in the introduction and subsequent "Jamaicanization" of North American religious practices, such as the Baptist and Pentecostal movements (Austin-Broos 1997; Chevannes/Besson 1996). Besides, many Jamaican immigrants returned to Jamaica from the United Kingdom throughout the 1970s because of unstable economic conditions. Others became "twice migrants" (Bhacchu 1990), moving to the United States and Canada under their British passports. Accord-ing to De Haas (De Haas/Fokkema 2011: 22), "migration processes tend to become partly self-perpetuating, leading to the formation of migrant networks and mi-gration systems". As networks and systems become strong, it becomes easier for migrants to overcome obstacles to migration, and thus, migration is likely to be-come self-reinforcing (ibid.). As migration from a community or society becomes common, this behaviour is normalized and expected. Returnees do not use the word "transnational", but they nonetheless understand themselves as people who have "travelled" (Chamberlain 1998; Goulbourne/Chamberlain 2001; Olwig/Hastrup 1997). While they share the experience of 'travel', they generally desire to 'return' to Jamaica and enjoy a returnee lifestyle in their homeland. To return to one's place of birth or place of 'origin' is a complex decision-making process that reflects migratory life in general, but also cultural values and strategic choices made at a specific point in life. Before the actual return happens, there are complex sets of thoughts, ideas, aspirations, and intentions involved that form the final motives to move.

Family connections in the home country, dissatisfaction with current life in Canada, feelings of loyalty, nostalgia, or the perception that better life opportunities are awaiting them in Jamaica as well as lasting ties with kin and local life are important factors that prompt return intentions. Especially the maintenance of affective ties through holiday trips, the upkeep of traditional cultural practices and values, maintenance of the local language and staying up-to-date with local news via social media, music and the internet are also worth mentioning. Ultimately, all these factors become relevant when a high level of dissatisfaction with the actual place of living prevails due to issues such as economic instability, experiences with racism and limited access to full participation in the host society. Age (especially pre-retirement), climate, socio-economic status, and acquisition of dual citizenship are further combined catalysts of return. Sometimes life-transforming events such as death and the loss of a significant person are also aspects that catalyse into return decisions. Specifically relevant in the case of Jamaican returnees is, however, land ownership. Owning land or housing is often a precondition to returning to the island. It will be seen in the personal stories of the interlocutors that the influences leading to a return are a combination of two or more of the factors mentioned above. All decisions are highly emotional and filled with images of yearning and 'belonging' to Jamaica or a 'paradise home' once lost. The memories and expectations of the idealized homeland –that returnees departed from years ago or that they only know from vacation and family visits– generate both mental as well as practical hurdles in the process of return and resettlement to Jamaica. Hence, return migration is not the final moment of migration for some of the women in this study. However, before we take a closer look into future movements, it is necessary to examine the affective and imaginative desires that fuel return aspirations among the women of this ethnography: The desire of returning to a place where feelings of home, belonging, and acceptance await, regardless of social status and skin colour.

9.1   Nine Nights of Postmemory

For Elisha, her Jamaican identity was always an active component of her life. Her parents made sure she and her sister were firmly rooted in Jamaican culture. "I am Jamaican. I know where I am from, you understand, I know my roots", she claims. Growing up in a multigenerational house grounded her emotionally to her homeland as narratives from Jamaica and memories were omnipresent; primarily through the Jamaican cuisine of her grandmother and through her parents speaking affectionately about Jamaica, the climate, the food, the music and their childhood memories of growing up in a "stress-free" place. When Elisha was a child, her mother arranged regular holiday trips to Jamaica that caused her to have an excessively positive sense of nostalgia and feelings of belonging to the island. The intermittently practiced "home" return to visit family and friends while being on vacation in Jamaica constructed a complex imaginary of Elisha's local-to-local relation (see Duval 2002; Coles/Timothy 2004). Hannam, Sheller, and Urry describe how memories influence desires to return to an ethnic homeland. They state, "People and places are continually on the move, but images and communications are also intermittently on the move, and both actual and potential movements organize and structure social life" (Hannam et al. 2006: 11). Lived experiences such as her grandmother's 'soul food', her parents' glorified memories and the short-term periods of returning to Jamaica on holiday trips created imaginaries that inspire Elisha's will to return 'back to the roots' even though she never physically migrated or dislocated in the first place. Hirsch and Miller define the act of generational sharing of language, food, and folklore from the homeland as a way of installing "postmemory" (2011: 4), images that exist through actual discussions, but also via memories or historical knowledge from former generations that migrated. This generational memory is recalled in her own childhood experiences and displacement. The cognitive process of remembering here does not form linearly. The past is not given, but continuously reconstructed and represented. Believing and "self-spun webs" (Geertz 2003) of truths seem to be one of the confounding factors in recreating those narratives and positivistic stereotypes over time. The notion of postmemory elaborates this specifically strong bond as "being dominated by narratives and experiences that "precede their own birth" (Hirsch 2008: 103). Hence, the transmitted narratives operate so powerfully that memories are constituted as if they were one's own. Postmemory here is defined as an intergenerational transmitted form of knowledge that functions as an affective force, whereby "post" signals its temporal belatedness (ibid. 106). However, the involvement with the past is less mediated by acts of remembering, but rather by "imaginative investment, projection and creation" (Hirsch 2008: 107). Thomas-Hope sets forth: "The spheres of contact established historically and maintained by Caribbean countries through political and economic linkages determine the overall framework of the national information field" (2002: 7). This statement gives further rise to the assumption of postmemory not only being interconnected with familial remembrance and personal mental journeys into the past, but also to a "national" memory culture of migration and displacement. Taking into account the global connection of Jamaican people all over the world, travelling and living in other nations and cities, Elisha's lifestyle reflects Appadurai's notion of the significance of imagination through the production of cultural aspects such as "[...], songs, fantasies, myths and stories" (Appadurai 1996: 49). He argues further that globalization, media, and new technologies embrace the interchanging and imaginary process across time and space (ibid. 55). Through contemporary social media and messenger services, Elisha stays in daily contact with her Jamaican friends who greatly support her idea to come to Jamaica. An ongoing process of information gathering and exchange via communication networks between planners, movers and those who stay behind further contribute to the differing perceptions of what goes on "abroad" and "a yard[1]". Thomas-Hope outlines: "[...] migration has become deeply embedded in the psyche of Caribbean peoples over the past century and a half" (Thomas-Hope 2002: 1.2.1). Elisha explains her decision to return to Jamaica equitably as an emotional move, a journey of yearning that exists before her actual physical relocation. Sheller and Urry (2006) describe this act as a "virtual return" while still living in the host country. Additionally, through staying in touch with family abroad via technological services and engaging in touristic mobility, women like Elisha create individual aspirations and opinions about Jamaica that exist only in their very own particular cognitive, imaginative worlds. Through Elisha's connections, the importance of simultaneity across geographical borders is again emphasized. Continuous social interactions through what Appadurai (1996) calls "technoscapes" are one of the processes of transnational mediation and translation that structure interactions in spaces of diversity (Lehmkuhl 2019). The social, cross-cultural relationships and communication networks are the key to the movement of transnational migrants (Levitt et al. 2004).

Moreover, the creation of Jamaica as 'home' is not only constructed through the story-telling of her parents, but also her engagement in female spaces in Montreal, her interest in Jamaican music, food, fashion, and Rastafari. Clifford reminds us, that "practices of displacement might emerge as constitutive of cultural meanings rather than as their simple transfer or extension" (Clifford 1997: 3). Therefore, spatiality functions as a reflection of the interlocutor's agency in the process of becoming 'othered' or of being intentionally different (see the previous chapter). Black diversity existed in Canada long before immigration waves from the Caribbean emerged in the 1960s. However, up to now, they are not part of a broader Canadian mental landscape or national 'master narrative', especially not in Quebec. Therefore, migratory experiences of being "different" to "other" people from one's "own" peer group or relatives are striving forces of a recreation of or longing for an authentic 'homeland' space. The longing for the homeland is characteristic for all women accompanied in this study. Therefore, feelings of, e.g., "homesickness"

---

1   Note: "yard" is a Patois synonym used for Jamaica.

seem by far more deeply rooted than a simplistic view of a linear, modern-day migration to a Canadian exile. The feeling of displacement or separation from the homeland is, therefore, less a physical than an emotional condition and grounded in what Patterson describes as "natal alienation" (Patterson 1982: 13). Separated from an 'African' homeland through transatlantic slave trade, the dispersal and with it an emotional mourning continues through the event of economically necessary migration to the northern hemisphere. While living in the diaspora, the exchange of information and images via various networks and "-scapes" (Appadurai 1996: 34f.) reconstruct an idealization of Jamaica and are vital components of distinctly constructed "Jamaicanized" identity formations. Plaza describes that imaginative mobility is embodied in memories, nostalgia, and geographic locations to stay connected with home and in the host society, in which migrants uphold a mental, physical and emotional network with relevant locations (Plaza 2008: 5). Longing for a place consistent with their identity constructions uncovers 'home' less as a category of assignment than as a notion of meaningful place.

When Elisha's grandmother died four years ago, the family transported her mortal remains to the family gravesite in Jamaica according to her last will. "Granny always said, 'mi nah go sleep inna dis soil yah'"[2], recollects Elisha. Hirsch and Miller (2011) explain that specifically second and third generation immigrant children consume homeland narratives repeatedly through language use, culture, music, and stories of their relatives. Here postmemory is again relevant as Elisha's aspiration to leave Montreal for Jamaica strengthened through the experience of her grandmother's death. As Hirsch states, "Familial structures of mediation and representation facilitate the affiliative acts of the postgeneration. The idiom of family can become an accessible lingua franca easing identification and projection across distance and difference" (Hirsch 2008: 115). Such a 'projection' can be found in Elisha's experiences of her grandmother's nine night, a ceremony held before the burial in Jamaica at their family home in Montreal. Elisha reflects on the procedure as follows, "When grandma passed away, my mother wanted to do a traditional nine night. That was the moment I really wanted to know more about my family's past, about our heritage. It was overwhelming. I realized how little I did know", Elisha reflects contemplatively. The traditional Jamaican ceremony is an event where family and friends gather on the ninth[3] day (and night) after the passing of the deceased

---

2   Translation: Grandma always said, 'I do not want to be buried in Canada!'.

3   Note: The symbol of the 'nine' derives from the belief that a person's soul stays 'on earth' for nine days after their death. On the ninth night, the spirit of the deceased passes through the 'dead yard' to 'saying goodbye' to the family and friends. For many Jamaican families, it is an important ritual so the deceased spirit will not be trapped or turn into a 'duppy' (Jamaican word for ghost). Therefore, some people, for example, cover mirrors, stop clocks from running or move furniture.

to mourn, exchange stories, eat and drink. It is a procedure of standing guard until the departing spirit is ready to leave the house to go to its ancestral 'roots' in Jamaica (or at times Africa) and eternal peace. Like many children of immigrants, Elisha realized even more strongly that she knew little about the proceeding itself, neither what people expected of her nor what was required in general. The number of people who came to mourn for her grandmother was an overwhelming experience, similar to the amount of food, drinks, and the numerous talks that felt like an emotional roller coaster. "There were people from Grandma's church and different jobs, all those 1950s and 1960s immigrants with so much to share. Women who last saw me decades ago were insulted that I didn't know who they were", recollects Elisha. Their stories, some memories from childhood days, others more recent were the highlight of the evenings. "I heard for the first time about her life in Jamaica, the jobs she did there, how she met my grandfather, about going to parties here in Montreal in the 1970s, about walking home because no taxi driver would take them because they were Black", related Elisha.

The differences regarding rituals between a traditional Euro-Canadian and Afro-Jamaican death ceremony was new ground to Elisha, who had been only to one or two traditional Christian funerals in Montreal before. Enduring the ninth night brought her to an emotional "boiling point", especially since the ceremony is not only about the passing person's spirit, but also about the relatives who grieve and stay behind. "When my mum and aunty came and asked my sister and me to rearrange the furniture in granny's bedroom, I was mortified and didn't want to do it [...]". Nine night traditionally involves moving pieces of furniture, which belonged to the dead person, e.g., the bed and other personal items to cause the leaving spirit to be disoriented and depart from the house. This inner conflict created by her mother's wish marked a turning point for Elisha. "I was so disconnected from this tradition and did not understand what it meant to my mother. I realized [...] I had to wake up out of my Canadian bubble". From that day on, Elisha's wish to return to Jamaica intensified. The loss of her grandmother was a catalysing event that also confronted her with her own mother's traditional belief systems, which she had never noticed as strongly up until this day. Elisha's return is therefore highly influenced by her parents' support who hope that Elisha can have their way to a comfortable retirement by reinstalling networks with local friends and relatives and reactivating their old links.

Elisha's knowledge about Jamaica that her parents tried to install through holiday trips served to prevent a feeling of alienation in the event of possible return. Therefore, a multi-layered process of yearning for reconnection, for the community, for traditions and geographies is perceptible. Places become symbolic of specific life experiences, expectations, and people that make sense of memories, imaginaries, and affective ties. Homeland, like any other place, is, therefore, a fabricated project that changes over the course of life and deals with ever-new formations

(Gupta/Ferguson 1992; Massey 1995). Although places are geographically locatable, home, as in the case of Elisha, can prove to be imagination or projection of personal ideas and expectations (Morley 2000). Her mother and grandmother's romanticized homeland narratives together with family visits in Jamaica nurtured her with the image of Jamaica as an alternative home; a distinct cultural geography imprinted in her psyche like a cognitive plan. The caretaking of her homemade Jamaican shrine that stands near to the window of her little one-room apartment is representative of this plan; filled with souvenir collections, Caribbean-inspired decor, maps and photo collages, Rastafari literature and concert tickets from her favourite Jamaican musicians. Furthermore, her bodily practices and art are a reflection of her inner self-construction, her yearning for home and the glorification of an idealized homeland. Home is then, for example, similar to a metaphorical umbrella that protects Elisha as she states from "the coldness of the heart in this city".

9.2   A Taste of Home

The feeling for Jamaica as home also seems like an unquestioned affiliation in Ms. Brown's life. This affiliation depicts individualized perspectives on a home-space that go beyond the field of the nation-state itself. It is a space connected to the people who continuously create it as such, a space of hybridity. Interpreting her daily practices about home reveals the vexed and changing relationships she has with various locations showcasing that each location subsequently depends on interpersonal networks to friends, kin, neighbours, and links to church or community members. Rapport and Dawson debate 'home' as a concept that "brings together memory and longing, the ideational, the affective and the physical, the spatial and the temporal, the local and the global, the positively evaluated and the negatively" (1998: 26f.). It becomes clear that 'home' therefore can take on a multitude of interpretational levels, which in combination provide information about, e.g., identity, connections between dwelling and home and, of course, time and space. Ms. Brown's home-making practices in Montreal are a symbol of the experienced loss of her childhood home and the absence of a familiar, meaningful place. Much of her identity construction bases on this experience of loss and the desire to reverse or improve it soon. Home here lies in the smell of her Jamaican food, traditional recipes from her grandmother and in the conserved stories, which she also passed on to her children about their 'authentic' homeland. As Assmann and Czaplicka state,

"[...] cultural memory is characterized by its distance from the everyday. [...] Cultural memory has its fixed point; [...]. These fixed points are fateful events of the past, whose memory is maintained [...]" (1995: 129f.).

Informal talks and sharing food at the kitchen table were, not only important key elements of building a trustworthy relationship with a woman like Ms. Brown, but also led to relevant "rich points" (Agar 2008) of understanding the cultural subtext and the connection between cultural memory and food cooking practices. Hence, taste and smell as part of an indispensable "sensory" ethnographic practice (Pink 2006; 2013) became pertinent.

Ms. Brown's kitchen is a rather small, but practically organized space in which she devotes a lot of her time. Even though she has long working shifts, she will always make time to prepare her dinner. Eating outside her house or taking out food is out of the question unless it is from a Jamaican chef in Montreal that she truly trusts. On a Saturday morning, I visit Ms. Brown for another in-house meeting. Approaching the stairs that lead to Ms. Brown's upper apartment complex, I smell the typical flavour of boiled beans (called peas in Jamaica), pimento and garlic. It is nearly 10 a.m., and the meal is already bubbling in the large silver aluminium pot (Dutchie pot) under a small flame on Ms. Brown's stove. The red beans, which are a main component of Jamaican cuisine, had been soaked overnight and serve as the ingredient for her soup today. Tomorrow a share of the pre-boiled legumes will be combined with white rice and coconut milk to make a typical Jamaican Sunday dinner of rice and peas (as a side dish served with meat or fish). "If you don't cook your food in a Dutchie pot it no taste Jamaican", Ms. Brown says while she gently drops a whole Scotch bonnet pepper in the pot. "If the pepper buzz[4] the whole soup will spoil, so you have to know how to stir the soup, [...] when I was a young girl my grandmother taught me how to cook real red pea's soup". While she grinds some more spices on a chopping board, Ms. Brown visits her memories. When she was 13 years old, she lived on her grandmother's farm in rural Jamaica. Her mother had left for Canada several years before. Even though she remembers missing her, living in the countryside was the best part of her childhood. Especially during school holidays, Ms. Brown and her sister had endless possibilities. A small stream behind the house was their bathing spot; there were goats and chickens on the farm and numerous fruit trees that the children could climb and eat from as well as vegetables that her grandmother harvested. The slightly yellowed picture that I saw days ago in her living room showed her grandmother's house and the land she inherited together with her sister. The puzzle finally came together. Ms. Brown spent most of her childhood time helping outside in the garden or the kitchen. Cooking with her grandmother is one of Ms. Brown's fondest memories. "Our food is a reflection of

---

4   Translation: If the pepper bursts, the whole soup will be ruined [...]".

our heritage; I am very protective when it comes to my culture. Everything I know comes from my grandmother's tradition", she states. Ms. Brown remembers her grandmother as a resolute, strong, and caring woman who instilled morals, spiritual guidance, and kindness in her. "She used to share out food to poorer people as well; she gave everyone a handout, used to help raise children for others. She was an important part of her local community, and the only thing she feared was God", Ms. Brown explains thoughtfully while stirring up the soup again. "When we were sick, she went outside to the bushes and picked herbs; she had this knowledge about the plants and the land, you know. We didn't have no pharmacy [chuckles]; she knew how to cure anything; she was a powerful woman, my grandmother". Ms. Brown's memory of her grandmother takes on the form of an archetypal figure whose strength and teachings are worshipped. While Ms. Brown's mother was also an essential part of her later life, her grandmother was much more influential in the formation of her belief systems and in the foundation of socio-cultural practices that Ms. Brown passed on to her children. The children were raised "in the tradition of my grandmother", as she puts it. Ms. Brown's grandmother comes across as an idealized figure. The grandmother with her remembered knowledge about healing, food practices, and her generosity and spiritual teachings as well as community-oriented life, is an energetic, spiritual as well as an emotional connection with Ms. Brown. The return to 'grandmother's land' serves as a strong part of her own identity and self-understanding. The search for a place consistent with these memories is reimagined in moments of leisure, of food cooking and of "nurturing the soul" as Ms. Brown says. Her weekly meal plan of authentic Jamaican dishes, which repeat in almost the same running order, on the one hand generate daily routines, which offer security, and on the other hand, produce spaces of yearning and remembrance, sentimental journeys across the ocean of memories. Norbye describes this nostalgia of migrants as "a deep longing for a lost wholeness. [...] for another time, for [...] completeness" (Norbye 2010: 160). Ms. Brown's furniture, the decoration of her living room, the exclusive cooking of Jamaican cuisine, and the repetitive anecdotes of her childhood memories in Jamaica construct a life unliveable in Montreal. It is significantly unliveable, because experiences outside of the safe spaces are quite harmful and, together with work-related stress and racialization and the cold climate that affect Ms. Brown's health increasing with age, life seems better in Jamaica.

Her social network in Montreal, which mainly consists of English-speaking, Afro-Caribbean women in similar life circumstances (similar age group, similar job, and similar recreational activities), offers little resistance to her plans. Thus, Ms. Brown is aware of the fact that, after all this time abroad, a recovery of her "authentic" homeland is impossible, she still hopes to regain the feeling of being at home, at her place of 'heart', as she puts it. Homeland as a meaningful place marked by multiple temporalities is woven together through feelings of belonging

(Easthope 2004: 135). One is at home when one inhabits a cognitive environment in which one can undertake the routines of daily life and through, which one finds her identity best mediated or in that, sense 'homeless' when such a cognitive environment is missing (Silverstone 1994; Hannerz 2004). However, her high expectations of having a quick and easy return to her homeland and her beloved childhood memories will result in a painful and disappointing process.

9.3   Partner Banks and Homeland Ties

"Living in Montreal also means having a good network of people; it is not like anywhere else. You need help, especially help from other women who go through or experience something similar. My mother was not there; I had no relatives, no aunt, nothing. So you make a network that works like family and makes you feel at home", Carol remembers, talking about her first years in Montreal. For her, being, living and working in the city without her mother, grandmother, or any other maternal or paternal female relative was difficult at the beginning. Even though she left Jamaica by choice and although she had a professional network that was work- and career-related, she remembers how it felt to be on her own. "My mother she taught me how to live with people, she was a rigorous woman, who showed her love in a tough way, you know, she gave me common sense", reflects Carol. The first contact that Carol found locally in Montreal was through church. In church service, she met other Afro-Caribbean women who served as a social anchor in her first years in Montreal. "I realized many of us newcomers had monetary issues and extreme problems to open up official bank accounts, especially without secure employment that was well paid for. Most of the women I met were domestics; some did not have legal documents or overstayed. [...] So we started doing a partner. Me and one of my friends who also had a better education and a regular income started it. The idea was not ours, though, my grandmother, my mother, many people that I knew from home used to do it. My grandmother used to be a partner because she was known to be smart and trustworthy. I knew how it works from my family. [...]. People trusted us!".

The partner bank is a collective saving scheme popular in Jamaica. The idea behind this traditional socio-economic system is simple. A group of people, so-called 'partners', agrees to pay a regular amount of money to a trusted person, the so-called 'banker', every week. Weekly, one member of the group receives the total sum contributed by all partners. Therefore, if ten partners save 50 dollars a week over ten weeks, each one will receive 500 dollars, either at the beginning of the scheme in the form of a loan or at the end of the scheme in the form of accumulated savings. For the system to work efficiently, the number of partners and the number of weeks have to be even. The banker is a trustworthy person, who

decides which partners are paid their 'hand' or their 'draw' in which order, generally selecting the more trustworthy ones first, while more unreliable partners get
paid at the end of a term. This informal economic system of pooling money has
its roots in the impoverished communities of Jamaica's urban and rural population (Hossein 2018: 86f.). This community aiding activity is primarily in the hands
of women or "banker ladies" (ibid.). In Montreal, the low access or even exclusion
that immigrant women from the Caribbean had to face at mainstream banking
institutes fostered a socio-economic security system amongst themselves in line
with their socio-cultural heritage and networks of care. Using 'partners' offered
the possibility to save money and to enable them to survive by infiltrating the local
financial system without attracting further attention as many partners were undocumented immigrants. "Most people prefer partner banks because there is no
paperwork involved. I remember as if it was yesterday when she [here referring to
her grandmother] sat at the kitchen table counting the bills with quick fingers and
writing everything in her little booklet. Interesting how such small things you see
as a child take on great importance in your later life", Carol says lost in thought.
"The knowledge that I had from my grandmother really jumped start my career
and my life in Montreal as a young woman without connections. She helped me to
reach where I am today". Even though Carol no longer runs a partner bank today,
she explains that the system remains popular amongst Afro-Caribbean people in
Montreal to this day. The informality that allows more impoverished or undocumented members to draw cash, for example, in emergencies or when their credit
status would make them ineligible for loans from conventional banks, keeps the
partner banks alive, and the system has long since reached the middle class (Hossein 2018: 86). Similarly, to Jamaicans at home, Jamaicans in Montreal here exclude
themselves by choice from regular commercial institutes since they trust and know
the people in their collective. Jamaican banker women can bridge precarious situations by offering their financial services, which ordinary people can trust (Hossein
2018: 87).

After Carol met her husband who was born in Montreal to a Barbadian family
background, life became a little easier. She could rely on his family networks to
help with daily needs or with the child rearing, while she was at work. Marriage
and the local inclusion through her partner bank endeavours were strong pillars
that aided Carol's integration and access to society. The knowledge from her 'foremothers' and the upkeep of the traditional, informal Jamaican economic system
provided for monetary needs and linkages with other Afro-Caribbean women in
her local environment in Montreal. The feeling of hominess ("Heimatgefühl") and
connection to Jamaica and the friendships and 'trust-networks' shared with other
women prevailed through these practices. Therefore, Carol wanted her children to
have a vital connection to Jamaica. By narrating her childhood memories to them,
and via the anecdotes she shared about her mother and grandmother, she fostered

in them a sense of connection to her country of birth. She made sure that they enjoyed summer holidays on the island and is proud that her adult children have secure connections with their relatives in Jamaica and engage in travels there until today. "I could have never imagined raising my children as solely Canadian", states Carol. "They have to know their roots and background. Their nationality will always be questioned here; it is fragile", declares Carol. Moreover, she says, "Jamaica will always be there; it is our cultural identity, the knowledge, the practicality. When you go there, you can charge up again for a couple of months and get away from the winter [laughs] that is how we always did it. You need this energy. It doesn't mean you need to live there [...], no not at all, but without it, you cannot live in Canada either. It nurtures the soul!".

Even though Carol engages in homeland vacations every year, she would never return to Jamaica. The homeland serves to contrast the negative experiences of living in Canada: Racial discrimination, separation from stay-behind family and hectic day-to-day life. Jamaica is a fond memory that serves as a place of great experiences, beautiful vacations, and romantic notions of cultural belonging (cf. Said 1985). A place that charges up her batteries, as she says and an affective connection across time and space. The nostalgic imaginaries that Carol holds to her place of origin also give rise to an 'essentialization' of Jamaica. Examples of such are, i.e., in Jamaica, things are still soulful, people are always friendly, food still tastes like food, and the weather is always good, which are significant imaginative factors in Carol's recurrent homeland travels. As Hirsch and Miller describe, while living in host countries many migrants become "roots-seekers" (2011: 13). Although Carol is highly reflective of herself not being able to live in Jamaica permanently anymore, her well-organized holiday trips and her longstanding absence from living a regular life in the country of her birth constructed a somewhat sanitized version of Jamaica. Even though all of the women in this study have their own or second-hand affective memories that mark important points of their own or familial histories, in the event of returning to Jamaica the character of these memories and the way how they clash with local facts show similarities in all cases.

10 Take Off: Mobile Perspectives

With this chapter, we leave the Montreal-based ethnography behind. In the following, we will travel to or return to Jamaica with the women of this study. Here we look into the mobility process itself that raises questions such as "Which preparations occurred before departure? Who needs to be notified before coming home? How was the traveling process itself?". The experience of accompanying the interlocutors on their homeland travels and returns was a multi-layered, yet, holistic process that involved a broad range of before, during and after communication and interconnected dynamics involving various people, anticipation, moving to Jamaica, on-site experiences, going back and post-travel recollections. As Watts and Urry state, "Mobile ethnography involves traveling with people and things, participating in their continual shift through time, place and relations with others" (2008: 867). Here the ethnography again follows the actual course of the fieldwork, which started in the urban environment of Montreal and then took off via plane from Montreal or Toronto to the Jamaican island. Watts and Urry (2008) identify the traveling time as a 'liminal space' between 'here' and 'there' that needs consideration when researching migratory mobility. This liminal space of traveling brings the anticipations to a climax while pre-communications and preparations are silenced or finished. Moving together with the interlocutors enriched the analysis since a broader understanding of their mobility strategies evolved.

Instead of just meeting them at specific points in time, I was part of an entire process. The sites I observed and visited resulted in field notes and photographs. The photographs were again relevant for the discussion of the post-travel recollections with the research partners. Anticipation, memories, and expectations constructed before traveling and returning, strongly influence the 'local knowledge', for example in terms of the ways my interlocutors experience Jamaica, its people, and their (extended) families. As we will see post-traveling, individuals then remember only particular events or situations and tend to forget or overlook negative experiences after some time passes by, which results in recurring travels. In this sense, local experiences altogether influence future travel and migratory intentions as well as future anticipation and expectations.

10.1   Flying Home

In two years, Ms. Brown will receive her well-deserved pension and can follow her dream to return to Jamaica. Even though she is still indecisive about leaving behind her friends and beloved apartment in Notre-Dame-de-Grâce. Today, 23 years after her last trip to the island, Ms. Brown finally flies back home to her place of 'heart'. On this trip, she will find out if her family used her longstanding payments and remittances to further build, maintain and furnish her part of the "dream house", the inherited home of her beloved grandmother and place of retirement. Ms. Brown arrives at precisely 4:30 a.m. in front of the Air Transat section of Toronto Pearson International Airport. She waves excitedly and screams my name while making her way through the crowd. Behind her "a cousin" as she refers to the young man, who pushes a luggage cart with three huge suitcases and a large handbag piled so high he could hardly be seen. Stylish as ever, in a lime green two-piece dress suit, golden sandals, her hair, and nails freshly done and decorated with jewellery and with a nervous look on her face, the 63-year-old woman stands before me. Today December 9, 2016 marks over twenty years that she has not been 'home' to Jamaica.

"I'll have to pay for overweight", she laughs while we make our way to the check-in counter and continues in deep Jamaican Patois in which she often changes at will: "Mi cyan reach from foreign and no bring nutten fi dem"[1]. "Dem", her younger sister Jodi and her entire family have been anticipating her arrival for months in the little countryside town where she grew up with her grandmother. The waiting area is jam-packed with tourists and Jamaicans, who are all ready to escape the Canadian winter. The noisy airport loudspeaker announces a 45-minute delay shortly before boarding. Ms. Brown's smile fades "typical" she grunts and shows her disapproval with a sound made by sucking air through her front teeth. This "kissing of the teeth" is a typical non-verbal communication form in Jamaica that many people use when they are not pleased with a situation or person. While we wait, suddenly they roll in. The first one is hardly noticeable, then the second, the third one strikes our attention until sixteen elderly people in sixteen wheelchairs park in front of the priority-boarding lane of our flight. "Dem fly home fi dead", whispers Ms. Brown in my ear, "you see, that's why mi waan go from early mi nah waan do dis"[2]

The turbines howl loudly. "Oh pupa Jesus, please make this plane yah reach safe!" Ms. Brown prays nervously with folded hands as the plane starts to get ready for take-off. We are seated like Jamaican 'tinned mackerels', under my feet Ms. Brown's oversized handbag because her seat neighbour, a Jamaican engineer from

---

1   Translation: I cannot come home from Canada and have no gifts for the family.

2   Translation: They fly home to die, you understand, that's why I want to leave Canada now I don't want to do this.

Mississauga, also brought several different sized pieces of luggage, similar to the rest of the passengers who all seem to be traveling with overweight luggage today. Ms. Brown talks a lot, not only to the engineer, who is flying home for Christmas, but also with an older Jamaican man sitting on the next aisle seat beside us and with a young mother sitting in the seat in front of her. The flight is one merry, loud chatter of small talk. The topics are diverse, but are certainly about Jamaica. After a short and uncomfortable three hours and fifty minutes, we belatedly touch the ground. "You smell it, darling? We reach, we reach!" hums Ms. Brown cheerfully right after stepping out of the aircraft. "Yeah, Jamaica" winks the old man from the aisle seat, a big smile on his wrinkly face.

At the baggage claim area, Ms. Brown heaves her three suitcases from a wild cluster of luggage stacked upon each other. Before that, we had to wait almost an hour in the seemingly never-ending line of immigration control. "Welcome to Jamaica", she chuckles "what a mess". After we finally got through with our search for luggage and the sheer never-ending waiting time at immigration, a solid wall of sultry-hot air confronts us as we leave the airport building in Montego Bay. "Wha gwaan foreigner?"[3] Jodi shouts cheerfully, running towards Ms. Brown, who instantly starts to weep for joy when she sees her sister, followed by joyous hugging and chattering. "We see us, next week girl, thanks for coming along", Ms. Brown waves to me out of the moving vehicle and drives off to the countryside, while I make my way to the taxi stand.

10.2   The Festive Season

"I am so glad it's this time of the year again", Carol sings happily, bending down over a large suitcase stuffed with a variety of food containers, clothes, shoes and wrapped up presents. It is nearly two weeks until Christmas. Carol is packing her 'souvenirs' for her stay-behind family in Jamaica. At least twice a year she travels 'home', for vacation and visiting her family and friends. In the winter, their dates to 'go down' are always fixed a year in advance. Carol's family has to leave the 'freezer', as she calls Toronto during winter, at least for three weeks during the Christmas season.

While wrapping up some t-shirts in paper printed with snowflakes, she talks non-stop about the beach, the warm climate, the sunshine, mangoes, pears (the Jamaican word for avocados), fried fish, curried goat and her need for relaxation and enjoyment. "On top of everything I need to know what a gwaan[4]", Carol declares

---

3   Translation: How are you/ What's new foreigner?
4   Translation: Above all, I need to know what's new/ what's going on.

zipping up one of her suitcases while sitting on top of it. Her periodic visits to Jamaica do not only serve as homeland and roots vacations but also foster meaningful relationships she has with local friends and extended family, whom she misses a lot. Similar to Ms. Brown's case the buying of gifts is essential before departing, not only during the Christmas season. "I always support my family, I mean, I send money and it's only appropriate to bring some gifts, you see [...]. Jamaica is hard, trust me, we need to help", says Carol.

Carol explains that her stay-behind family more or less expects the 'foreigners' to bring things from abroad to support the local part of the household with various items from clothes, school materials, foreign food products, cosmetics to toys and baby articles. Carol's return visits are well prepared and organized as she even has the most distant cousin on her checklist of gift receivers. Gifts and monetary support both function as reciprocal payments for the caring and hosting of Carol and her husband during their stay on the island. Furthermore, these ties are relevant if Carol wanted to return permanently one day. "You never know what happens", she always says. Hence, roots traveling facilitates future return intentions and reconstructs the local benchmark against what is 'heard' or remembered while being in Canada. In that sense, Carol's seasonal visits are not only crucial for herself and her family, but also for others in the Canadian diaspora whom Carol informs about local news. "Here, help me with that one", commands Carol and points at the next large piece of luggage, "this is the one with the presents from other people". Puzzled, I ask her what she means by "other people", it quickly becomes clear that Carol does not only carry items for her own family but also additionally brings gifts and remittances (cash) on behalf of others, who are unable to travel to Jamaica, for example, due to their immigrant status. "Without these lists [points at three different neatly hand-written papers], I would completely lose track of everything that I have to bring. So now help", she urges, "take this nice watch from aunty Ruby and roll it in a pair of socks, immigration does not need to find everything we bring", she chuckles and continues packing. We organize the luggage until late at night. The next morning we leave for the airport early to check in six huge suitcases, three of which are packed with presents, and take off to Kingston's Norman Manley airport.

10.3   Coming Here to Stay

"I am boarding now, so see you at the airport in a few", Elisha shouts through the WhatsApp video, calling me from Montreal's airport. Five hours later, I'm waiting in front of Montego Bay's crowded airport exit gate, making my way through many suitcases, travellers, tourists, hotel concierges and shouting taxi drivers. I arrived in Jamaica a week prior to Elisha and today marks the starting point of her endeavour to 'return' to the land of her ancestors. Before her and my arrival in Jamaica, we coordinated our trip and Elisha laid out plans about all the things she wanted to do during her first four weeks on the island, which seemed like a task for a lifetime. Even though Elisha knew the island from regular holiday trips with her family as a child and teenager, it quickly became apparent that organizing the trip and traveling alone in Jamaica was something that worried her a lot. The preparations and also the process of 'who to inform ahead of time' was of great significance before she travelled. Especially her maternal aunt was a crucial part of her arrangements, which meant the conducting of numerous phone calls, texts as well as video messages. Two weeks before her departure, she asked me to take over the planning of the first two nights and the organization of our rental car. Firstly, because I was already there, and secondly, because Elisha was not sure if she wanted to drive by herself since she feared Jamaican roads. I quickly realized that I had more local knowledge in terms of infrastructural and contextual knowledge of, e.g. bargaining with vendors. However, as best as I could, I held back this knowledge in most situations on our travels in order to not affecting her experiences and the overall course of the trip.

"I'm here", Elisha screams across the airport hall, which leads some people to crane their necks in her direction to see what happened. After meeting, we made our way to the car rental, which is located directly inside the airport hall. After a waiting time of nearly one and a half hours, we drive off to our first stop on the North Coast.

11 Frictions in Paradise: Facing Facts

"Yes: if, owing to the work of oblivion, the returning memory can throw no bridge, form no connecting link between itself and the present minute, if it remains in the context of its own place and date, if it keeps its distance, its isolation in the hollow of a valley or upon the highest peak of a mountain summit, for this very reason it causes us suddenly to breathe a new air, an air which is new precisely because we have breathed it in the past, that purer air which the poets have vainly tried to situate in paradise and which could induce so profound a sensation of renewal only if it had been breathed before, since *the true paradises are the paradises that we have lost*" (Proust 1999 [1927]: 259-261, emphasis added).

This chapter follows four interlocutors of this study as their imaginations and aspirations about Jamaica are confronted with local facts and experiences that result in unexpected boundaries. For these women, cultivating the dream of returning to their homeland, actual return migration and return visits become a reality check. Here, return aspirations are also intertwined with female desires for social mobility and living the 'good live' in Jamaica upon return. The return intentions that started from an inward wish and process to leave Montreal due to negative experiences will, for some women, be interrupted or shifted in the light of the emergence of new socio-cultural boundaries, differences that ground in being alienated from local social life and certain customs. While in Montreal, the interlocutors rarely feel a sense of belonging, they construct their identity around images of belonging to an ethnic homeland. However, upon return, some experience ethnic marginalization because they are seen as foreigners (see Kim 2009). Similar to Kim's study on Korean Americans, the women's returns result in the process of re-experiencing their "struggles with race, ethnicity, nationality, and culture" (ibid. 306). Their 'otherness' (cf. Spivak 1985) here is primarily based on cultural differences. Therefore, the study explores the frictions and adjustments made by the interlocutors under these circumstances. Several aspects hereby emphasise the 'in-between' positionality (Bhabha 1994) and 'special' status of these women. Thus, difficulties in making friends, problems regarding their accents, loneliness, feelings of being an outsider, financial pressure, familial responsibilities, culture shock and aspects of resentment as well as having to accept things as they are will be analysed.

11.1   House of Horror

Her voice sounds hollow over the phone as if she is calling from a faraway place. "I am coming to town next Monday", she grunts into the telephone. A long, deep sigh came from the other end of the line when I asked her if everything was all right. When I picked her up at the bus stop on Monday afternoon, nothing was left of her happiness and motivation at our 'goodbye' at the airport. "I am so frustrated [...]" she affirms. Her family reunification was not going as she expected. She arrived at the property in a happy mood, feeling great to be back home. When she got there, her sense of well-being was quickly shattered after she realized that the house was not in good condition: The roof and some tiles needed urgent fixing, the water pipes were leaking, and the formerly beautiful garden looked more like a neglected jungle. Above all that, the expensive kitchen appliances that Ms. Brown had shipped to Jamaica were not in the house. Her sister had never cleared them at the wharf, which requires paying customs charges and handling fees. The monthly money transfers (remittances) to her sister were no longer used for the house since Jodi had lost her job recently. Instead of telling Ms. Brown about her difficult economic situation, she used the money to pay her expenses. As a result, the mortgage payment as well as the electricity bill had not been made for two months. To make things worse, her cousin's family moved (without paying rent) in the other side of the two-story residence, which was thought to be Ms. Brown's upon her return. After confronting her sister, they had a great quarrel that left her feeling rejected in her own house. "They want me to pay for everything [...]. I'm honestly in shock", she goes on in a broken voice. Ms. Brown's family was not expecting her to 'really' coming back to the house they built through her income. They ridiculed her, teasing her with questions about her intention to come back to this countryside place full of hardship and struggles for everyone and where she, after all, would be treated as an unknowing 'foreigner'. No, she was supposed to stay in her nice place 'up North', where everything was provided for her. Her sister finally reminded her that it was Ms. Brown's moral responsibility to take care of the problematic financial and familial circumstances since she was the only one in a successful living and monetary situation. The reminder of her being the 'foreign' breadwinner for her family hurt Ms. Brown deeply since she had never neglected her duty to provide and send money to her kin. She was left with feelings of guilt and a heavy heart: "The title [of the land] is in both mine and my sister's name, so that is a roadblock I have to face", acknowledges Ms. Brown. "I really thought they would make something out of themselves with all the money that I sent; dem just spent it on nonsense [...]. I tell you, dawg say him won't work, him wi' siddung an look fi him mus get a libin[1] [...]. No, I have the right now to come back and stretch my foot after all these years of hard work", she says. Realizing that being absent while her sister was supposed to build, renovate, and refurbish their grandmother's old house was a significant mistake. Seeing the house as being far from the romantic state she had wished it to be in was one thing, yet the experience of being back in her childhood village was another.

The flourishing area where her grandmother used to reside is impoverished and crime-ridden today. The former quaint little village was struck with unemployment and rural depopulation. Therefore, many houses were "for sale" or had been abandoned and most locals dream of getting away as fast as possible. Ms. Brown's sister who was ashamed about the situation, had not informed her because of the fear that Ms. Brown would have stopped sending monetary support or worse, might have looked around for a house somewhere else. After the disastrous effects of Hurricane Gilbert in 1988 and due to national and foreign policy changes that were introduced after the 1989 elections by the *People's National Party*, local demographic changes in the village occurred. Young people were trying to make it in the urban centre of Kingston or trying to get a visa to migrate to North America. In the following years, even at the time of Ms. Brown's last visit in 1993, the former peaceful countryside shifted. Infrastructural problems and crime rates significantly increased until the millennium while property values and school ratings decreased. Hence, many families that Ms. Brown knew moved away and the people in the village felt strange to her. Ms. Brown, who thought she was well aware about the local situation, had to realize that her family had not informed her about the new conditions. After she fought with her sister, Ms. Brown decided to walk through the town, down the road to the local police station to talk to the officer on duty; however, the answers there were also not pleasing and aggravated the overall picture of the problematic situation. In addition, Ms. Brown knows that locals, who move on to better areas and leave behind people of lower classes, commonly abandon impoverished places. "Jamaicans don't gentrify places", she lets out with a heavy sigh. "I should have been more careful, you know, ask around and also try to read local news online or so, but I have to confess I feel like an alien. It seems like all this is a nightmare, as if I had driven into the wrong village", Ms. Brown stops after letting out the tirade about her sister. We walk, awfully quiet, on our way down the village road, both absorbed in thoughts.

Two days later at a bank institute in Kingston, Ms. Brown draws a number at the entrance and sits down to wait her turn. Only one cashier is open, and a young

---

1 Translation: The dog says he will not work; he will sit down and look, for he must get a living. Meaning: Some people prefer to wait on others to give them handouts instead of working for their own money.

woman is being served. Senior citizens are generally being offered the privilege to be seated until served instead of having to stand up in the often incomprehensibly long line at the counter. Ms. Brown wipes her face with her handkerchief and sighs with relief at the cool air spreading through the air conditioning system. She takes out her phone and waits. After half an hour, Ms. Brown starts to get annoyed. The line is not moving. When another half hour passes, the next cashier becomes available, who seems to be absorbed with logging into her computer. The line still does not move and there is no signal of her number on the small, flat screen. Ms. Brown gets up abruptly and heads right to the desk, "Excuse me what numbers are you serving here?" she asks in a clear voice and proper English. Other people from the queue agree, nod, or make comments about the incredible length of the waiting period. The cashier holds her head down and continues organizing her belongings. "Give me a moment, Miss," she says. Now furious, Ms. Brown demands to speak to the manager who, upon arrival, states, "Of course, you will be served next, Miss. Just take a seat, please". Another 30 minutes pass, and the young woman finally leaves the counter. The screen releases a clear 'beep' and, regrettably, does not display Ms. Brown's number. An elderly woman behind us gets up and makes her way to the desk. Ms. Brown whispers "Jesus have mercy" and sinks back into her chair. That day, Ms. Brown and I spent four hours at the bank to finish her account business. After leaving the institute, Ms. Brown is still angry and rants that she will file a complaint to the banking institute's headquarter about the waiting time and the unfriendly staff.

Another incident happened when Ms. Brown and I went to a local wholesale store, where Ms. Brown wanted to shop for some Jamaican products to take back to Montreal. It was Saturday morning, and many people were out for their week-end shopping. Accordingly, the line was relatively long. After standing nearly 20 minutes in line, finally, it was Ms. Brown's turn to be served. Suddenly, two men come into the wholesale store. With their hectic gestures and loud talking, they attract immediate attention. They stop and then they are standing right next to Ms. Brown. A blink of an eye later, one of them waves to the cashier, smiles and passes Ms. Brown by stretching himself around her and loudly ordering several items from behind the counter. Ms. Brown, seemingly overpowered by this bois-terous behaviour, interjects, "Excuse me, I'm next in line". Before the sales clerk can give her an answer, the man turns around and barks, "Where you think dis is? Foreign? Me a get served now!"[2] While long lines are nothing unusual in Jamaica, it is also commonplace that people will bend themselves over or around you to be served or interrupt you to talk to an employee. From a Euro-Canadian perspective, this behaviour should be blocked or at least excused by the sales representative

---

2   Translation: Where do you think you are? Abroad? It's my turn now!

or the shop owner. Often, especially when a person protests, staff members pretend that they were not aware of who was there first. It can happen that someone will stretch his or her arm across your face while attempting to jump the line. At times, this can happen so subtly and fast that one might not even realize it. Often an individual appears, ignores the queue, orders, or puts money in front of the cashier, takes the products and disappears. The salesperson will proceed while not even looking up to see who is next in line to be served. These practices of serving customers who are not there are prevalent in certain places in Jamaica. If Ms. Brown had been more accustomed to the local procedure at the bank, she would have known the waiting time that comes with opening an account. Similarly, the situation at the wholesale store would not have seemed so strange to her or better; she would have known a different way of addressing the man and his 'line-jumping behaviour'. The act of being or behaving what Jamaicans call "street smart" could have saved her a lot of nerves and frustration. Furthermore, the incidences show that she is no longer used to specific customs and is estranged from claiming her right to be served (which is intimately interconnected with the skilful negotiation of the 'right' local price). The years of absence from Jamaica showed her that she has to readjust to current socio-cultural practices in her homeland.

While lines in Jamaica are slow, driving in Jamaica is fast. Ms. Brown never drove herself and insisted on only driving with official drivers who work for established taxi companies. In the countryside, where only minivans or route taxis[3] operate, this is not an easy task. Similarly, it is hardly possible to order a regular taxi from a company in the middle of Kingston's rush hour. After several unsuccessful attempts to call a driver, Ms. Brown decided on taking a regular route taxi. As we walk in the direction of the stand, a rushed conductor appears in front of Ms. Brown, "forward Miss, dis way, mi ave di best seat fi yuh"[4]. We take our seats in the back of the car, with a middle-aged worker already sitting in the front passenger seat. After exchanging greetings with her, we waited for the conductor to fill the last remaining seat. The engine of the car powered up the air-conditioning system that blew strongly while the back door and the driver door were still open. The route taxi driver, a 30-something man, scolds the conductor for robbing him of his money while not bringing in enough customers. He drops into his seat and steps on the gas pedal to let the engine roar, holding in his hand a sizable and carefully folded stack of Jamaican 100 dollar[5] notes. Finally, the conductor found more customers and a mother with two young children squeezes into the car. Ms. Brown, who sighs deeply, tries to fasten her seatbelt, but reaches behind her into

---

3   Note: Route taxis are cheap cabs that drive only one specific route from point A to point B. If
     passengers want to come off somewhere along the route they usually call for a "one stop".
4   Translation: Come on Miss, this way, I have the best seat reserved for you.
5   Note: 100 JMD (about one USD) is the regular route taxi fee.

a void. All the seat belts have been removed from the vehicle. The driver wipes his sweaty forehead with an old rag, mumbling some curses about the conductor and drives off honking his horn and wildly gesturing into the congested traffic. "Yo, move di vehicle now, boss", he screams to another driver and swings down the road, around potholes, and passes, whenever possible, at an incredible speed. The loud music is still hammering the newest Dancehall music out of the speakers in the trunk. He had been driving on the wrong side of the road for a good while and had driven across several unbroken white lines when Ms. Brown, seemingly afraid, asks the driver to slow down and keep to the traffic regulations. The driver, obviously amused, passes another car in a blind bend and only grunts "time is money, seen". Kindness is not something drivers have in dense traffic, and they cannot afford to sit back. Whoever is first at the route taxi stand will get the next full load of customers. For one drive the taxi driver earns 500 Jamaican dollars (100 JMD from each customer), minus the fee he has to pay for the conductor and minus the cost of gasoline. During rush hour, traffic moves slowly and rushing is the only way to make more money faster. Whoever can manoeuvre their car between two others in the adjoining lane the best is the winner. This can be a very hard-earned win as neither driver wants to be the loser. In general, route taxi drivers earn very little for a relatively demanding job, especially as some of them have to share the pay with the owner of the vehicle they drive. One thing is clear: Ms. Brown will never set foot in one of Kingston's route taxis for the rest of her life. Finally, we reached our destination safely, though shaken and Ms. Brown sweaty with fear.

Due to her rosy imaginaries that she nurtured through her memories about the 'good old days' in Jamaica, Ms. Brown had certain expectations before going back to Jamaica. These expectations clashed greatly with local 'realities' which gave her an immense 'culture shock'. Even though Montreal has its challenges, Ms. Brown now reflected on living with proper socio-economic institutions that, for the most part worked, as they should. In Jamaica, she experienced numerous situations in which she felt helpless or confused as a citizen. Whether running necessary errands at the bank, shopping, or simply walking by the roadside, many incidences showed her that she was used to a much more advanced infrastructural environment. After her return to Montreal she stated disillusioned, "I can't remember my people being so rude to one another". The lack of a feeling of community or a collective sense, which she had often described as such a significant traditional value and which she carried in her nostalgia all these years seemed to be lost, especially in her beloved village. The unforeseen rejection she faced on her revisit to Jamaica and specifically the quarrel with her sister and the state of the house deeply traumatized her. This was nothing that she would have expected nor anticipated from her relatives. The situation in Jamaica put her quickly expected return to the island into question.

11.2   Begging and Giving

"No, they beg too much, it's getting worse every year", Carol rants while I accompany her to the grocery store. We are on our way to shop for some spices and groceries for her Christmas dinner, and she is furious about an incident that happened on the street corner next to her holiday home yesterday morning. While we are driving past the street corner, her eyes darken and she recalls yesterday's eventful morning: She usually likes to walk down to the nearby fruit seller enjoying the morning sun. A group of young men sits lazily on the wall of the narrow corner road next to a gully, drinking rum shots from the nearby bar, listening to music and smoking. The area is typical of Kingston, where uptown neighbourhoods with exclusive townhouses are side by side with smaller, impoverished ghetto areas. However, this one is not a 'bad' one. In Jamaica, this means that no real crime or shootings happen, and Carol always carries a few coins for the youths. "Of course I want to help, you know. I think it is our duty to help where we can. But, this time I just said to myself, 'no'! So, I said, 'why are you just sitting around here? Get up and try to find a job, you're too young just to do nothing!' And you know what this rude boy said to me 'Mi no work fi people, Miss'[6], she exclaims, taking a deep breath. "Can you believe this? So I tell him, 'so where you think this money I give you is coming from?'", she says and begins a tirade about the ambivalent relationship that some local Jamaicans have to employment and receiving money for free, 'handouts' as Jamaicans say. While many work hard to improve their living situation, to send their children to school or to escape poverty, some seem satisfied with their current living conditions. Carol got angry about the situation on that day. However, visitors and returnees like her unintentionally preserve this culture of "begging and giving". The understanding is that as a Jamaican foreign national, if you come from abroad, you have the responsibility to give back to the local population. The belief that making money overseas is easier and quicker is common amongst locals and especially family members who stay-behind foster the belief that foreign family members are responsible for them.

Many returnees like Ms. Brown and seasonal travellers like Carol continuously hear anecdotes of suffering and desperation by the people they left behind and this often results in guilt-infused obligations to send money or give money away. In addition, many returnees or foreign nationals who come as tourists exaggerate their wealth and stage their pride of 'having made it' by displaying foreign consumer goods, extravagant clothing, and generous donations of money. Carol belongs to the first category of annually returning visitors who want to help. She knows the difficult socio-economic situation in her country through these visits and is informed about ongoing struggles with the economic and political disorder. Fur-

---

6   Translation: I don't work for people, Miss!

thermore, migrants such as Carol or Ms. Brown will never forget who helped them and gave them monetary and emotional support when they left Jamaica; especially Carol, who feels responsible for many relatives and villagers (and their descendants) who back then gave her money for her flight to Canada. Carol is what Paerregaard (1997) defines a returnee with a "moral" motivation driven by the wish to see her country better in the future or as she contextualizes "I really hope our small island can improve, and you know, mi still gi dem[7], because they don't even know how it is abroad! They only believe what they see on TV, mi cyan blame dem[8]". Carol is referring to a phenomenon that explains why many local Jamaicans firmly believe that 'foreign' is more desirable. This concept of 'foreign-mindedness' is strongly related to the TV shows aired, reports, and documentaries as well as social media channels and their positive images of wealth and a modern, urban lifestyle sent from North America to the Caribbean. Here, Carol always mentions the popular "Bill Cosby Show" as an example. These shows and similar formats transported the idea of the global North as a place of luxury, readily available consumer goods, and easy access to money into Jamaica's mental landscape.

With many Jamaicans aspiring to leave the country and seeking socio-economic opportunities in North America, it can be a challenging undertaking to explain to local people the returnees' desires to come back to the island. There is a stigma about coming back to Jamaica; it tries to identify if a person returns successfully or has failed abroad. Failure is closely tied to returnees who have been deported[9]. Success comes in the form of accumulated wealth and status. A Jamaican saying to a person who comes from abroad is 'watch that you don't get stale' referring to foreigners as typically being 'fresh', well dressed, well fed and well off. Therefore, not only the remittance sending culture to family and kin but also the local hand-ing-out of money strengthens the image of the 'rich returnee'. While Carol's initial choice to migrate brought her into the category of a foreign national with a higher socio-economic status in Jamaican society over time, many of her family members and social relations, as well as material assets such as her holiday home, stay be-hind on the island. These cross-border ties and international relationships that she fosters every year through her travels also involve interdependencies between her-self, her family abroad and her family and kin in Jamaica. Even though her interest in returning to Jamaica permanently no longer exists, her motivation to stay con-nected with those left behind remains, whereby 'guilt, responsibility and morality' are altogether effective and strengthening aspects (Waldinger 2017: 11). Carol lives a lifestyle that creates a fluid concept of 'home'. Through regular reconnection to her homeland, Jamaica, she upholds and refreshes her contextual knowledge about

---

7   Translation: I give them money nevertheless.

8   Translation: I cannot blame anyone for not knowing how it is outside of Jamaica.

9   See further on the phenomenon of Jamaican deportees (Plaza/Henry 2006).

significant changes and shifts in the local society each time. Therefore, Carol can manoeuvre herself in both the Canadian and Jamaican environment with relatively little friction. Hence, the identification of migrants who find themselves in a "space of liminality" (Turner 1969) does not hold for Jamaican women like Carol. There are no fixed spaces of transition; instead, there are oscillations of knowledge around an equilibrium point that is Jamaica (see chapter 12). The homes that her life encompasses are constantly recreated and bring together material, imaginative, and actual knowledge through mobility, transforming her into a "transcultural" (Welsch 1999) sojourner and citizen. When I asked Carol about home, she said, "You know there is still a difference between comfortable homes and homeland [...] the more you know a place, the more accustomed you are, the more you feel at home. I feel at home in Toronto, I feel at home in Montreal, and I feel at home in Jamaica. But Jamaica is the place I feel most at home, although I prefer to live in Toronto".

11.3   Pitfall Expectations

The little takeaway shop stands out. The multi-coloured hut on the beachfront lures customers with the cliché that many know about Jamaica. "Cold Beer - Joint" is written in hand-painted letters on the board wall. We park our rental under a large Mahoe tree while several young men loudly argue about who may take charge of our car while we are at the beach, for a fee of some Jamaican dollars, of course. After Elisha negotiated the price, which seemed a little too high, we walked past the booth, down to the seaside. The dreadlocked bar owner behind the counter smiles cheerfully: "Just tell me when you're ready to order ladies". Elisha immediately books beach chairs, umbrellas, fried seafood, and drinks. Today, on her first day at the beach, everything should be perfect. "Oh my Gosh, look at this beach! I'm in paradise [...]", Elisha sings animatedly. While a young employee drags our beach chairs and umbrella through the hot sand and a friendly waiter delivers the drinks, the tall, well trained bar owner casually approaches to talk to Elisha. "Where are you from pretty lady?" he asks with an alluring smile, "if mi was Babylon mi would a haffi charge yuh with the crime of sweetness cyan done![10]" The small talk at the beach that seemed to be nothing more than a regular flirt turned out to be Elisha's major field of interest in the next couple of weeks. Although I tried to add some healthy scepticism about his sweet promises, she was utterly fascinated by his casual manner, his appearance, and his dealings with her, calling her his "Nubian Queen". Elisha's previous romantic interactions in Montreal were mostly rooted in

---

10   Translation: Where are you from pretty woman? If I were a police officer, I would have to charge you for your never-ending sweetness!

her extended friends' network, and she dated exclusively men who had an Afro-Caribbean or African background. Over the course of the fieldwork, it dawned on me that for Elisha moving back to Jamaica not only had an ideational motivation of going back to the land of her ancestors to start her new life and her own business, but also had the purpose of finding a 'real' Jamaican man. Eventually, getting married and having children –who also felt a connection to their homeland– where important considerations. However, I kept out of this matter for the time being in the sense of non-intervention in the course of the field research.

Two weeks later, we visited her relatives. Driving up to the gated-community complex where her aunt and uncle reside, shed some light on why Elisha's image of Jamaica, besides her holiday trips as a child, is transfigured into white sandy beaches and high-end communities. Her maternal aunt excitedly waves before greeting us at the footsteps of their exclusive villa. The impressive interior design and lush garden behind the house together with the veranda and outdoor swimming pool merged into an overall luxurious impression of the 'good life'. "I'm so glad you're taking this long holiday to come to see us, darling", her aunt speaks with an accent that I identify as British. While we're taking a tour of the house, Elisha immediately explains to her aunt that she is not on holiday, but here to stay permanently in Jamaica and to start her own business. Her uncle, who just came from the garden, overheard the explanation and laughed, "Can you believe this child?" he says to his wife with a good amount of disbelief in his voice. "Well I'm glad you're here darling, at least for the time being", he finishes the conversation with a smile. After Elisha finished her extended road trip around the island, to waterfalls, beaches, resorts, and musical events as well as extensive nightlife events in Negril and Kingston, she stayed her last weekend with her relatives. From there she returned to Montreal with an ample set of positive traveling experiences, continuously enthused about her trips and all the 'beautiful people' she met. Over time her relationship with the bartender became more and more serious, and she texted and video-chatted with him and her 'new' local friends as often as possible. When she told her parents about her new friends, they were content to hear that their daughter integrated well into Jamaican society. Her sister remained sceptical and did not like the idea of Elisha being involved with a Jamaican man in Jamaica or as Debby said herself "Dem island boy gi too much trouble[11]". After returning to Montreal, Elisha infused her daily activities with the planning of her next trip to Jamaica. It was the sole topic of conversation. She worked overtime in the salon and even got a little side-job in a friend's bar, where she started working as a waiter to save money for the flight.

---

11   Translation: These 'island boys' will give you a lot of trouble. Meaning: Local Jamaican men will give you a hard time.

About six months later, Elisha called me with the 'good news' that she had saved enough money and prepared enough ideas for her next visit which was to determine where and how she would live and start her business. We were able to coordinate our travels again and Elisha came while I was already in Kingston. She landed in Montego Bay and started her trip by visiting her aunt again. From there, she tried to get into contact with numerous people to realize her idea of a business that sells organic and hand-made products from Jamaica to tourists. However, she recognized that getting access to Jamaican society outside of the fun and rather touristic endeavours of her previous trip was harder than she had initially thought. People often promised they would ask around and make contacts for her. Nevertheless, all these promises fizzled over time. Her accent always revealed her as an outsider, which resulted in uncomfortable situations such as overpricing in taxis, at local shops as well as monetary expectations of new 'friends' who thought she was rich. What bothered her the most was, however, the fact that no one identified her as Jamaican. The 'starting difficulties', as she called these incidents at first, were becoming more and more unpleasant. After a month, which Elisha spent in different parts of the island to inquire about her idea, she stayed in Kingston to get in touch with local retailers who already sell similar products. She thought she could maybe get a job there; unfortunately, these attempts were unsuccessful as well. Most of the time, people told her that they already had enough staff or that they were not interested. Elisha began to have self-doubts and was sure that she could not get a job because everyone perceived her as a foreigner. This feeling of being an 'ethnic outsider' made her vulnerable to the status of what Brubaker (2015: 30) labels as "ethno-cultural separation". Brubaker describes how ethno-cultural insiders intentionally single out specific characteristics such as accent or appearance to exclude newcomers from an opportunity they would be appropriate for in terms of education or know-how as a "deliberate strategy of insulation from surroundings" that are like in Elisha's case "economically disadvantaging" (ibid.). Accordingly, she was happy when her aunt and uncle invited her to visit them for the weekend. She hoped they were inviting some other younger people or even supporting her with an idea and asked me to join her.

Upon arrival, we met a retired couple, the Reid's, who were direct neighbours and also invited for dinner. Likewise, they were returnees, whom Elisha's relatives knew from Birmingham. The Reid's immigrated to the UK in the late 1950s. Mrs. Reid worked as a nurse; Mr. Reid was in logistics. They had been back for six years now and bought a house in the same community as her aunt and uncle. Their pensions, savings and children who still live in the UK secure their future and the Reid's annually travel to Birmingham to spent time with their grandchildren. However, their lives in Jamaica seemed to be filled with church and returnee association schedules that organize trips to see the island and to meet new people. Elisha's aunt adds, "We have at least two excursions each month, one with the church and one

with the association". Returnee associations provide significant support in re-inte-
grating their foreign nationals back into society. However, especially in the case of
English returnees, they often create exclusive spaces in their returnee enclaves (see
further Horst 2013). Some returnees, so Horst, cultivate their "Englishness" and,
therefore, socio-economic distinction from the main society, especially in terms of
class and mannerisms (ibid.). Elisha's uncle and aunt were the generation of the migrants who emigrated to England following the "Windrush" (Hall 1999) generation.
Before independence, many Jamaicans, who respected the Queen and England as
the 'mother country' at that time came back with what Jamaicans call 'royal properness' and being 'more British than the English'. These returnees live in the hills of
Jamaica so Goulbourne,

> "In a prosperous ghetto characterized by some English pastimes: tea in the after-
> noon, the cultivation and display of well-manicured lawns and gardens ordered
> for more aesthetic pleasure than practical use, which stand in sharp contrast to
> the utilitarian kitchen and fruit gardens of rural Jamaica" (Goulbourne 1999: 164
> qtd. in Horst 2013: 1).

Similar to Elisha's uncle, Mr. Reid spends much time in his garden. He boasted
about how green his lawn was this season and how many different varieties of
fruits and vegetables he was growing. While having dinner on the terrace, with a
view of the sunset over the Caribbean Sea, Elisha's aunt repetitively emphasizes the
beauty of life in Jamaica, "It's just sad how some people have to live here", she says.
Elisha asks what she means by this comment. Her uncle paraphrases, "My dear,
there are good people in Jamaica like us, but they hide away behind their security
guarded houses, you don't see them much as long as you are not part of this class.
And then, there is a majority of bad people in Jamaica [...]. That you should not mix
and mingle with, it's dangerous", he closes. Elisha looks puzzled and Mrs. Reid continues, "When we came here, I always used to invite local people that I knew from
earlier days to dinner, no one ever invited us back [...] you can just wonder why they
keep everyone so distant, especially the good ones". "And you have to protect yourself", adds Mr. Reid, "everyone thinks you have something to give. Fake friends will
surround you with open arms and open hands telling you about their hardships".
Hammond exemplifies in her research on return migration to Somaliland that returnees make strict distinctions between the mentality of locals who never lived
outside the country and locals who spent time abroad, which can advance into a
feeling of superiority (Hammond 2015: 44f.). Further, the distinction between successful and unsuccessful returnees holds here again. When Elisha's aunt brings the
dessert, the stories continue about 'foolish returnees' who show off their wealth in
public spaces, advertising their 'foreignness' and inviting people they hardly know
into their lives. "Most of them come from America", Elisha's uncle states and I pick
up a little contempt in his tone. In her article about transnationalism, Horst (2007)

points out that despite sharing an identity as 'returning residents', Jamaican migrants in England who returned to Jamaica re-established themselves on the island by committing to the community, i.e., through the involvement with returning resident associations, whereas United States returnees continue to travel between Jamaica and the United States. "And worse, darling, you cannot find a husband out here [...] you would really have to look in the right places", her aunt adds as she refills the wine glasses. "Seriously aunty?", interjects Elisha angrily. She told me later how intolerable she found the debate about the two-class society and the lesson she was receiving through her relatives and their friends. "Most of the men here are really not on your level, hun, not like the men you know from Canada, their stage of thinking about women here is not the same", her aunt urges. The conversations continued along those lines over the entire weekend and Elisha was glad when we left Sunday evening. She was irritated by her relatives' debates and the "set-up" as she called the dinner with the Reid's. Throughout the weekend, she was frequently trying to shift the conversation to aspects that are more positive since she was still filled with the excitement of starting her new life in Jamaica. Elisha could not grasp why her aunt and uncle, as well as their friends were living pleasantly in Jamaica and at the same time trying to convince her not to come back. Unable to change the ongoing lectures, she just kept silent.

On our drive back to Kingston she says, "It's just because they're old, they're just grumpy and negative. It will be totally different for me!". Therefore, she was looking out for a local job, which she quickly found in an NGO in Kingston, where she was able to get to know many new people. Through her aunt's contacts, she found a small apartment where the rent was relatively low and the area was safe, but it was different from what she was used to before; frequent electricity cuts and sometimes a whole day without running water caused a sense of uncertainty for Elisha. In addition, the warnings from local people not to walk anywhere, also not near her apartment after dark, which can be as early as 6 p.m. depending on the season, frightened her. After she found out from her aunt that she needed to activate, the water tank supply in her apartment complex and learned how to save water in containers for dry days and to always having candles at the apartment, the romantic idea of living in paradise Jamaica slowly faded. Meanwhile, the voluntary job at the local organization, which provided after-school programs for children from marginalized inner-city communities, brought her eye-to-eye with the oftentimes harsh, local realities of Kingston's urban poor. There, Elisha encountered young children who grow up with the prevailing mind-set that everything from overseas is better and who dream of going to 'foreign' one day. "These children are completely brainwashed", exclaims Elisha one afternoon over coffee, "I tried to explain to them that the image they have about the USA is complete nonsense, but they won't listen". She could not understand that the "American dream" still existed in Jamaica. Besides being confronted with local ideas about North America, developing genuine friendships was, other than going out to party, a complicated undertaking. Unfortunately, it turned out that her aunt's warnings contained some truth. The love affair with the handsome bartender, which she had never mentioned to her relatives, ended after a few weeks back on the island as Elisha quickly became aware of the fact that it was far more complicated to navigate affairs of the heart than she had anticipated. The short interlude with the bartender unpleasantly showed her that he was less interested in a love affair, as his primary focus lay on her foreign accent, passport, and monetary support. This experience, which I cannot delve into further in this study, deeply shocked Elisha who thought so highly of him, his attitude and his appearance. The concept that she had in mind about local realities, specifically about local men who claim to be Rastafari, made her feel like she was a total stranger. "The first thing he asked me was, 'where are you from?' That's when I should have known better", she reflects on the phone one morning. It was less problematic 'to lose the guy' than it was to be continuously treated like an outsider, someone who did not belong and, worse, was seen as a source of income as well as a 'trophy' woman from foreign lands.

Being treated as a 'foreigner' deeply hurt Elisha. She had never imagined herself becoming 'othered' in the process of homecoming to Jamaica. While being marginalized and racialized for her blackness in Montreal, she expected to find a feeling of belonging in her ancestors' country. This "authenticity dilemma" (Kim 2009: 305) hails not from 'otherness' based on skin colour, but rather from cultural differences and inexperience with the changing local context. Even the local people, whom Elisha had known before coming back to Jamaica via her Facebook channels, were all of a sudden barely reachable or slowly alienated themselves from her the longer she stayed on the island. Although she liked her colleagues at work, she noticed after a while that she had little in common with most of them. As she said, they are all quite different "in outlook and in mind-set". Despite Elisha's initial expectation of an easy homecoming due to her ethnic affiliation and love for Jamaica, the actual course was different. The more she tried to live a local life, the more she felt excluded as an outsider. Adaptation difficulties are heightened for ethnic return migrants such as Elisha, "because they were born and raised abroad and are essentially strangers in an ethnic homeland that has become a foreign country for them" (Tsuda 2009: 4).

Elisha returned to Montreal after almost six months in Jamaica. Although she received a certain amount of rejection in her 'home' country, she has not lost her affinity for her place of 'heart'. However, she is already contemplating a next 'move' and considers traveling to Ghana visiting relatives of her paternal family. Drawing on Okphewo (2001: xiv), the diasporic life worlds and search for 'home' of third generation immigrant children such as Elisha cannot be detected in only one place, but rather in their engagement in a 'worldwide web' of entangled diasporic spaces. As previously mentioned, the creation of an idealized version of Jamaica through her childhood memories and parental narratives created a romanticized picture of living on the island in contrast to the live she lives in Canada. Ms. Brown, Carol and Elisha perceive themselves as 'home comers'. However, their claim to the homeland is often called into question, not only by local Jamaicans, but also through their own realizations of socio-economic, cultural and infrastructural challenges. The gap between the nostalgic imagery and the "real-life space" (Norbye 2010: 145) is hereby varying for each individual. Therefore, the next chapter will show how experienced boundaries can again become 'porous' (see Faist 2011) through the privilege of holding dual citizenship and the possibility of ongoing cross-border activities.

11.4   Returnee Life: Riches and Regrets

Josephine Bailey sits on the large veranda of her two-story house looking across the flourishing green of her backyard. Mango season is just about to start, and she will soon taste one of the first Julie mangoes. Josephine is retired and returned to Jamaica five years ago and, in moments like these, she feels happy to be back home after facing all those rough, cold winters in Montreal. The garden was a long-term project in which she had put all her effort and money in the past few years. Her neatly mowed lawn just reached its perfection. Surrounded by colourful Bougainvillea and Hibiscus flowers and packed with numerous Jamaican fruit trees, the garden finally reached its most satisfactory condition. To the far end of the garden, near the herb beds, she arranged a little house for her chickens that she bought two years ago. The afternoon sun, which she likes to watch set sitting in her comfortable armchair, covers the backyard with a golden glow. After sitting me down with a big glass of homemade lemonade, she tells me about her new plans to rent out one part of her house to tourists, "so I could fly up for the summer", she explains in a pensive mood.

Before returning, Josephine was relatively aware of the fact that the Jamaica she had left behind would not be the one she was going back to. Concerning being aware of being an 'outsider' at first, she says "I'm in contact with my sister every day, she lives in Montreal. We write WhatsApp or talk on the phone. I do not like to miss out on what my friends in Canada are up to. They come to visit me too. I also talk to my relatives in England. I can call a lot of people if I need to". In his anthropological work on "Kinship and Class in the West Indies" (1988), Smith claims that Jamaicans are less concerned about typical 'western' definitions or normative rules of kinship or descent that characterized most of the early anthropological studies. He further suggests that kinship serves as an extensive network of possible connections expressed through the recognition of persons as relatives. As an example, his participants' collections of comprehensive lists of all those whom they viewed as relatives outnumbered with an average of 284 the number calculated by Schneider for white Americans (Schneider 1968: 49). Smith's study bridges classical scholarly research done by e.g. Clarke (1966) and recent studies, e.g., Besson (2002), which analyse unrestricted descent and ego-centred bilateral kinship. Research suggests that kinship relations in Jamaica are rather extensive and multiple than rigidly structured. Horst and Miller's (2005) study on cell phone usage in Jamaica, presents similar findings concerning the prominence or significance of kinship in their respondents' cell phone usages. "Although kin was included, it was in much the same way as friends and acquaintances, all of them representing potential connections that were usually operationalized only at the time of a specific need" (Horst/Miller 2005: 760). How Josephine utilizes her phone and social connections resembles these findings, which can be understood as a virtual way of 'staying connected' (see her statement above) (ibid.). Her calls, text messages, or conversations are mainly used to have a friendly chat and maintain potential connections with family and friends over time, whereby conversations often consist of rather short exchanges and are hence less extensive. Here a virtual connection to a person can be direct or via a mutual friend and can be activated at any given time or whenever needed. Horst and Miller further state that "the only real difference between friendship and kinship" is that kin connections are latent and can be revived after long intervals, while with friendship "a minimal degree of sociality to preserve the relationship is preferred" (ibid.). As research on transnational Jamaican families suggests, telephones are crucial in maintaining connections with the more extensive family and social network over time and space, sometimes merely as a means of keeping in touch (cf. Horst 2006; Goulbourne/Chamberlain 2001). Josephine repeatedly confirmed the importance of "not missing out" and staying in touch with her friends and family locally and in various destinations abroad. Studying transnational families further reveals the importance of friends in providing mutual aid and support and the strategies used to create an extensive network not just locally, but also globally. As in Josephine's case, the virtual connectedness is a cultural practice of sustaining cross-border networks that establish visibility and support systems, which may prove useful to one's future needs. Here, the phone has been proven a vital tool in coordinating migratory moves and travels for all interlocutors. Before returning to Jamaica, regular trips to the island as well as regular phone calls were her primary means of staying connected to contractors who built her house, the gardener she initially hired, and friends who helped her move as well as her family. Like Carol, she knew the importance of staying connected and knowing sociocultural happenings. Local returnee associations that she frequently visited at the beginning of her re-adaptation process were not the right place for her to meet new friends. "I know this kind of people now, these people are all about their community, [...] they are mostly home comers from England, they only want to stay amongst themselves, you know, [...] and they have all these rules and activities. It's like in the associations in foreign, but with a better climate [laughs]. No, it's not my thing. I still have my life outside of Jamaica". As Horst demonstrates, Jamaican returnees coming from North America are more prone to travel between both worlds, whereas Jamaican returnees from England tend to stay in Jamaica permanently and most likely amongst themselves (Horst 2013). Since air travel to Canada is relatively cheap, Josephine considers a relocation every now and then or when "paradise Jamaica gets boring" as she puts it. Especially in the hot summer months, when neither family nor friends are visiting from abroad, life can get lonely and tedious at times. "It's just the garden, the chickens, the sun, you know. It's too monotonous. [...] I'm used to going out and meeting people. Here it's harder to do that. [...] It's mostly church or funerals [laughs] or bingo nights. It's not the culture, you know". Additionally, Josephine likes to fly out and see her children, who live across Canada and the United States and often invite her to stay at their homes.

When Josephine left Jamaica as a child, she first migrated to England to live with her aunt for a few years. Married life brought her to Canada later on, where she lived, raised her three children and buried her husband. The ethnographic descriptions of the encounters that I had with Josephine and the narration of her migratory life pathways, provide insights of the transformations in the returnee's sense of ethnicity, namely being English, Canadian, or Jamaican. From firstly perceiving England as the 'mother country' and Canada later in life as the land of "possibilities and work-related success", to the final frustration felt about both countries post-migration resulting in a sense of belonging neither to England nor to Canada. She further stated that "being a Black woman" facing linguistic hurdles and racism while living in Montreal gave her a severe feeling of alienation and displacement. However, Josephine still feels a strong sense of connection to both countries since she spent many wonderful years of her life there, raising her children and living with her husband. "The racism was pure stress I admit, but as long as we stayed in our circles and I had my family surrounding me I was good", she reflects. The rebuilding of a new life in her 'homeland' Jamaica was a long-term project consisting of hard work, endurance, and saving money whenever possible. As in Ms. Brown's case, the task of building a house was a life's work, which accompanied her through all life stages. Returning to Jamaica was initially a dream she wanted to fulfil together with her husband, who sadly, passed away two years before Josephine was retired. Before her return to Jamaica, she sold her apartment and all her personal belongings in Montreal, including her car, and she shipped furniture as well as various kitchen appliances to the island. While living abroad, Josephine frequently travelled to Jamaica together with her husband to oversee the construction process of the house and the installation of utilities as well as the layout of her garden, which resembles –unlike other typical Jamaican back yards– a well-groomed park. Now that she is here, she sometimes regrets that she did not rent out her apartment in Montreal instead of selling it because she would have had a place to return to every now and then. However, at the time, shortly before returning, she was very enthusiastic about leaving Canada and wanted to cut all ties. Besides, she thought it would be too much work to cater to the needs of tenants while being absent and in Jamaica. Thinking about another life model, she now wonders where to reside while in Montreal and what to do with her incredibly large Jamaican house.

Josephine's mansion has five bedrooms, three bathrooms, one large kitchen with a front room, one large representative living room and another smaller kitchen on the other side of the house. Surprisingly, she only uses one-third of her house, which entails the large kitchen, the veranda, and her bedroom, which she also utilizes as her living room. The other two-thirds of the house are 'untouched'. The large living or representative room that one enters through the front room when visiting the house, displays Josephine's prized possessions. Three different sized, plastic-covered sofas with a large mahogany coffee table, a large dining table with six matching upholstered armchairs, a crystal glass chandelier with eight arms, a set of open shelves filled with expensive-looking ornaments, vases, and decorative items such as fairy tale figurines and oversized decorative fruits, a buffet with crystal platters and artificial flower arrangements, on top a large ceramic swan figurine an animal not even native to Jamaica, which is the showpiece of the dining table. On the walls, paintings of woodlands and rivers together with a picture of 'The Last Supper' and a golden wall clock that does not work; all together with matching brownish carpets, pillows, blankets, and curtains that block out the outside world and wrap the room in a time capsule. Only rare occasions would allow the usage of the room, e.g., family visits during the Christmas season. The reason to go into such detail concerning the material objects in this room is to focus on the socio-cultural practice of accumulating objects of wealth and social status in preparation for the homeland return (see Miller 2008). The exclusionary status of the room with its shrine-like quality is something Josephine had fought for, a major accomplishment of her life, a sacred place of her success and respectability. Not only possessing this house and garden, but also having this decorative interior shows clearly that she 'made it' abroad, as she says "I did not waste my time". Similar utilization of material culture such as in Josephine's living room are also described in other studies on Caribbean returnees (e.g. Plaza/Henry 2006). They can be interpreted as markers of a process of trespassing, a sense of alienation from land and people in Jamaica, and highlights the relationship between particular objects of material culture and the inherent politics of identity.

Often she would say something like "you know, local people are hard to deal [...], it's not like before that I can just casually meet with someone, there are always these expectations from the other side". There was a distinction she made between herself and the "local people". So, who was local in the end? The ones who never left Jamaica? I realized that Josephine's homecoming was more challenging for her

than she had initially thought. Even though she thought her connectedness via social media, telecommunication, travel, and her affinity to the country would make
her reintegration easy (see Kim 2009) the opposite was the case. She had problems
making friends as she did not like the exclusionary returnee associations, and she
was always on the careful lookout for extended family member's expectations. As
Cook-Martin and Viladrich (2009: 133) claim in their study on Spanish migrants, the
materialization of social acceptance, or the absence of such, can become a source of
deep frustration. The living room highlights not only her accumulated wealth and
social status as a successful returnee but also her distinction from local 'others'.
However, the objective criteria displaying successful adaptation or reintegration
into Jamaican society are not congruent with her inner adaptation. Focusing on
Josephine's perceptions of her adjustment and the extent to which the homeland
has filled self-defined needs, show that readapting can also remain unfinished.
Josephine finds herself in a space neither wholly Canadian nor entirely Jamaican.
In her anticipated 'homeland' Josephine finds herself in a constant space of temporal and spatial "in-betweenness" (cf. Bhaba 1994) living "somewhere between foreign
and local" (Wang/Liu 2016: 2). Returnees like Josephine seek to construct lifestyles
that balance the years of hard work endured to return and retire in Jamaica. Large
houses, lush gardens, and consumer goods assert and assist in the creation of a
lifestyle of leisure and enjoyment. Nonetheless, reintegration into Jamaican society can be harder than initially perceived, which results in feelings of loneliness,
boredom, and otherness. Hence, many returnees seek a mobile lifestyle that better
reflects their individual needs and practice oscillating between Jamaica and North
America.

As this chapter has shown, potential and actual returnees and frequent homeland travellers like Carol grapple with unforeseen difficulties, frictions, uncertain-
ties, and issues of distrust when going to Jamaica, some to a larger and some to
a lesser extent. People like Carol can manoeuvre themselves with relative ease between different life worlds since they have enough knowledge that makes them
insiders in different localities. Staying actively connected with Jamaica and North
America simultaneously is an integral part of Jospehine's and Carol's lives that
comes with responsibility, morality, favours and caring commitments. Individuals
such as Elisha and Ms. Brown can have a hard time finding out "what to believe and
whom to trust" or simply how to get to know, and adapt themselves in a country
that feels more different and difficult than they had perceived or imagined. Due
to their childhood memories, nostalgia, intergenerational narratives, and online
friends, the realization of local realities and conditions in Jamaica contrast sharply
with the romanticized and rosy imaginaries about the homeland. A local family
in Jamaica is, therefore, a sometimes-harsh reminder of actual local living conditions, whereby, perplexity, trauma, loneliness, and a great deal of annoyance result
from being disconnected of local occurrences and information networks. In this

event, the understanding of ethnic belonging to Jamaica can become vulnerable and affects future planning and mobility.

12 Roots, Pathways and Trajectories: Processes of Oscillation

"A lot of people will say, 'mi hear say yuh live a foreign'. Unno can gwaan! Any which part mi live: Toronto, London, Florida [...] a Jamaica mi deh. Jamaica mi deh all the time!" –Miss Lou[1]

In times of increased migration and mobility research, it seems as if people, images, objects and culture are in constant flux. Attempts to describe these flows and fluctuations are manifold, with people being dispersed, displaced, deterritorialized (Glick Schiller et al. 1992; 1995; Appadurai 1990), reterritorialized, in '-scapes' (Appadurai 1991; 1996), 'hyper-mobile' (Gössling et al. 2012), cosmopolitan (Vertovec 2009), fluid, altogether nomads 'on the move' (Cresswell 2006; Gupta/Ferguson 1997). As a result, various studies about movement are closely linked to globalization processes, which challenge the idea of the interconnection of culture, people, and places. However, quite contrary to contemporary assumptions, movement and mobility are not new phenomena of the globalized world. Historical events give rise to the assumption that border crossing migration and mobility have long been a norm and survival strategy (see Jónsson 2008) to many people, including Jamaicans. Jamaica has a longstanding and ongoing "culture of migration" (see Thomas-Hope 2002; Cohen 2004; Hahn/Klute 2007), which makes studying mobility central to analysing its cultural meaning and measuring socio-cultural changes over time.

Even though neoliberalism and capitalism both enhanced mobility in terms of socio-economics, governments worldwide often recognize mobility as a threat that needs to be ordered, regulated, and restricted (Scott 1998). In the Jamaican case, these regulatory policies are felt due to, e.g., new immigration laws by the United Kingdom in 2003, by the United States after 9/11 and constant changes in

---

1 Translation: Many people will say, 'I hear you live abroad'. You can continue to gossip! No matter in which place I live: Toronto, London, Florida [...] I am in Jamaica. I am in Jamaica all the time! Transcribed quote from a stage performance of Jamaican comedian, poet and writer Dr. Louise Simone Bennett-Coverley (1919-2006) who is lovingly called 'Miss Lou' (Caribbean Insight TV 2018).

Canada, e.g., the recent implementation of Bill 9 and Bill 21 (2019) by Quebec's government. Therefore, mobility not only brings about constant movement and innovation, but is also distributed unevenly and excludes certain people (Salazar/Smart 2011). Hence, mobility is not only a necessity (e.g. in the case of refugees), a strategy to better one's livelihood (e.g. in the case of labour migrants) or a tool of global markets, but ultimately a privilege, which is still not an all-encompassing standard. The same processes that enhance mobility and global interconnection also produce immobility and exclusion (Tsing 2011). The aim here is to express that neither the mobility paradigm nor the fixation with the nation-state and territorial borders help in understanding the contemporary context of mobility and migration within and across conventional borders (Ong 2006). Therefore, this study considers movement not to be unravelled or in constant flux, but instead informed, regulated and distributed across different generations and shaped by various actors, places as well as political and socio-economic structures. Again, the women followed in this ethnography are privileged by holding dual citizenship. However, in the event of Jamaican migration to Canada and other countries, there is also a large number of undocumented and trapped immigrants, over-stayers, and deportees. These facts are mentioned here to acknowledge that the world is far away from being borderless. Socio-cultural and spatial differentiation is a complex process of historical and current political construction that has gained a lot of strength quite recently (e.g., refugee crisis in the EU-Schengen area or the building of the US-Mexican border wall, to name a few) and is, above all, a normative charged instrument. Certain groups, e.g., migrants with an illegal residence or deportees were purposely neglected in this study because their individual life pathways would have opened up different analytical as well as methodological criteria. Moreover, other trajectories that I am unable to discuss more in-depth in this study were, e.g., stay behind family or people who recently emigrated from Jamaica to Montreal.

Throughout the fieldwork, it was essential to pay attention to how the mobility of the interlocutors is structured through their imaginaries, intergenerational narratives, socio-cultural practices as well as the frictions and interdependencies that occur from these dynamics, especially if the place one has left years ago has changed. For anthropological research, it is accordingly not so relevant to only replicate patterns of mobility and migration that fit the paradigms of transnationalism or mobility studies (cf. Hannam et al. 2006; Larsen et al. 2007), but much more to understand and to describe how mobility is imagined and experienced as well as why movement is meaningful. From an anthropological perspective, it is therefore necessary to keep in mind the continual significance of locality as a mode of knowledge and practice that continuously recreates culture and society. As Salazar and Smart state, "Mobility creates tensions and the distinct trajectories of movement that individuals adopt shape their life, but also the places where they live" (2011: 6). Hence, a renewed focus on both mobility and the places that shape these movements is presented.

This part of the ethnography is dedicated to the various forms of movement that can be seen through my interlocutors' migratory life pathways. Their mobility and crossings of borders are permeated with cultural meanings and imaginaries. Moving between different places and the necessity to adjust to varying socio-cultural, multi-layered contexts produces alterations, ruptures and, at times, silences. Studying migratory mobility between homeland, host society, and diaspora does not only give insights into existing socio-cultural networks, but also into the production of new knowledge (Treiber 2013) and connections in order to navigate shifting conditions; instead of focussing on bipolar local-to-local relations. Movements and personal decisions, therefore, do not form linearly but have shown to be an ongoing process of mediation and negotiation that structures interactions in spaces of diversity (Lehmkuhl 2019). To describe this dynamic process the term oscillation seems to be a fitting notion.

Oscillation as a term is generally used to describe repetitive variations, usually in time, of measures about a central value, often a point of equilibrium or balance between two or more different states. Oscillations commonly occur in mechanical systems, but also in dynamic systems in almost every area of scientific research, e.g., business cycles in economics, geothermal geysers in geology or the beating of the human heart in biology. Typical examples of oscillation include the swinging pendulum or the alternating of current. This chapter highlights how oscillation processes occur that mediate cultural belonging beyond national borders. In scholarly research and theory, the term oscillation has been undervalued as a tool to describe migratory mobility and cross-border phenomena. Commonly used in studies about animal ecology, geophysical or medical research, oscillation, as a term has not yet been sufficiently used to describe migratory trajectories, whether these trajectories take shape in actual physical or mental or virtual mobility. Moreover, some scholars have used the term to describe that people's migration can oscillate, however, the literature hereby rather engages with seasonal labour migrants', temporary commuters, who are literally sitting on their packed suitcases and never settle in the 'receiving' countries (see Hawkins 1999; Rees et al. 2010).

However, I understand migratory oscillation processes not only in terms of physical movement, but also in terms of a mental, virtual and socio-cultural practice of constantly swinging (albeit in different degrees of strength) around an equilibrium point similar to the motion of a pendulum or random as the movement of a tire on a rocky road. For this study, I argue, that this equilibrium point is "Jamaica". With that I mean, Jamaica not as a physical object that one can hold, but rather an imaginary or an affective notion that has individual characteristics for each person. The picture that I want to evoke here is that of a sand pendulum suspended and moving in various directions from a point of reference. The traces the pendulum leaves in the sand symbolize the tracks that the interlocutors of this study leave behind on their pathways, in varying places and with other people. Whether roots traveling or returning semi-permanently or permanently, Jamaica as a romantic 'homeland' image plays a crucial role in the lives of all interlocutors. For example, in the case of Elisha, who was not born there, Jamaica serves as a point of identification and reference, as an idealized space of belonging. Belonging to a country because of this identification is less bounded by a national terrain as it rather entails an ethno-cultural affiliation. Although there is (notably when absent from Jamaica for a longer time) a "conditionality of belonging" (Laoire 2009: 42), meaning that belonging in Jamaica has to be approved by the local society, their own conviction of ethno-cultural affiliation and identity of being Jamaican remains unbroken. Feelings and frictions of being excluded, not knowing certain local customs and attempts to counteract local perceptions, therefore, are part of a process of mediating and negotiating modes of belonging to Jamaican culture and society. This process is dynamic and can last throughout one's entire life course, which is shaped by historical and contextual dimensions produced via individual, temporal and spatial (im)mobility that constructed certain meanings concerning places, people and socio-cultural particularities. These assumptions or expectations often cause frictions, silences, ruptures, and traumas that ultimately bring the interlocutors back or closer to their central value or self-defined place of 'heart'. This closeness can be physical, but it is finally rather an affective intimacy as in times of physical immobility, a simultaneous mental static is not given. Instead, in times of standstill, the mind, thoughts and mental preparations for the next journey and possibilities of future movement to Jamaica are the priority.

In addition, not a bipolar oscillation between two places alone should be considered, but also the possibility to swing back and forth between different options and third spaces as was shown for example through Ms. Brown's trip to Miami. While these options might reduce direct travels to the island for a while, they never remove Jamaica from its central position of the 'mental maps' of the interlocutors. Therefore, various modes of oscillation, which are not unilineal nor completely fluid, best illustrate Jamaican women's migratory trajectories that swing about a central point of value (Jamaica). Related to the idea of oscillation is, for example, the concept of seasonality, the presence of variations that occur at specific regular intervals (e.g. annually, quarterly, monthly), which are caused by various factors of which the most common ones are weather or vacation time. Seasonality consists of repetitive, periodic and generally predictable patterns of a series in time, e.g., a seasonal oscillation process, which comes in the form of ongoing homeland travels and vacations to Jamaica while generally living in Canada.

12.1   The Roots Traveller

Regular seasonal movements maintain not only a smooth socio-cultural re-adaptation in Jamaica, but also simplify daily life in Canada. Jamaica serves as a source of energy, recreation, and a familial place where Carol, for example, recharges her 'empty batteries' and gets to know the latest local happenings. The holiday home, an upscale apartment in one of Kingston's upper-class areas, was an investment and her attempt to stay connected to her Jamaican family, local friends, and the island overall. The flat that one of her cousins takes care of is rented out for the rest of the year, to tourists or business people who come to visit the capital city. The rental fees create a local income for her family members who take care of the place, e.g., paying maintenance bills for the air-conditioning, gardening, electricity and water as well as doing other tasks that are involved in times when the apartment is empty. As Clifford (1997) suggests in tracing the "routes to the roots", through uncovering the mobile life pathways of women such as Carol culture is re-produced through both "dwelling and traveling". Furthermore, Carol made sure that her family in Canada (also her children) would have a place to stay any time they want to visit Jamaica. Her involvement in local matters through her holiday home ensures she stays up-to-date with local, socio-cultural changes, occurrences, and shifts.

Therefore, Carol was the only research partner with a relatively small amount of frictions or ruptures. Even though she faces situations in which she is perceived as a foreigner, Carol can reflect on why local Jamaicans treat her that way, as she knows of the influence of external media such as American TV that enables locals to imagine 'greener pastures' in foreign lands. Carol understands that her status as a returning foreign national, who can swing back and forth between North America and Jamaica, is not only high due to her dual citizenship and mobility, but also that this status is an immense privilege. This privilege gives her a moral impetus to help locals and donate money to local charity organizations. Her desire to revisit the country of her birth at regular intervals is her way of tracing roots and "re-grounding" with her homeland (cf. Olwig/Sørensen 2002; Ahmed et al. 2003; Stefansson 2004). Her specific type of mobility problematizes not only spatial and cultural essentialisms, but also advances the understanding of 'transcultural' exchanges (Welsch 1999) of knowledge and identity constructions, which are related to a seasonal temporality. Here, a too-long absence from the homeland is equated with a loss of local context knowledge, hence, an increase in frictions and social alienation.

Carol's seasonal attempts to stay connected shows furthermore that "place matters" (Foner 2005: 174) as the highly desired reconnection with the homeland cannot be met alone through, e.g., the usage of the internet or remittance sending practices. The ethnography thus shows that Carol's personal migratory experiences are tied to an ongoing discursive and cross-border cultural web of Jamaican social networks, which mediate ethno-cultural alienation or belonging. Moreover, Carol recently chose to relocate her family to Toronto, which exemplifies how internal border-crossings, inside of the broader nation of Canada, already make a massive difference in terms of quality of life for people like her. Her personal considerations guiding this movement were powerfully intertwined with the wish for and knowledge about better living conditions in an Anglophone metropole such as Toronto that already hosts a considerable number of Jamaican immigrants and has less segregation on a communal level. The value of a more prominent and more condensed Jamaican community, with restaurants, grocery stores, market places, leisure activities created by churches, associations and local groups, was the significant key for moving to Toronto. Additionally, Carol said, "You know, the flights from Toronto to Kingston are more regular, and I have more choices when it comes to traveling, it's just more convenient and cheaper too. [...] After all, the children were also fond of us moving to Toronto; you know since they come to visit us from the States".

After Carol's migration to Montreal, she engaged in several border-crossing movements, travels and post-migratory mobility practices over the years that expanded beyond Jamaica, Canada, or North America. She was never a classical migrant who came, assimilated, and stayed grounded. All her mobility across internal and external boundaries were infused with cultural meanings and knowledge about people and places. As a result, all these elements are relevant in her current mobility and important for her self-understanding and realization of 'being and belonging' to a contemporary, diverse world that offers her the possibility to navigate and negotiate life in different places. Hence, in her seasonal mobility practices Canada and Jamaica are simultaneously intertwined. As countries of migration, Canada and Jamaica are products of a wide variety of processes of exchange and border-crossings that trigger ongoing processes of internal discourses about differences and otherness. Roots travellers such as Carol strengthen these cross-cultural exchanges of images, narratives, and practices through their migratory agency. However, Quebec as a 'distinct' province inside of Canada seems to have many difficulties with the inclusion of cultural 'others'. Difficulties that cannot only be seen in the life courses of the interlocutors of this study, but also in ongoing, historically grown, language controversies, exclusionary tendencies, pressing issues with racism as well as many political exclusionary decisions with regard to immigration (Bill 9) and cultural (religious) differentiation (Bill 21).

12.2   The Aspiring Returnee

After Ms. Brown returned from Jamaica and was back in her apartment in Montreal, she was very depressed. Weeks went by without me hearing from her. Silence. Then at the end of June, she gave me a call. "I was a little bit out of the loop, to be honest with you, but now I found back my balance", she explains on the phone. The quarrel with her sister and the situation at the house had left her in shock. Her initial thought was that she was unable to go back and live in a situation like that: A rundown house with broken tiles and water leakage as well as electricity outages now and then. This was not the retirement life Ms. Brown had imagined. Therefore, she made some phone calls and sent out some text messages to relatives as well to her children in the hope of finding an alternative solution.

"So I went down to Miami, you know to visit Norma [one of her cousins] and she lives pretty nice there", Ms. Brown, explains. South Florida in the United States is home to the second-largest Jamaican population outside of Jamaica. Political un-rest in Jamaica in the 1970s resulted in a mass exodus of Jamaicans to Miami. What makes South Florida especially attractive to pensioners is the year-around warm climate, which is similar to Jamaica, as well as its geographical proximity to the is-land. Most airlines fly daily between the USA and Jamaica with a flight time shorter than 60 minutes. "I tell you Jamaican food is everywhere, Norma said there are over five hundred restaurants, even in the supermarket there was an aisle with Jamaican products, laawd god[2], I tell you, it's like a dream come true", Ms. Brown continues. Additionally, the cultural hybridity through the existence of other Caribbean and Latin American immigrants, as well as the affordable cost of living, seem like at-tractive prospects. Lauderhill, where cousin Norma lives, is fondly called 'Jamaica Hill' due to its distinct Jamaican community in the area, where, amongst other recreational possibilities, many churches with Jamaican pastors are located; also, an Anglican service that cousin Norma attends regularly. Further, several Jamaican-born representatives run the city commission, and Jamaican professionals are well represented in the health sector. "The beaches are wonderful too, long, white sand, [...] and I loved South Beach and Ft. Lauderdale", Ms. Brown emphasizes whole-heartedly. "I considered it, you know, it's really nice, and you know I love Norma, but after all, it's not Jamaica", she sighs from the other end of the line. While I was already starting to believe that Ms. Brown had changed her mind and was intro-ducing her next retirement idea to me, her last comment left me confused. After her field trip to Miami and her local research about retirement homes, Ms. Brown decided to speak again to her sister: about "what had happened" and the condition of the house.

"You know, blood ticka dan wata"[3], she justifies her intention. Together, they finally had found a suitable solution for how to ease the situation and realize a plan that ensures Ms. Brown's return as well as socio-economic benefits for the family of her cousin. First, Ms. Brown called one of her oldest local friends to buy a cheap car in good condition, which her cousin will use as a route taxi in the countryside. In an

---

2   Translation: Lord God (Jesus).
3   Translation: Blood is thicker than water.

attempt to get her cousin off the couch and into a job, she gave him a functioning vehicle. The income he now generates is used for the urgent fixing of the house, maintenance of the car, incoming bills, and the support of his family. When the construction is finished, he will then pay a share to Ms. Brown upon her return. The wife of her cousin was sent immediately to get her paperwork sorted out since she needs a passport to follow Ms. Brown's invitation to Montreal. In Montreal, Ms. Brown organized a domestic job for her with an older woman who needed help in the household. "Over time, she will get by and can save much money to send for the family. I will help her sort out the paperwork and introduce her to some people, so she can stay for a while and realize a living, maybe she can even send for them [referring to her family] when she got settled". The young woman who will leave behind two teenage children is eager to follow Ms. Brown's offer and leave behind the troubled situation in the countryside as well as prospectively increase the standard of living for her entire family, especially her children before they turn 18 years old[4]. The children themselves will be left in the care of Ms. Brown's sister Jodi and their father for the time being. As the children are used to go to a secondary educational institution, which is farther away from the countryside village, they often stay with different relatives (in the next bigger city).

Finally, Ms. Brown and her sister agreed on a different monetary support system. Jodi sends Ms. Brown all the receipts for the bills via photo messages and will then be reimbursed for the expenses. Ms. Brown, who wants to stay more connected to local tasks concerning the house, set up new control mechanisms, saying, "I need to supervise this whole process now; otherwise they slack off too much, you will see with my help things soon run back the way it should". Not giving up on her dream of returning, Ms. Brown already planned her next trip to Jamaica, which she will use to check on the renovation of the house and the transfer of her new kitchen appliances, which are still sitting at the harbour. The next two years, will be used to thoroughly plan and structure her return. Now that she knows what had been going on locally, she will be more cautious and take things into her own hands. "Believe me, I had to do some straight talking with my sister, I told her I'm going to come and live in my house, and no one can stop me from doing so" Ms. Brown related.

Her physical stasis over the years and her sparse travels, due to her economic situation in Montreal, caused her to face significant problems upon her return to Jamaica. Even though Ms. Brown's memory of Jamaica was highly present in her daily life, her mental mobility and connection to the island was solely focused on another time (past) and only on a singular, romanticized place that sharply clashed with the actual situation. Her mental and emotional fixation infused by

---

4   Note: It is substantially harder for children to join their parents via family reunification programs after they are considered adults by law.

glorified and mythologized memories presupposed knowledge about Jamaica that was densely filtered by her ultimate aspiration of reconnecting to the homeland. Therefore, these imaginaries of 'fixity' influenced her mobility experience tremendously (see Easthope 2009). Similar to first-time migrants who anticipate their new and better life in modern cities of the global North; Ms. Brown's anticipations were extremely optimistic and expected to be a compensation for all her hardships and frustrations in Montreal. Hence, imaginaries build a strong foundation for the cultural meaning of migration and mobility. After fantasy and facts clashed, her inner world was shattered. She realized that the state of marginalization and exclusion, that she so urgently wishes to escape in Montreal, could be repeated in Jamaica.

However, her resilience and also the new socio-cultural context knowledge that she had gained supported her in seeking and finding alternative solutions. Even though her initial understanding of the local situation had dramatically changed, she transformed and renegotiated her new local life through active involvement and agency. Throughout her lifetime, she learned how to cope with roadblocks concerning various people and different structures. Moreover, her social networks allowed Ms. Brown to look into other directions and options before making her final decision, which additionally helped aid her initial traumatic experience after coming back from Jamaica. Her familial "network-mediated" migration (Wilson 1998: 395) further facilitates the migration of one of her extended family members, which also significantly benefits the local household in Jamaica. After Ms. Brown presented the solutions to her sister, Jodi assured Ms. Brown to be supportive of her homecoming. Therefore, while one migrant might leave the 'host country', a new one emerges from the same social structures supported by familial networks of reciprocity. Hence, returnees like Ms. Brown hold a lot of social capital that allow newcomers to be successful in Canada and Jamaican conditions to better.

Currently, Ms. Brown is only a few months away from receiving her pension. She has already sold and given away several miscellaneous items from her apartment in Notre-Dame-de-Grâce. Her preparation process of leaving Montreal is in full effect. New tiles have been added to the front patio of the house, the utility bills have been paid for, and the electricity and water supplies have been reactivated. The taxi she bought for her cousin is running well and contributing relevant funds to the house. The only point Ms. Brown is still unsure about is selling her apartment; maybe behind her resolute personality and certainty there is still a small doubt or fear of permanently returning to her grandmother's house. Maybe she just wants to be smarter this time, or maybe she wants to generate income from keeping the apartment and renting it out to tourists in Montreal. Over the three years' time of accompanying Ms. Brown, her formerly 'unidirectional' thinking about a permanent resettlement in Jamaica has changed. In today's WhatsApp video call, I can see her face lighting up while she imagines possible new routes for her future life: "You know, most importantly mi ago go back home, no matter what [...]. But why not visit Norma from time to time or go to Montreal for a couple of weeks, you know, Betsy is still here. [...] And the children, mi waan go see dem too. As long as Jesus provides me with good health and time anything is possible, don't it?[5]"

12.3   The Glocal

Even though Debby, as an important interlocutor, was excluded from the last two chapters, she is still relevant for the understanding of various processes that accompany the migratory experience. Debby does not intend to return to Jamaica although she engaged in familial holiday trips to Jamaica like her sister Elisha. It is also not her primary goal to repeat these vacations in a consistent form. However, Debby is still intensely involved with Jamaican culture and people in her daily life. Through her salon, Debby became an important local, socio-cultural institution in Montreal. Through her agency, the love for her customers and her job, she created a sanctuary space through which many socio-economic networks of the city flow. Her work supports not only community ties, but also connects different generations of Afro-Caribbean immigrant women that find a safe space in Debby's salon. Here, one can stay informed about the newest trends and latest gossip and talk about Montreal and Jamaica. Debby eagerly and regularly informs herself about fashion, hair and styling trends in Jamaica via online and social media channels, but also via friends, she has on the island. Through her regular trips to Brooklyn (NYC), she is further connected to another part of the Jamaican diaspora in the United States that she uses for styling updates, to purchase her products (especially products, which are not available in Quebec, e.g., specific make-up shades) and as an exchange with other hairdressers and fashionistas. Therefore, Debby works hard to satisfy her customers with exclusive products, up-to-date styling, competitive prices and a 'reproduction' of a Jamaican beauty salon in Montreal that has no peer. As Debby says, "This is where I live; my mother and grandmother earned all of what I do so that we can be fully engaged in life here in Montreal. There's a lot of Jamaican people who are successful in what they do on the ground level, you know. I believe we can make this place our own and find some happiness in that". The local demand in Montreal for places like Debby's strengthen her belonging to the city which is, however, closely interconnected to a continuation of Jamaican socio-cultural practices that are at times distinctively overemphasized as 'Jamaican'.

The concept of "glocalization" put forth by Robertson (1998) is used to analyse how social actors construct meanings, identities, and institutional forms within the socio-cultural context of globalization, conceived in multi-dimensional terms.

---

5   Translation: The most important thing is that I will be going back home. [...] and the children, of course, I want to visit them as well. [...].

Through her own and familial migrant experience, she inherited and further constructed her 'original' Jamaican culture to a new context, in which intracultural and intercultural identities and practices intermingle; she so consistently reinvents her own "glocal" self-understanding. Debby's employees and business partners are strictly Jamaican. Even though she has clients from different parts of the world, her business is family-owned. Her salon is a location that embodies cultural meaning, in its composition of furniture, decoration elements, music played and hairstyles created, altogether offering a specific ethno-cultural Jamaican 'aesthetic experience' that bases in familial memories, intergenerational work ethics and diasporic imaginaries of Jamaica. This aesthetic can also be found on Debby's own body, on which she cultivates practices and bodily features that resemble the aesthetic of an 'authentic' Jamaican Dancehall queen.

Through Debby, this study was informed about beauty, hair, and the body being a racialized subject in Montreal. It was shown that questions of who fits into society in terms of certain 'white' standards of appearance are a pressing issue, especially when it comes to work-related racialization. Hereby, Debby also caters to Afro-Caribbean 'natural' hairstyles, which makes her beauty salon an exception compared to similar salons in Jamaica. Even though styles like afros or dreadlocks are often seen as "too ethnic", Debby wants to make sure she includes everyone, no matter which hairstyle they wear, in her surrounding community. In general, Debby's job is not only collective work, but also a genuine service, a "pink-collar job" (De Mello 2013: 160f.) performed primarily for women. She offers women of all ages an emotional support structure, through her hair-, make-up- and nail-styling practices as well as the respect she has for her clients. Debby ultimately gives people a feeling of companionship and makes them "feel better" (more beautiful, sexy, proper, to name a few terms that came up during the study) as she puts it. By attending to her own body and the bodies of her customers and their feelings, she performs high-quality body and emotional labour (ibid.). Debby's life experience is not only articulated through her salon, but also her engagement with a wider Jamaican diaspora, the city of Montreal, and her body: Many dimensions that communicate, inform, and fortify each other into a holistic picture of Debby's life world as a child of Jamaican immigrants.

Because of this, the relationship with her mother from whom she took over the salon is crucial when talking about her work in the local Afro-Caribbean community in Montreal. Her salon mirrors this intergenerational relationship and history through pictures, décor, and the clients who come to get their hair done. For example, a photograph of her mother braiding hair in their old apartment in Little Burgundy has a prominent spot at the salon, which not only shows Debby's story, but also her feelings and the way she inhabits space in Montreal. The interconnection between the space and her familial migration history that she considers a success story. Therefore, the salon can be understood as a "glocal space", not a binary site between Montreal and Jamaica, but rather a communal space that serves as an intermediary in which Debby is the 'cultural broker'. Insofar, the salon becomes a relevant Jamaican diasporic hotspot on Montreal's city map in which women practice, narrate, embody and negotiate socio-cultural values, traditions, narratives, obligations, inclusion and exclusion, experiences with marginalization and racialization as well as various forms of knowledge about migration. Hence, they influence the local setting in Montreal inconspicuously through their ongoing agency and existence.

12.4   The Wanderer

After Elisha returned to Montreal, she plunged into work. In less than five weeks, she reactivated her pop-up shop network and found a new place to sell the Jamaican-inspired jewellery that she created right after coming back. Whenever I spoke to her about Jamaica, Elisha seemed too busy with her new project to delve into any negative experiences or simply did not want to talk about them. Probably a part of it was shame, especially in front of her local friends and her sister; she did not want to lose face. While she admitted that she was naïve to think she could go to Jamaica without 'real' preparations and stay there forever, she says, "I think it's good to take a little distance, for now, you know, but I will try it again for sure. I just have to have a better plan". Obviously, this plan did not only involve money for her, but also becoming more accustomed to local circumstances. Therefore, her new plan for the future was to travel to Jamaica regularly to get to know local customs better and to stay personally more in touch with her new friends on the island.

The newly found inspiration that she immediately put into her art and jewellery gave her a feeling of success since her collection was displayed at several Afro-Caribbean fashion shows together with works from local fashion designers. Her mobility to Jamaica mediated artistic impulses that inspired her work tremendously. "I must say, I also missed my community here, the sisters and the art network, I feel like I got a fresh start here after coming back and people were really interested in my travel and the whole experience!" explains Elisha. Specifically, Elisha's social network in Montreal and Jamaica supported and facilitated her mobility processes by providing her with local support structures and context knowledge in both places. In Montreal, her art network provides a safe, collectivistic space within her Afrocentric cultural orientation against racism and negative experiences. Her art network showered her with great respect for her trip 'back to her roots' and supported this reunification with the ethnic homeland. This space of an informal ethno-cultural community creates solidarity amongst young Afro-Caribbean art entrepreneurs such as Elisha and entails a shared diasporic consciousness of oppression. Staging the historically grown presence of this oppression through her art reveals how her identity and existence in Montreal is informed by the past and present simultaneously. Here, this network of third and fourth generation immigrant children developed a communal self-understanding by emphasizing and staging their cultural distinctiveness, which heightens their wish to preserve certain socio-cultural customs and affiliations. Mainly concerned with keeping their cultural symbolism alive, they create a positive and at times, politicized image of their identity. The active involvement of using art against racism and for the acceptance and visibility of Black diversity in Montreal's society are here worth mentioning. Though externally often ascribed a minority status, this network claims their cultural and ethnic presence in terms of a "we" consciousness and as "Canadian-born" Black people. The construction of their otherness creates "sameness" within the group context. As Hall states, group cohesion and Pan African or Afrocentric identity constructions support to align "subjective feelings with the objective places" (Hall/Du Gay 1996: 597f.) that they occupy in the city of Montreal.

The positive outcome from her travel experiences in Jamaica also explain why Elisha is already planning her next trip, this time to Ghana. "Africa is always on my mind, so I guess this is the right time to see it". Since she has Ghanaians in her paternal family, "local support would be no problem", as she said. While Jamaica remains to be the main constant in her daily life and aspired future destination, at the moment Ghana serves as a new locality of getting to know her 'roots' and herself. Elisha's life continuously crosses national boundaries and actively puts together Jamaica, Canada, and now Ghana into one social field (Glick Schiller et al. 1992). While Jamaica and Ghana serve –although weighted differently– as destinations of psychological comfort, sites of ancestry and ethno-cultural belonging, the positive connection to Montreal is solely based in her familial as well as her art network, which she both identifies as "emotional homes". As Louch states, "relations therefore cannot be thought anymore as totalized, fixed or absolute sites. Relations need to be considered in flux and movement and our research becomes a study of travelers as well as by travelers" (Louch 1966:160). Elisha's mobility does not take linear paths, but shows rather "relational ways of entanglement and translation between transnational locations, nations, and human beings developed out of historical encounters and displacement" (Clifford 1997: 7f.). Whether or not Elisha returns to Jamaica or if she finds her happiness in Ghana or if she stays in Montreal, her life course cannot be pre-determined and has an open ending at this point and for this ethnography. Despite this limitation, this study illustrates the continuous mediation and reinvention of social realities and identity constructions that play a role when researching present-day mobility and migratory trajectories.

Therefore, it is crucial to take into consideration the multiple layers of identification and connection through practices and intergenerational narratives that inform diasporic individual (and group) consciousness. The demonstration of how

vital dynamic, affective, and communicative ties and networks to friends and family motivate Elisha to be mobile and stay connected to, e.g., Jamaica was central
in this study. Networks are mainly maintained through images or imaginaries
(Salazar 2011: 576f.) that Elisha keeps and nurtures through her own and second-
hand memories of the Jamaican homeland and opinions about and experiences in
their present place of living. Her daily life in Montreal is infused with a yearning
for connection and belonging in which Jamaica plays a crucial role as a glorified or
romanticized "point of suture" (Hall/DuGay 1996) or equilibrium point. Migration,
mobility, and immobility are all aspects of Elisha's trajectory that explore relational
and structural frictions across time and space. As Hillman and Van Naerssen state,

> "People on the move look for immediate solutions to their problems and needs,
> […]. […], the way people think about their situation also frames their migratory
> agency. Their agenda is itself a reaction to the answers that people have already
> given to the situation of crisis and uncertainty they find themselves in" (2018: 5).

Accordingly, the emotional ability to deal with unforeseen challenges and changes
as well as an individual's socio-cultural and gender-based experiences or demands
were of specific relevance. I end this section about Elisha with a quote from Ju-
dith Butler that sums up the limitation of the prediction of individual migratory
mobility and the connected identity formations:

> "In this sense, identifications belong to the imaginary; they are phantasmatic
> efforts of alignment, loyalty, ambiguous and cross-corporeal cohabitations, […].
> Identifications are never fully and finally made; they are incessantly reconsti-
> tuted, and, as such, are subject to the volatile logic of iterability. They are that
> which is constantly marshalled, consolidated, retrenched, contested and, on
> occasion, compelled to give way" (Butler 1993: 105).

12.5   The Commuter

Even though Josephine has developed a rather pragmatic approach of becoming
used to new local conditions in Jamaica, she is at the same time frustrated about
loneliness and alienation from local, social life and has difficulties understanding locals' implicit principles of behaviour. Similar to Ms. Brown, Josephine is also
bothered by the long waiting times and poor customer services, for example, at
banks or restaurants. Together with frequent light shortages at her house and the
overall different pace of life, living permanently in Jamaica seems more challenging
than she had initially thought. After five years in Jamaica, she realized that she had
romanticized living there and that solely being on the island is not her idea of an
entirely satisfying returnee lifestyle.

In addition, local Jamaicans requests for money, accompanied by media portrayals of crime, further produce feelings of anxiety. These feelings result in a heightened use of security, e.g., security services such as alarm systems to protect her house. Since her Smartphone connects her with friends and family abroad daily, she only has a small number of local friends and acquaintances that she occasionally meets in church, at funerals or at specific events. Besides these local circumstances, a recent event catalysed her new idea of moving between Jamaica and Canada into reality.

"Shelly is pregnant, can you believe it, they told me last week", Josephine tells me with a big smile and water filling up her eyes. "I already booked my flight to go see her, no what a blessing, finally", she laughs while continuing to talk about her daughter's pregnancy. Never used to wasting her time, Josephine has already called her old contractor who she asked to plan and realize the reconstruction of her Jamaican mansion into two or three large apartments. "After all, I don't need so much space when I travel back and forth, so I get my private space and then I can rent out the rest of the rooms", she explains, excited about her new project. In Toronto, where Josephine's daughter lives, she already called and texted some of her local contacts to inquire about renting a flat. "Of course, I can stay at Shelly's house, but no, the children need their privacy, you know, it's a new adventure, and they need mi now, [...] without help you can't raise children [...] and I can always be there for the summertime for sure", Josephine declares while imagining her new life. "Plus I can go and visit my friends in Montreal, and you know, Delroy's grave is there, so finally I can go and revisit him more often. It did not let me go the last years that he is there and I am here", she explains with a sad tone in her voice. To learn that Josephine's husband was buried in Montreal (and not in Jamaica) changed my understanding of why she was not fully content with her life on the island. The person with whom she planned and realized her retirement home and return aspirations with, was no longer there and beyond that, not even buried somewhere close, so she could be able to visit his resting place. Together with the news of welcoming an additional family member soon and through the support of her family and friends network, Josephine decided to adjust her life accordingly.

As this study has shown, mothers and grandmothers play a crucial role in the imagining and construction of the family. One significant phenomenon to emerge from this household construction is reflected in mobile, cross-border care taking activities of grandmothers. Plaza (2000) describes the existence of "transnational grannies" moving between the US, Canada, and the Caribbean, offering their children child rearing support, gifts, and help with household duties. As Josephine's case demonstrates, return put her into a conflictive state. On the one hand, her love for Jamaica, Jamaican food, the climate, her beautiful and comfortable retirement house as well as the overall relaxed lifestyle were there, but on the other hand, she frequently felt overwhelmed by local problems and guilt about leaving behind her adult children in Canada and the USA. The return to Jamaica that was initially prompted by her deceased husband was much harder without him than she had anticipated; in particular, because she felt as if she could not fulfil her role as a mother (and now a grandmother) other than via phone calls or text messages. The restructuring of her previously held gender roles (e.g. wife, mother) and the difficulties that occurred through being absent from her children is also reflected in other studies about Caribbean female returnees (see Bauer/Thompson 2006; Olwig 2007; Horst 2007). As Horst states,

> "The availability and ownership of mobile phones has in many ways collapsed the distance between Jamaicans at home and abroad due to their ability to create a sense of involvement in each other's everyday lives. It has also enabled Jamaicans at 'home' to communicate their care and concern for their friends and family 'in foreign'" (2006: 159).

However, the mobile phone and virtual communications alone are not enough to fulfil Josephine's need of genuine connections. It helped her bridge emotional and physical gaps between Jamaica and her family and friends only for a while. Josephine landed in Toronto at the beginning of July 2019. By that time, her daughter's pregnancy had reached the final stage. She stayed until the baby was born and is the "happiest grandmother alive" as she told me in a text message. She also found a pleasant, small apartment not too far from her daughter's house. Additionally, she was able to visit Montreal, her friends, and her husband's grave, which made her feel extremely relieved. While she was gone, her contractor in Jamaica started to put in new doors into her house and took care of the refurbishing of the bathrooms, which are necessary preconditions for the rental. Before leaving Toronto, she called me to update me on her newly found life pathway between Jamaica and Canada. She said, "This is exactly what I needed, I feel brand new; finally I have a new task to attend to, [...] this is the life I always wanted to live, being with my family and being in Jamaica".

13 Conclusion

This study provided ethnographic insights into the life worlds of Jamaican women in Montreal. In particular, the analysis of socio-cultural practices in relation to local appropriations of female spaces, home-making strategies and the maintenance of social networks on a local as well as a global level were important aspects of the ethnography. The ethnographic depictions of Jamaican women's lives in the city, their experiences and aspirations, as well as their strategic mobility to Jamaica have been proven an ongoing process of mediation and translation; for many women this becomes a steady cross-border as well as transcultural residential and livelihood pattern.

Historically, Jamaican immigrants mainly migrated to Anglophone cities in Canada, the United States or the UK. The government in Quebec began to recruit nurses and domestic workers from the Caribbean as guest workers through the *West Domestic Scheme* from the 1950s onwards. This labour migration, mostly involving women from Jamaica, has so far received little attention in the academic literature on Quebec. Hence, this study offered a first approach to comprehend the motives, narratives, practices and perspectives of second and third generation Jamaican women in Montreal/ Quebec. The narrated biographies of five different women, together with the analysis of their current life situations, illustrated the importance of family relationships across time and space. Especially female relatives and their stories about the Jamaican homeland provided insights into socio-cultural affiliation, identity and highlighted the self-understanding of these Jamaican women.

In the context of a 'multi-sited' ethnography (Marcus 1995), through actively accompanying the women on their journeys to their Jamaican homeland, strategic mobility perceived to be important. The temporary or final return to Jamaica turned out to be a life-long, multi- layered process that reveals the longing for childhood memories, traditions, places and people. The sustained and active social relations with family, friends and acquaintances across cultural, geographical and national borders has proven to be an important means to survive the dynamic process of return migration. The study gave access to a different geographical sense of Jamaican women, in which Montreal is an important old and new contact zone.

The study acknowledged the specific historical and socio-cultural impact that female immigrants from Jamaica have had on the province of Quebec. Women have
dominated Jamaican migration to Montreal. This gender distribution has been an
ongoing phenomenon for now 65 years and shows how labour market demands and
historical circumstances in the province of Quebec have been partly influenced by
post-colonial migratory inflows. Second and third generation immigrant women
alike share, personally or through a close female relative, this history of migration
to Montreal. Settling structures in Montreal show that there is no typical Jamaican
immigrant enclave as in other prominent diasporic cities such as New York City or
Toronto. Jamaicans live scattered across town without being bordered by an ethnic neighbourhood and are, therefore, in a way invisible to many people in Montreal. Hence, they built strong social networks and webs of community ties through
which they connect themselves locally and, as a result, are able to assimilate themselves 'inconspicuously' into the urban environment.

Quebec's integration policy of interculturalism envisages that immigrants
should develop a feeling of belonging and a comprehension of Quebec society with
the help of the host society. However, the current political momentum in Quebec
promotes a nationalist ideal of culture being homogenous, which strengthens
markers of difference between cultural 'others' and 'native' Quebecers. Hence,
language-based discrimination due to Quebec's French language policy is an
issue in Montreal. Here, Jamaican women intentionally exclude themselves from
French areas or even refuse to speak French in general. The ongoing language
debates are restrictive and divisive conditions in their daily and work-related
activities. Hence, the challenge of spatial and cultural division exists. In addition,
Jamaican women report racial discrimination and police-based racial profiling as
major problems in Montreal. Thus, Jamaican women feel no personal connection
to Quebec society, stay largely among themselves, and cultivate identities that
are strongly connected with their individual ethno-cultural affiliation. Jamaica
is a very important constant in their daily lives and community life is mainly
structured through social networks and meetings in important key spaces in the
city: Local place-making activities, exclusive meeting points or semi-public and
private home spaces strongly correlate with the conservation of Jamaican socio-
cultural practices. For example, cooking food, listening to Jamaican music, following Jamaican news and politics, participating in Jamaican-based cultural events,
keeping the Jamaican language Patois alive, attending Afro-Caribbean church services, holding onto Afro-Caribbean stylizations of the hair and beauty ideals, are
all important aspects of maintaining connections with Jamaica, even though they
are physically absent from the island. Socio-cultural practices found in important
female key spaces exemplified women's socio-cultural identity constructions and
self-understandings as Jamaicans. For example, Ms. Brown's church network and
the women's association were significant anchors of her local life and of belonging

to Montreal. Elisha's pop-up shop network and friends in the music and arts scene create temporal Afro-Caribbean diasporic places in the city of Montreal that function not only as sanctuary zones, but also as a source of income for the younger generation.

Looking further into Jamaican women's social spaces, quickly led to Debby's beauty salon as an important community institution in Montreal. Here, beauty and 'body discourses' as well as reinterpretations of traditional Jamaican gender roles and power relations were important key aspects of this study. Female bodily practices imply meanings and constructions about socio-cultural interaction between Jamaican female bodies and Montreal's (Quebec's) socio-cultural environment, such as the Dancehall events, where Debby and her fellow fashionistas gave the reader an idea of gender role negotiations and the translation of beauty ideals. The analysis of Jamaican women's bodily practices also answered questions about the negotiation and mediation of home, cultural identity and feelings of belonging to Montreal and Jamaica. Hair straightening practices, concepts of the ideal female body shape and weight, bodily modification in the case of nails and lashes, stylization practices and female communion through body work reconstruct not only a familiar 'home-space', but also serve to neutralize experiences with racism, discrimination and feelings of exclusion as well as othering. Ms. Brown's "work wig" and her daily transformation before leaving for work is an example of such a mediated experience. The dissatisfaction with their actual living situation in Montreal, the discontent with their social status as well as the unfamiliarity with life in Quebec results in the creation of such exclusive Jamaican spaces.

However, functioning social networks did not only structure community life in Montreal, but were also a crucial aspect of reconnecting with the Jamaican homeland. The study demonstrated that women who stayed in Canada for a long time without making return visits, for example Ms. Brown, had more difficulties reintegrating in Jamaica. The social connection to local family and socio-economic resources over time and space were prerequisites for successful returns. Virtual connections via mobile phones and social media were helpful tools of structuring mobility through social networks. Daily virtual connections to Jamaica as well as remittance sending practices to their family that stayed behind or ownership structures in Jamaica strengthen cross-border identification and connection with the homeland. Additionally, many women engage in recurrent trips to Jamaica and live mobile lifestyles that give them a different mind-set in contrast to other immigrants who have to remain stationary. These seasonal travels are also used to socialize Canadian-born children to Jamaican cultural values. For example, being seasonally present and aware of changing conditions in Jamaica is a powerful motive in Carol's life, as she manoeuvres family interests, information and movement between Canada and Jamaica, easily moving and readjusting to differing places, spaces and understandings of life. Her experiences also showed sharp differences between life in Montreal and life in Toronto. Racialization here seems to be flatter in Toronto than in Montreal, possibly due to a larger Jamaican immigrant enclave in Toronto and, of course, in terms of a common language in daily life activities. Josephine supposedly reached her goal by returning to her homeland Jamaica, but ended up constantly missing her old life and friends in Canada. Therefore, she altered her temporal and spatial presence through social networking in a way that enabled her to feel more at ease with her original decisions. Here, social networks, family bonds and feelings of care responsibilities were relevant factors about the women's decision-making processes.

Mediating belonging and negotiating connection to Jamaica and Montreal over time requires constant translation work across and beyond real and imagined borders. The concepts of space and place, meaning the focus on specific interconnected localities in the case of Jamaican female migration strategies, cannot only be seen through a temporal lens, e.g., historical migration waves or new technological advancements of globalization; migratory movements were shown to be embedded in the cultural context of the interlocutors' familial histories and an overall 'culture of migration' in Jamaica. Here, time was an important aspect in the discussion of the interlocutors' memories and experiences as necessary points of departure to interpret their present-day lives and future aspirations. The importance of discourses about ethnic 'roots' and memories about a Jamaican 'homeland-space' connected to intergenerational narratives was traced in this study. Narratives of female relatives about migratory experiences, culinary and cultural traditions, religious teachings, socializing practices and answers to life's challenges were important aspects of the women's biographies. The analysis of childhood memories and remembrances of grandmothers, mothers and sisters revealed the significance of family bonds. Memories and stories that have been preserved over time often translated into actual socio-cultural practices. For example, Carol's memory of her grandmother sitting at the kitchen table, counting the bills for the 'partner bank', helped her during her initial integration phase in Montreal. This intergenerational knowledge supported her in finding a local, social network of trustworthy peers. Another example is Ms. Brown's memory of her grandmother standing inside her tiny Jamaican countryside home, dropping spices into her Saturday soup pot and later sharing it with a needy neighbour. Acts like these and other related memories of her grandmother mean a lot for her self-understanding of being a "God-fearing" Jamaican woman, for her willpower and survivability in Montreal as well as for her devotion in her job as a geriatric nurse. The upkeep of the "soup cooking" tradition over time counteracted feelings of alienation and homesickness. The ethnographic examples found in this study explain how mental mobility into the past can function as a present-day coping mechanism of living in a completely new environment, where language, customs, the climate and the rhythm of life differ greatly from those at home.

As examples of the third generation, Canadian-born women's lives have shown that intergenerational memories and stories can leave significant marks on the younger generation. For example, Elisha's experience of the desperation of her grandmother who was unable to return to her beloved Jamaican homeland until she died. Being part of the traditional nine night and realizing what it meant to her grandmother to be buried 'in Jamaican soil', left her with a generational mark. Additionally, Debby's non-negotiable Jamaican pride became known each time she picked up her half-moon shaped needle. A hairstyling tool that evokes the memory of her mother who made a minimum living wage with her "hair salon" in the early days in Little Burgundy. Furthermore, the birth of Josephine's grandchild, for example, catalysed into a new life purpose that not only counteracts her loneliness in Jamaica, but also shows how intergenerational narratives and practices of care continue to be relevant across borders.

Jamaican women have agency and are able to overcome visible borders. The research with interlocutors "on the move" revealed a distinctive Jamaican cultural understanding of migration and the simultaneous relevance of time, space and place for mobile people. Due to their personal flexibility, resilience and redefinitions of space, Jamaican women were able to develop altered routes towards a desired future in or with Jamaica. The strategic mobility and trajectories of the women of this study called for a temporal and spatial awareness of the interconnection of narratives, memories and practices to certain 'yearning spaces', places and people. In this sense, imagined and "real-life" spaces are interrelated and intersected by the social actors who move through and within them. The mental, virtual and physical mobility of this study's interlocutors made clear that return migration is not the endpoint or outcome of mobility after initial migration.

The analysis of female patterns of migratory mobility also included moments of immobility. However, this study proposed to not assuming that in times of physical immobility, a simultaneous mental stasis is given. Instead, in times of stasis, the thoughts and mental preparations for the next movements to Jamaica are the priority. In addition, not a bipolar travelling between two poles alone should be considered, but also the possibility to move back and forth and swing between different localities and third spaces. Even though frictions and traumas occurred along the women's pathways –both practical and psychological difficulties, mainly compounded by the women's memories and expectations of an idealized homeland– they found alternative ways to overcome developing obstacles. Elisha, for example, is now off to new shores (Ghana), while still believing in the possibility of going back to Jamaica at a later point in time. Ms. Brown sorted out almost "en passant" her chaotic and socio-economic precarious family situation after her visit to Miami, which has helped her to realize that her future life is in Jamaica. Future returnees will increasingly live a life of 'here' and 'there', moving based primarily on personal and familial circumstances as well as social networks. Ageing returnees might become ailing or ill and their movement may be restricted. For others in good health, younger and mobile, movements are unpredictable and complex. For the numerous ways of constructing belonging to Jamaica beyond the confines of national borders, the concept of oscillation was introduced.

Migratory oscillation processes here revolve around the equilibrium point 'Jamaica', which are composed of mental, virtual and physical mobility practices with individual characteristics for each person. At the same time, the affective intimacy with Jamaica remains the relevant component for all. The study was able to present a diverse collage of the multi-dimensional and multi-layered experiences, practices, narratives, memories and imaginaries of past, present and future that conceptualize a "mobile mode" of these women's 'being' in the world. A mode highly privileged through holding dual citizenship, being visa-free movers that enable them to recreate their existence, identity and belonging. This privileged form of migratory movement plays a crucial role in Jamaica, where returnees greatly contribute to the island's society. However, Jamaican migrations to Canada also entail a large number of undocumented, trapped and less fortunate people, over-stayers and deportees. Again, it is necessary to acknowledge that 'our world' is far from being borderless or fluid as 'transnationalist sophistry' oftentimes suggests. Sociocultural and spatial division and differentiation is a complex process of historical and political constructions that have gained a lot of strength in recent times, both publicly and academically.

In the future, the number of first and second generation "original" returnees will decrease and the phenomenon of return migration might become irrelevant. However, this study revealed that desires of returning can also spark in the third and fourth generation as racism, discrimination, and alienation in metropolitan areas such as Montreal prevail. Based on these realities, many young people might continue to hold onto the aspirations and dreams of their ancestors: The desire to return to a place where they will be accepted, belong, and feel at home regardless of language, social class, skin colour and ethnicity. Above all, this study highlighted one of the most crucial aspects of the human existence, which is the yearning for a place of 'heart', a place that feels like home. I conclude this book with a line of Bob Marley's song "Rastaman Chant[1]". This song is a popular anthem in Jamaica and expresses the idea of yearning for a reconnection with an ethnic homeland. Elisha used to sing this song on our road trips in Jamaica:

---

1   Original source: Bob Marley & the Wailers, Rastaman Chant, Capitol Records, 1973.

"One bright morning when my work is over
Man will fly away home
[...]
I say fly away home to Zion, fly away home
One bright morning when my work is over
I will fly away home [...]"

References

Abu-Lughod, L. (1991). Writing Against Culture, In: R. G. Fox (eds.) Recapturing Anthropology: Working in the Present, Santa Fe, N. M.: School of American Research Press, pp. 137-61.

Agar, M. H. (2008). The Professional Stranger: An Informal Introduction to Ethnography. Howard House: Emerald Group Publishing Limited.

Ahmed, S., Castañeda, C., Fortier, A. M. & Sheller, M. (2003). Uprootings/ Regroundings: Questions of Home and Migration, Oxford: Berg Publishers.

Ahmed, S. (2007). The Language of Diversity, In: Ethnic and Racial Studies Journal, Volume 30, 2007, Issue 2: Feminism and Postcolonialism: Knowledge/Politics, pp. 235-256.

Allaire, B. (2013). Jacques Cartier, In: The Canadian Encyclopaedia, n.p., retrieved from https://www.thecanadianencyclopedia.ca/en/article/jacques-cartier [01.02.19].

Appadurai, A. (1990). Disjuncture and Difference in the Global Cultural Economy, In: Theory, culture & society, 7 (2-3), pp. 295-310.

Appadurai, A. (1991). Global Ethnoscapes: Notes and Queries for a Transnational Anthropology, In: Fox, R. J. (eds.): Recapturing Anthropology: Working in the Present, Santa Fé: School of American Research.

Appadurai, A. (1996). Modernity at Large. Minneapolis/London: University of Minnesota Press.

Appadurai, A. (2000). Grassroots Globalization and the Research Imagination, In: Public Culture 12 (1), pp. 1-19, retrieved from https://www.muse.jhu.edu/article/26176 [24.08.18].

Assmann, J., & Czaplicka, J. (1995). Collective Memory and Cultural Identity, In: New German critique, (65), pp. 125-133.

Austin, D. (2007). All roads led to Montreal: Black Power, the Caribbean, and the Black radical tradition in Canada, In: The Journal of African American History, 92 (4), pp. 516-539.

Austin, D. (2013). Fear of a Black Nation: Race, Sex and Security in Sixties Montreal, Paperback, Toronto: Between the Lines Publisher.

Austin-Broos, D. (1994). Race/class: Jamaica's Discourse of Heritable Identity, In: New West Indian Guide/ Nieuwe West-Indische Gids 68, No. 3/4, Leiden, pp. 213-233.

Austin-Broos, D. J. (1997). Jamaica Genesis: Religion and the Politics of Moral Orders. Illinois: University of Chicago Press.

Bachelard, G. (1994). The Poetics of Space. Boston: Beacon Press.

Bakare-Yusuf, B. (2006). Fabricating Identities: Survival and the Imagination in Jamaican Dancehall Culture, Fashion Theory, Volume 10, Issue 3, pp. 1–24, Oxford: Berg Publishers.

Barnes, A. (2009). Displacing Danger: Managing Crime through Deportation, In: Journal of International Migration and Integration/ Revue de l'integration et de la migration internationale, 10(4), pp. 431-445.

Barone, L. (2015). Montreal Reimagined: Luca Barone - What makes Montreal different? In: Montreal Gazette, April26,2015,http://montrealgazette.com/new s/local-news/montreal-re-imagined/montreal-reimagined-luca-barone-what-makes-montreal-different [10.08.17].

Basch, L.; Glick Schiller, N. & Szanton Blanc, C. (1994). Nations Unbound. Transnational Projects, Postcolonial Predicaments and Deterritorialized Nation-States, London and New York: Routledge.

Bauer, E., & Thompson, P. R. (2006). Jamaican Hands Across the Atlantic, Kingston: Ian Randle Publishers.

Beck, U. (1998). Perspektiven der Weltgesellschaft, Edition Zweite Moderne. Frankfurt am Main: Suhrkamp.

Beine, M.; Docquier, F. & Schiff, M. (2008). Brain Drain and its Determinants: A Major Issue for Small States, pp. 1-23, retrieved from, http://ftp.iza.org/dp339 8.pdf [02.07.17]

Bennetts, L. (2014). The Breakthrough: Lupita Nyong'o. Glamour Magazine, n.p., retrieved from, https://www.glamour.com/story/lupita-nyongo [22.05.18]

Berger, P. L. & Luckmann, T. (1984). The Social Construction of Reality. A Treatise in the Sociology of Knowledge, London: Penguin Books.

Besson, J. (2002). Martha Brae's Two Histories: European Expansion and Caribbean Culture building in Jamaica. Chapel Hill and London: University of North Carolina Press.

Bhabha, H. K. (1994). The Location of Culture. London & New York: Routledge.

Bojadžijev, M & Römhild, R. (2014): Was kommt nach dem Transnational Turn? Perspektiven für eine kritische Migrationsforschung, In: Labor Migration (eds.): Vom Rand ins Zentrum. Perspektiven einer kritischen Migrationsforschung. Berliner Blätter, 65. Berlin, Panama Verlag, pp. 10-24.

Bouchard, G. & Taylor, C. (2008). Building the Future, A Time for Reconciliation, Abridged Report, Bibliothèque et Archives nationales du Québec, retrieved from https://red.pucp.edu.pe/wp-content/uploads/biblioteca/buildingthefutu reGerardBouchardycharlestaylor.pdf [12.07.17]

Bourdieu, P. (1983). Ökonomisches Kapital – Kulturelles Kapital – Soziales Kapital. In: Pierre Bourdieu (1993): Die verborgenen Mechanismen der Macht, pp. 49–80.

Bourdieu, P. (1998). Practical Reason: On the Theory of Action. Redwood City: Stanford University Press.

Brand, D. (1984). Black Women in Toronto. Gender, Race and Class, In: Fireweed: A Feminist Quarterly of Writing, Politics, Art & Culture (Summer), pp. 26-43.

Breidenbach, J. & Zukrigl, I. (1998): Tanz der Kulturen. Kulturelle Identität in einer globalisierten Welt. München: Rowohlt.

Brettell, C. B. (2017). Marriage and Migration, In: Annual Revue of Anthropology 46 (1), pp. 81-97.

Brubaker, R. (2015). Difference and Inequality. Grounds for Difference, Cambridge: Harvard University Press.

Brown, D. (1997). Work force losses and return migration to the Caribbean: A case study of Jamaican nurses, (ed.) Patricia Pessar, In: Caribbean Circuits: New Directions in the Study of Caribbean Migration. New York: Center for Migration Studies.

Brown-Glaude, W. (2013). Don't Hate Me 'Cause I'm Pretty: Race, Gender and The Bleached Body in Jamaica. Social and Economic Studies, 62(1/2), pp. 53-78, retrieved from www.jstor.org/stable/24384496 [16.10.18].

Buckridge, S. O. (2004): The Language of Dress. Resistance and Accommodation in Jamaica–1760–1890. Kingston: University of the West Indies Press.

Burman, J. (2002). Remittance; Or, Diasporic Economies of Yearning, In: Small Axe 1, 6 (2): pp. 49-71.

Burman, J. (2011). Transnational Yearnings: Tourism, Migration and the Diasporic City, Vancouver, Toronto: UBC Press.

Bush, B. (1981). White 'ladies', coloured 'favourites' and black 'wenches'; some considerations on sex, race and class factors in social relations in white Creole Society in the British Caribbean, In: Slavery and Abolition, 2 (3), pp. 245-262.

Busque, A.-M. (2015). Québec Language Policy. The Canadian Encyclopaedia, retrieved from http://www.thecanadianencyclopedia.ca/en/article/quebec-language-policy/ [16.01.19].

Butler, J. (1993). Bodies That Matter, London: Routledge.

Caribbean Insight TV (2018). Caribbean Comedian, Episode #4, Miss Lou, 1919-2006, retrieved from https://www.youtube.com/watch?v=JF1FmpDrLWU&t=5 23s [10.12.19].

Carling, J. & Erdal, M. B. (2014). Return Migration and Transnationalism: How Are the Two Connected? Connections between Return Migration and Transnationalism, In: International Organization for Migration International Migration, Vol. 52 (6), pp. 3-12.

Carter, P. (1992). Living in a New Country, London: Faber.

Cerwonka, A. & Malkki, L. H. (2007). Improvising Theory: Process and Temporality in Ethnographic Fieldwork. Chicago: University of Chicago Press.

Chamberlain, M. (1998). Caribbean Migration. London: Routledge.

Chann, W. & Chun, D. (2014). Racialization, Crime, and Criminal Justice in Canada, Toronto: University of Toronto Press.

Charles, C. A. D. (2010). Skin Bleaching in Jamaica: Self-esteem, Racial Self-esteem and Black Identity Transactions, In: Caribbean Journal of Psychology, 3, pp. 25-39.

Chevannes, B. (1996). Rastafari: Roots and Ideology (Utopianism & Communitarianism, Syracuse: Syracuse University Press.

Chevannes, B., & Besson, J. (1996). The Continuity-Creativity Debate: The Case of Revival, In: New West Indian Guide/ Nieuwe West-Indische Gids, 70 (3-4), pp. 209-228.

Chiasson, M. (2012). A Clarification of Terms. Canadian Multiculturalism and Quebec Interculturalism Multiculturalisme canadien et interculturalisme Québécois, n.p., retrieved from http://canadianicon.org/wp-content/uploads/2014/0 3/TMODPart1-Clarification.pdf [06.02.19].

Clarke, E. (1966). My Mother Who Fathered Me: A study of the family in three selected communities in Jamaica, 2nd Edition, London: George Allen and Unwin.

Clifford, J. (1986). Introduction: Partial Truths, In: Writing Culture. The Poetics and Politics of Ethnography, (eds.) James Clifford & George E. Marcus, pp. 1–26. Berkeley: University of California Press.

Clifford, J. (1994). Diasporas. Cultural Anthropology, 9 (3), pp. 302-338, retrieved from http://www.jstor.org/stable/656365 [27.03.18].

Clifford, J. (1997). Routes: Travel and Translation in the Late Twentieth Century, London: Harvard University Press.

CNA: Canadian Nurses Association (2009). Eliminating Canada's RN Shortage – News Release, Ottawa, May 2009, https://cna-aiic.ca/en/news-room/news-rele ases/2009/eliminating-canadas-rn-shortage [27.11.16].

Cohen, J. H. (2004). The Culture of Migration in Southern Mexico. Austin: University of Texas Press.

Cohen, Ro. (1995). The Cambridge Survey of World Migration, Cambridge: Cambridge University Press.

Cohen, Ri. (2000). Mom Is a Stranger: The Negative Impact of Immigration Policies on the Family Life of Filipina Domestic Workers, In: Canadian Ethnic Studies, 32 (3), pp. 76–88.

Coleman, S. & Hellermann, P. v. (2013). Multi-Sited Ethnography, Problems and Possibilities in the Translocation of Research Methods, London: Routledge (Advances in Research Methods Series).

Coles, T. & Timothy, D. (2004). Tourism, Diasporas and Space, London: Routledge.

Cook-Martin, D. & Viladrich, A. (2009). The Problem with Similarity: Ethnic-Affinity Migrants in Spain, In: Journal of Ethnic and Migration Studies, 35:1, pp. 151-170.

Cooper, C. (1993). Emergency (Un)Dress, Lifestyle Magazine 27, (July/August), p. 42.

Cooper, C. (1995). Noises in the Blood. Orality, Gender and the 'Vulgar' Body of Jamaican Popular Culture, Durham, NC: Duke University Press.

Cooper, C. (2000). Virginity Revamped: Representations of Female Sexuality in the Lyrics of Bob Marley and Shabba Ranks, In: Owusu, K. (ed.) Black British Culture and Society: A Reader. London and New York: Routledge, pp. 347–57.

Cooper, C. (2004). Sound Clash. New York: Palgrave Macmillan US.

Couture, C. (2018). Quebec, In: The Canadian Encyclopedia, n.p., retrieved from https://www.thecanadianencyclopedia.ca/en/article/quebec [22.09.19].

Craig, M. L. (2006). Race, Beauty, and the Tangled Knot of a Guilty Pleasure, Sage Publications (London, Thousand Oaks, CA and New Delhi), Vol. 7 (2): pp. 159–177.

Crawford-Brown, C. (1999). Who will save our children?: The Plight of the Jamaican Child in the Nineties, Kingston: University of the West Indies Canoe Press.

Crenshaw, K. W. (1994). Mapping the Margins: Intersectionality, Identity Politics, and Violence Against Women of Color, In: Martha Albertson Fineman & Rixanne Mykitiuk (Eds.). The Public Nature of Private Violence, New York: Routledge, pp. 93-118.

Cresswell, T. (2006). On the Move: Mobility in the Modern Western World, London: Taylor & Francis.

Davis, A. & James, C. E. (2012). Jamaica in the Canadian Experience: A Multiculturalizing Presence, Nova Scotia: Fernwood Publishing.

De Genova, N. (2016). The 'native's point of view' in the anthropology of migration, In: Anthropological Theory 16 (2-3), pp. 227-240.

De Haas, H. (2009): Mobility and Human Development. Human Development Research Paper 2009/1. United Nations Development Programme Human Development Report, retrieved from http://mpra.ubi-nuebchen.de/19176/ [03.07.18].

De Haas, H. (2014): Migration Theory. Quo Vadis? IMI Working Papers, No. 100, International Migration Institute: University of Oxford, pp. 3-39.

De Haas, H., & Fokkema, T. (2011). The Effects of Integration and Transnational Ties on International Return Migration Intentions, In: Demographic Research, (25), pp. 755-782.

De Mello, M. (2013). Body Studies: An Introduction. London: Routledge.

De Walt, K. M. & De Walt, B. R. (2002). Participant Observation. A Guide for Field-workers, Lanham: AltaMira Press.

De Verteuil, G. (2004). The Changing Landscapes of Southwest Montreal: A Visual Account, In: Canadian Geographer, 48 (1), pp. 76-82.

Denzin, N. (1970). The Research Act in Sociology, London: Butterworth.

Docquier, F. & Marfouk, A. (2005). International Migration by Educational Attainment (1990-2000), retrieved from http://unpan1.un.org/intradoc/groups/publi c/documents/APCITY/UNPAN022366.pdf [15.12.16].

Duval, D. (2002). The Return Visit-Return Migration Connection, In: C. M. Hall & A. Williams (eds.), Tourism and Migration: New Relationships between Production and Consumption, Dordrecht: Kluwer.

Duany, J. (2011). Blurred Borders. Transnational Migration between the Hispanic Caribbean and the United States. Chapel Hill: The University of North Carolina Press.

Easthope, H. (2004). A Place called Home, In Housing, Theory and Society 21 (3), pp. 123-138.

Easthope, H. (2009). Fixed identities in a mobile world? The relationship between mobility, place, and identity. Identities: Global studies in culture and power, 16(1), 61-82.

Entwistle, J. (2000). The Fashioned Body: Fashion, Dress and Modern Social Theory, Polity Press, Blackwell Publishers.

Faist, T. (2000). The Volume and Dynamics of International Migration and Transnational Social Spaces, Oxford: Oxford University Press.

Faist, T. (2011). Transnationalism: Migrant Incorporation beyond Methodological Nationalism, Heinrich Böll Stiftung, Migrationspolitisches Portal Global, retrieved from https://heimatkunde.boell.de/de/2011/05/18/transnationalism-mi grant-incorporation-beyond-methodological-nationalism [19.04.18].

Fischer, W. & Goblirsch, M. (2006). Biographical Structuring: Narrating and Reconstructing the Self in Research and Professional Practice, In: Narrative Inquiry, Volume 16, Issue 1, pp. 28-36.

Foner, N. (1985). Race and Color: Jamaican Migrants in London and New York, In: International Migration Review, 19, pp. 708-727.

Foner, N. (2005). In a New Land: A Comparative View of Immigration. New York: New York University Press.

Galabuzi, G. E. (2011). Hegemonies, Continuities and Discontinuities of Multiculturalism and the Anglo-Franco Conformity Order, In: May Chazan, Lisa Helps, Anna Stanley & Sonia Thakkar (Eds.). Home and Native land: Unsettling Multiculturalism in Canada, Toronto: Between the Lines Publishers, pp. 58-82.

Gardener, G. (2001). Unreliable Memories and other Contingencies: Problems with Biographical Knowledge, University of Wales, Aberystwyth: SAGE Publications (London, Thousand Oaks, ca and New Delhi), Vol. 1 (2), pp. 185-204.

Gaye, A., & Jha, S. (2011). Measuring Women's Empowerment through Migration, New Diversities, 13(1), pp. 49-66. Retrieved from: https://newdiversities.mmg. mpg.de/?page_id=2094 [27.04.18].

Geertz, C. (2003). Dichte Beschreibung. Beiträge zum Verstehen kultureller Systeme. Frankfurt a. M.: Suhrkamp.

Giddens, A. (1991). Modernity and Self-identity: Self and Society in the Late Modern Age. Redwood City: Stanford University Press.

Gilroy, P. (1993). The Black Atlantic. Modernity and Double Consciousness. Cambridge, Mass.: Harvard University Press.

Glaser, B. G. (1999). The Future of Grounded Theory, In: Qualitative Health Research, 9 (6), pp. 836-845.

Glaser, B. G. & Strauss, A. (1967). The Discovery of Grounded Theory: Strategies for Qualitative Research, Aldine Transaction, New Brunswick and London.

Glick Schiller, N.; Basch, L. & Blanc-Szanton, C. (1992). Transnationalism and the Construction of the Deterritorialized Nation: An Outline for a Theory of Postnational Practice. New York: Gordon and Breach.

Glick Schiller, N.; Basch, L. & Szanton Blanc, C. (1995). From Immigrant to Transmigrant: Theorizing Transnational Migration, In: Anthropological Quarterly, Vol. 68, No. 1, pp. 48-63.

Glick Schiller, N. & Fouron, G. E. (2001). Georges Woke Up Laughing: Long Distance Nationalism and the Search for Home. Durham, NC: Duke University Press.

Glick Schiller, N. (2005). Transnational social fields and imperialism: Bringing a theory of power to Transnational Studies, In: Anthropological Theory, (5), pp. 439-461.

Glick Schiller, N. & Schmidt, G. (2016). Envisioning Place: Urban Sociabilities within Time, Space and Multiscalar Power, In: Identities 23 (1), pp. 1-16.

Golash-Boza, T. (2014). Forced transnationalism: transnational coping strategies and gendered stigma among Jamaican deportees, In: Global Networks: A Journal of Transnational Affairs, Volume 14, Issue 1, January 2014, pp. 63-79.

Goulbourne, H. & Chamberlain, M. (2001). Caribbean Families in Britain and the Transatlantic World, London: Macmillan.

Gopie, K.-J. (2012). Jamaicans in Canada: When Ackee meets Codfish, Toronto: Jamaica Celebration 50 Inc.

Government of Canada (n. d.), Project Browser, Jamaica, retrieved from https://wo5.international.gc.ca/projectbrowser-banqueprojets/filter-filtre#charts [22.01.20].

Gössling, S., Ceron, J. P., Dubois, G., & Hall, M. C. (2012). Hypermobile Travellers, In: Climate Change and Aviation: Issues, Challenges and Solutions (eds.), 1st Edition, Routledge, pp. 153-172.

Grasmuck, S. & Pessar, P. R. (1991). Between Two Islands: Dominican International Migration, University of California Press, Berkeley, Los Angeles: Oxford.

Grenier, G, & Nadeau, S. (2011). Immigrant access to work in Montreal and Toronto, In: Canadian Journal of Regional Science / Revue canadienne des sciences regionales, 34 (1), pp. 19-32.

Greverus, I.-M. (1979). Auf der Suche nach Heimat. München: C. H. Beck.

Gunew, S. (2004). Haunted Nations. The Colonial Dimensions of Multiculturalism. London & New York: Routledge.

Gupta, A. & Ferguson, J. (1992). Beyond "Culture": Space, Identity and the Politics of Difference, In: Cultural Anthropology 7 (1): pp. 6-23.

Gupta, A. & Ferguson, J. (1997). Culture, Power, Place: Explorations in Critical Anthropology, Durham, N.C.: Duke University Press.

Hahn, H. P., & Klute, G. (2007). Cultures of Migration: African Perspectives (Vol. 32), Münster: LIT Verlag.

Hall, M. C. & Müller, D. K. (2004). Tourism, Mobility and Second Homes between Elite Landscape and Common Ground, Bristol: Channel View Publications.

Hall, S. (1990). Cultural Identity and Diaspora In: Rutherford, J. (Ed.). Identity: Community, Culture, Difference, London: Lawrence & Wishart, pp. 222-237.

Hall, S. (1993). What Is This "Black" in Black Popular Culture? Social Justice, 20(1/2 (51-52), pp. 104-114, retrieved from www.jstor.org/stable/29766735 [12.02.20].

Hall, S. & Du Gay, P. (1996). Questions of Cultural Identity, Los Angeles: Sage Publications.

Hall, S. (1999). Un-settling 'the heritage', re-imagining the post-nation. Whose heritage? In Third Text 13 (49), pp. 3-13.

Hall, S. (2000). Who Needs 'Identity'? Questions of Cultural Identity. London: Sage Publications.

Hammersley M. (1992). What's wrong with Ethnography? Methodological Explorations. London: Routledge.

Hammond, L. (2015). Diaspora Returnees to Somaliland: Heroes of Development or Job-stealing Scoundrels. Africa's Return Migrants: The New Developers, pp. 44-63.

Hannam, K., Sheller, M., & Urry, J. (2006). Mobilities, Immobilities and Moorings, In: Mobilities, 1 (1), pp. 1-22.

Hannerz, U. (1996). Transnational Connections. Culture People, Places, London: Routledge.

Hannerz, U. (2003). Being there..., there..., and there! Reflections on multi-sited ethnography, In: Ethnography, 4(2), pp. 201-216, retrieved from www.jstor.org /stable/24047809 [06.11.19].

Hannerz, U. (2004). Cosmopolitanism. A Companion to the Anthropology of Politics, pp. 69-85.

Hawkins, B. (1999). Black Student Athletes at Predominantly White National Collegiate Athletic Association (NCAA) Division I Institutions and the Pattern of

Oscillating Migrant Laborers, In: Western Journal of Black Studies, 23 (1), pp. 1-9.

Hazan, H. & Hertzog, E. (2016). Serendipity in Anthropological Research. The Nomadic Turn. London/New York: Routledge.

Henry, F., & Plaza, D. (2019). Carnival is Woman: Feminism and Performance in Caribbean Mas, University Press of Mississippi.

Hepburn, S. Signalling the End of the Migration Journey: Exploring Transnational Ageing Narratives on Residential Selection, In: International Migration & Integration 21, pp. 1263-1278.

Hillman, F.; Van Naerssen, T. & Spaan, E. (2018). Trajectories and Imaginaries in Migration: The Migrant Actor in Transnational Space, Routledge, Taylor & Francis Inc.

Hine, C. (2000). Virtual Ethnography. London: Sage.

Hinkson, M. (2017). Precarious Placemaking, In: Annual Revue of Anthropology 46 (1), pp. 49-64.

Hirsch, M. (2008). The Generation of Postmemory, In: Poetics Today, 29 (1), pp. 103-128.

Hirsch, M. & Miller, N. K. (2011). Rites of Return. New York, NY: Columbia University Press.

Hope, D. P. (2006). Inna di Dancehall: Popular Culture and the Politics of Identity in Jamaica. Kingston: The University of the West Indies Press.

Hope, D. P. (2010). Man Vibes: Masculinities in the Jamaican dancehall. Kingston: Ian Randle Publishers.

Horst, H. & Miller, D. (2005). 'From Kinship to Link-Up'. Cell Phones and Social Networking in Jamaica, In: Current Anthropology, Volume 46, Number 5, pp. 755-778.

Horst, H. (2006). The Blessings and Burdens of Communication: Cell Phones in Jamaican Transnational Social Fields, In: Global Networks, 6 (2), pp. 143-159.

Horst, H. (2007). 'You can't be two places at once': Rethinking Transnationalism through Jamaican Return Migration, In: Identities 14(1-2): pp. 63-83

Horst, H. (2013). Landscaping Englishness: Respectability and Returnees in Mandeville, Jamaica, CRGS (Caribbean Review of Gender Studies), Issue 2, Kingston: University of the West Indies Centre for Gender and Development Studies.

Hossein, C. S. (2018). Building economic solidarity: Caribbean ROSCAs in Jamaica, Guyana, and Haiti, In: The Black Social Economy in the Americas, pp. 79-95, New York: Palgrave Macmillan.

Hunger, U. (2002). The "Brain Gain" Hypothesis: Third-World Elites in Industrialized Countries and Socioeconomic Development in their Home Country, Germany: University of Münster.

Huntington, S. (1993). The Clash of Civilizations? In: Foreign Affairs, 72 (3), pp. 22-49.

Hutton, C. (2016). 'I Prefer The Fake Look': Aesthetically Silencing and Obscuring the Presence of the Black Body, In: Boxill, I. (Ed.). Notions of Beauty & Sexuality in Black Communities in the Caribbean and Beyond, Ideaz-Institute for Intercultural and Comparative Research, Kingston: Arawak Publications.

Igenoza, M. (2017). Race, Femininity and Food: Femininity and the Racialization of Health and Dieting, In: International Review of Social Research, 7 (2), pp. 109-118.

Inda, J. X., & Rosaldo, R. (Eds.) (2002). The Anthropology of Globalization: A reader. Malden, MA: Blackwell Publishers.

Ingold, T. (2007). Anthropology is Not Ethnography. Radcliffe Brown Lecture of Social Anthropology, Proceedings of the British Academy, 154 (2008): pp. 62–92.

IOM (2015). World Migration Report 2015, Migrants and Cities-New Partnerships to Manage Mobility, retrieved from https://publications.iom.int/books/world-migration-report-2015-migrants-and-cities-new-partnerships-manage-mobility [18.08.19].

James, C. E. (2011). Multicultural Education in a color-blind Society, In: Intercultural and Multicultural Education: Enhancing Global Interconnectedness, (39), pp. 191-210.

Janoschka, M. (2009). The contested spaces of lifestyle mobilities: Regime analysis as a tool to study political claims in Latin American retirement destinations, In: Die Erde, 140 (3), pp. 251-274.

Jensen, S.Q. (2011). Othering, identity formation and agency. Qualitative Studies, 2 (2): pp. 63-78.

Jung, L. (2012). Die kulturelle Aneignung des jamaikanischen Reggae von deutschen Reggae-Interpreten. Fachbuchreihe Medien und Kultur, Band 19, WiKu-Verlag, Köln.

Jónsson, G. (2008). Migration Aspirations and Immobility in a Malian Soninke Village, International Migration Institute (IMI) Working Papers, No. 10, James Martin 21st Century School: University of Oxford, pp. 2-45.

Kannakulam, J. (2008). Hip-Hop im globalen Transfer: Subkultur, Ritualität und Interethnizität, Hamburg: Tectum Verlag.

Kebede, R. (2017). Why Black Women in a Predominately Black Culture Are Still Bleaching Their Skin, Investigating deep-rooted ideals in Jamaica, retrieved from https://www.marieclaire.com/beauty/a27678/skin-bleaching-epidemic-in-jamaica/ [27.07.19].

Kelley, N. & Trebilcock, M. (2010). A History of Canadian Immigration Policy, Toronto, Buffalo, London: University of Toronto Press.

Keown M., Murphy D., Procter J. (2009). Introduction: Theorizing Postcolonial Diasporas, In: Keown M., Murphy D., Procter J. (eds.) Comparing Postcolonial Diasporas. Palgrave Macmillan, London

Kim, N. Y. (2009). Finding our way home. Korean Americans, "Homeland" trips, and Cultural Foreignness, In: Tsuda, T. (eds.) Diasporic Homecomings. Ethnic Return Migration in Comparative Perspective. Stanford University Press.

King, R. (2012). Theories and Typologies of Migration: An Overview and a Primer, Willy Brandt Series of Working Papers, In: International Migration and Ethnic Relations 3/12, Malmö Institute for Studies of Migration, Diversity and Welfare (MIM), Malmö University, pp. 3-37.

King, R. & Christou, A. (2014). Of Counter-Diaspora and Reverse Transnationalism, In: King, R.; Christou, A.; Levitt, P. (Eds.). Links to the Diasporic Homeland: Second Generation and Ancestral 'Return' Mobilities, pp. 1-7, London: Routledge.

King, R. & Lulle, A. (2016). Research on Migration: Facing Realities and Maximising Opportunities, A Policy Review, Luxembourg: Publications Office of the European Union.

Krumer-Nevo, M., & Sidi, M. (2012). Writing Against Othering. Qualitative Inquiry, 18 (4), pp. 299-309.

Labelle, M. & Salée, D. (2001). Immigrant and Minority Representations in Quebec, In Aleinikoff, T. A. & Klusmeyer, D. B. (eds.) Citizenship Today: Global Perspectives and Practices, Washington: Carnegie Endowment for International Peace, Brookings Institution Press, pp. 278-315.

Labelle, M. (2015). Multiculturalisme, interculturalisme, antiracisme: le traitement de l'altérité, Revue Européenne des Migrations Internationales, 31 (2), pp. 31-54.

Labelle, M. & Larose, S., & Piché, V. (2019). Caribbean Canadians, In: The Canadian Encyclopaedia retrieved from https://www.thecanadianencyclopedia.ca/en/article/caribbean-canadians [04.02.19].

Larsen, J., Urry, J., & Axhausen, K. W. (2007). Networks and tourism: Mobile social life. Annals of tourism research, 34(1), pp. 244-262.

Lafont, S. (2000). Gender Wars in Jamaica, In: Identities: Global Studies in Culture and Power 7 (2), pp. 233-260.

Laoire, C. N. (2009). Return Migrants and Boundaries of Belonging, In: Globalization, Migration and Social Transformation, pp. 41-54, London: Routledge.

Lehmkuhl, U. (2019). Translating Diversity: A Conversation between Translation Studies and Diversity Studies, In: Lehmkuhl, U. & Schowalter, L. (eds.) Translating Diversity. Concepts, Practices and Politics, Diversity Vol.4, Münster: Waxmann, pp. 9-28.

Lehmkuhl, U.; Lüsebrink, H.-J.; McFalls, L. (2015). Spaces and Practices of Diversity: An Introduction. In: (eds.): Of 'Contact Zones' and 'Liminal Spaces'. Mapping the Everyday Life of Cultural Translation, Diversity Vol.1, Münster: Waxmann, pp. 7- 28.

Lesser, B. (2008). Dancehall: The Story of Jamaican Dancehall Culture, London: Soul Jazz Records Publishing.

Levitt P. (2001). Transnational migration: Taking stock and future directions, Global Networks, 1(3): pp. 195-216.

Levitt, P. (2004). Transnational Migrants: When "Home" Means More Than One Country, Migration Policy Institute, retrieved from http://www.migrationpoli cy.org/article/transnational-migrants-when-home-means-more-one-country [08.05.16].

Levitt, P. & Glick Schiller, N. (2004). Conceptualizing Simultaneity: A Transnational Social Field Perspective on Society, In: The International Migration Review, Vol. 38, No. 3, Conceptual and Methodological Developments in the Study of International Migration, pp. 1002-1039.

Livingstone, A. (2018). Le Profilage Racial dans les Pratiques Policières: Points de vue et Expériences de Jeunes Racisés à Montréal, Le profilage racial dans les pratiques policières, retrieved from https://drive.google.com/file/d/0B-8vqv_856jERzhfX2E4cWdVdkRqdEYoMGFkZ3NwNUpDckwo/view [14.02.19].

Louch, A. (1966). Explanation and Human Action, Oxford: Blackwell.

Magocsi, P. R. (1999): Encyclopaedia of Canada's Peoples, University of Toronto Press, Scholarly Publishing Division.

Malinowski, B. (1922). Argonauts of the Western Pacific. London: Routledge and Kegan Paul.

Malinowski, B. (1935). Coral Gardens and Their Magic: A Study of the Methods of Tilling the Soil and of Agricultural Rites in the Trobriand Islands. London: Allen and Unwin.

Marcus, G. E. (1995). Ethnography in/ of the World System: The Emergence of Multi-Sited Ethnography, In: Annual Review of Anthropology, Vol. 24 (1995), pp. 95-117.

Marshall, D. (1987). A History of West Indian Migrations: Overseas Opportunities and Safety-Value Polices, In: B. B. Levine (ed.). The Caribbean Exodus, New York: Praeger Publishers, pp. 15-31.

Massey, D. (1995). The Conceptualisation of Place. In: D. Massey & P. Jess, eds., A Place in the World? Places, Cultures and Globalisation. Oxford: Oxford University Press.

Massey, D. (2005). For Space. London, UK: Sage Publications.

McIntyre, N. (2009). Rethinking Amenity Migration: Integration Mobility, Lifestyle and Social-Ecological Systems. Die Erde, 140 (3), pp. 229-250.

McWatters, M. R. (2008). Residential Tourism, (De)Constructing Paradise, Bristol, Buffalo, Toronto: Channel View Publications.

Miles, R. (1989). Racism (Key Ideas Series), 2nd Edition, London and New York: Routledge.

Miller, D. (2008). Migration, material culture and tragedy: Four moments in Caribbean migration, In: Mobilities, 3 (3), pp. 397-413.

MICC: Ministère de l'Ìmmigration et des Communautés culturelles (2011). La planification de l'Immigration au Québec pour la periode 2012-2015. Document de consultation, Québec, retrieved from http://ville.montreal.qc.ca/culture/en/ag reement-ministere-de-limmigration-et-des-communautes-culturelles-du-qu ebec-micc [15.03.18].

Moi, T. (1992). Femininity revisited, In: Journal of Gender Studies, 1 (3), pp. 324-334.

MEI: Montreal Economic Institute (2018). Labour Shortage: Quebec has lost more than 230,000 Youths, retrieved from https://www.iedm.org/82906-labour-sho rtage-quebec-has-lost-230000-youths [25.10.18].

Morley, D. (2000). Home Territories. Media, mobility and identity, London and New York: Routledge.

Morton, D. (2012). Strains of Affluence (1945-2000) In Brown, Craig (eds.) The Illustrated History of Canada, 25th Anniversary Edition, Montreal & Kingston, London, Ithaca: McGill-Queen's University Press.

NHS: National Household Survey (2016). Statistics Canada, Profile Canada, Québec, Montréal, retrieved from https://www.statcan.gc.ca/eng/start [20.10.18].

Norbye, A. B. (2010). Eating Memories: A Taste of Place, In: S. Williksen and N. Rapport (Eds.). Reveries of Home: Nostalgia, Authenticity and the Performance of Place. Newcastle Upon Tyne: Cambridge Scholars Publishing, pp. 145-164.

Okphewo, I.; Davies, C. B.; Mazrui, A. (2001). The African Diaspora: African Origins and New World Identities, Bloomington: Indiana University Press.

Omi, M. & Winant, H. (2014). Racial Formation in the United States: From the 1960s to the 1990s. 3rd Edition, New York: Routledge.

Oishi, N. (2005). Women in Motion. Globalization, State Policies, and Labor Migration in Asia. Redwood City: Stanford University Press.

Olivier-Mensah, C. & Scholl-Schneider, S. (2016). Transnational Return? On the Interrelation of Family, Remigration and Transnationality - An Introduction, In: Transnational Social Review 6:1-2, pp. 2-9.

Olwig, K. F. & Hastrup, K. (eds.) (1997). Siting Culture: The Shifting Anthropological Object, London: Routledge.

Olwig, K. F., & Sørensen, N. N. (2002). Mobile Livelihoods. Making a Living in the World. In: (eds.) Work and Migration: Life and Livelihoods in a Globalizing World, London and New York: Routledge (Research in Transnationalism), pp. 1-19.

Olwig, K. F. (2007). Caribbean Journeys. An Ethnography of Migration and Home in Three Family Networks, Durham: Duke University Press.

Olwig, K. F. (2012). The Care Chain, Children's Mobility and the Caribbean Migration Tradition, In: Journal of Ethnic and Migration Studies 38 (6), pp. 933-952.

Ong, A. (1993). On the Edge of Empires. Flexible Citizenship among Chinese Diaspora, In: Positions: East Asia Cultures Critique 1 (3), pp. 745-778.

O'Reilly, K. & Benson, M. (2009). Lifestyle Migration: Escaping to the Good Life? In: Benson, M. and O'Reilly, K. (Eds.). Lifestyle Migrations: Expectations, Aspirations and Experiences, Farnham: Ashgate Publishing, pp. 1-13.

Ortiz, F. (2019). The Cuban Counterpoint, In: A. Chomsky, B. Carr, A. Prieto & P. Smorkaloff (Eds.). The Cuba Reader. New York, USA: Duke University Press, original Spanish edition published in 1940, pp. 222-226, retrieved from https://doi.org/10.1515/9781478004561-047 [16.06.18].

Oxford Dictionary (2015). "bling-bling", retrieved from, http://www.oxforddictionaries.com/definition/english/bling [05.12.16].

Oyěwùmí, O. (1997). The Invention of Women: Making an African Sense of Western Gender Discourses. University of Minnesota Press. Retrieved g

Paerregaard, K. (1997). Linking Separate Worlds. Urban Migrants and Rural Lives in Peru, London: Routledge (Explorations in Anthropology Series).

Patterson, Orlando (1982). Slavery and Social Death, Cambridge: Harvard University Press.

Pessar, P. (1999). Engendering Migration Studies, In: American Behavioural Scientist 42 (4), pp. 577-600.

Pessar, P., & Mahler, S. (2003). Transnational Migration: Bringing Gender, In: The International Migration Review, 37 (3), pp. 812-846, retrieved from www.jstor.org/stable/30037758 [12.02.10].

Pink, Sarah (2006): Doing Sensory Ethnography. London: Sage.

Pink, Sarah (2013): "Engaging the Senses in Ethnographic Practice", In: The Senses and Society, 8:3: pp. 261-267.

Plaza, D. (2000). Transnational Grannies: The Changing Family Responsibilities of Elderly African Caribbean-Born Women Resident in Britain, Social Indicators Research, 1 (1), pp. 75-105.

Plaza, D. (2008). Transnational Return Migration to the English-speaking Caribbean, In: Revue Européenne des migrations internationales, Vol. 24 (1), pp. 115-137, retrieved from http://journals.openedition.org/remi/4317 [17.09.19].

Plaza, D. & Henry, F. (2006). Returning to the Source: The Final Stage of the Caribbean Migration Circuit. Kingston: University of the West Indies Press.

Platonova, A., & Gény, L. R. (2017). Women's Empowerment and Migration in the Caribbean, In: Series Studies and Perspective (No. 59), ECLAC Subregional Headquarters for the Caribbean, International Organization for Migration (IOM), pp. 5-41.

Potter, R. B.; Barker, D.; Conway, D. & Klak, T. (2004). The Contemporary Caribbean, Pearson Education Limited, Dorset Press.

Preston, V. & Wong, M. (2002). Immigration and Canadian Cities: Building Inclusion, In: Andrew, C.; Graham, K. & Phillips, S. (Eds.). Urban Affairs: Back on the Policy Agenda, Montreal: McGill-Queen's University Press, pp. 23-45.

Price, C. (2015). Rastafari Movement. In: Stone, J.; Dennis, R. M., Rizova, P., Smith, A. D., Hou, X. (eds.) The Wiley Blackwell Encyclopaedia of Race, Ethnicity, and Nationalism, Hoboken: John Wiley & Sons.

Pries, L. (2001). Internationale Migration. Einsichten, Themen der Soziologie, Bielefeld: Transcript.

Proust, M. (1999 [1927]). In Search of Lost Time, Volume IV, Time Regained (À la recherche du temps perdu), (transl.) Andreas Mayor and Terence Kilmartin, Modern Library Classics, Penguin Random House.

Rapport, N., & Dawson, A. (1998). Home and Movement: A Polemic. Migrants of Identity: Perceptions of Home in a World of Movement, pp. 19-38.

Rapport, N. (2014). Social and Cultural Anthropology. The Key Concepts, Third Edition, London and New York: Routledge.

Reckwitz, A. (2001). Multikulturalismustheorien und der Kulturbegriff: Vom Homogenitätsmodell zum Modell kultureller Interferenzen, In: Berliner Journal für Soziologie 2, pp. 179–200.

Rees, D., Murray, J., Nelson, G., & Sonnenberg, P. (2010). Oscillating migration and the epidemics of silicosis, tuberculosis, and HIV infection in South African gold miners, In: American Journal of Industrial Medicine, 53 (4), pp. 398-404.

Reichertz, J. (1999). Gültige Entdeckung des Neuen? Zur Bedeutung der Abduktion in der qualitativen Sozialforschung. Österreichische Zeitschrift für Soziologie 24 (4): pp. 47–64.

Reynolds, T., & Zontini, E. (2006). A Comparative Study of Care and Provision across Caribbean and Italian Transnational Families, In: Families & Social Capital ESRC Research Group Working Paper No. 16, pp. 2-28.

Reynolds, T. (2008). Ties that bind: Families, Social Capital and Caribbean Second-generation Return Migration. University of Sussex, Sussex Centre for Migration Research, Working Papers, 46, pp. 2-29.

Robertson, R. (1998). Glokalisierung: Homogenität und Heterogenität in Raum und Zeit, In: Beck, Ulrich (Ed.). Perspektiven der Weltgesellschaft. Edition Zweite Moderne, Frankfurt a. M.: Suhrkamp, pp. 192-220.

Rose, D. (2010). Local State Policy and 'new-build' Gentrification in Montréal: The Role of the 'population factor' in a fragmented Governance Context, In: Population, Space and Place, 16(5), pp. 413-428.

Rose, J. (2016). Immigrant Identities and Geographies of Belonging: Jamaican Immigrant Organizations in Toronto, Electronic Thesis, Geography, Toronto: York University, retrieved from http://hdl.handle.net/10315/32659 [29.07.18].

Rubinstein, R. (eds.) (1990). Anthropology and Aging. Comprehensive Reviews, Kluwer Academic Publishers.

Said, E. W. (1982). Opponents, Audiences, Constituencies and Community, In: Critical Inquiry 9, pp. 134-159.

Said, E. W. (1985). Orientalism reconsidered, In: Race & Class, 27 (2), pp. 1-15.

Salazar, N. B. (2011). Tanzanian Migration Imaginaries, In: Cohen, R. & Jónnson, G. (eds.) Migration and Culture, An Elgar Research Collection, International Migration Institute, Cambridge: University of Oxford, pp. 673-687.

Salazar, N. B. & Smart, A. (2011). Anthropological Takes on (Im-)mobilities: Introduction, In: Identities: Global Studies in Culture and Power, Taylor & Francis Group, LLC, pp. 1-8.

Sassen, S. (1991). The Global City: New York, London, Tokyo. Princeton: Princeton University Press.

Sassen, S. (2003). The State and Globalization, In: Interventions, 5: 2, pp. 241-248.

Schneider, D. (1968). American Kinship: A Cultural Account. Chicago: University of Chicago Press.

Schlehe, J. (2008). Formen qualitativer ethnographischer Interviews, In: Methoden ethnologischer Feldforschung, In: Beer, B. (ed.) Methoden ethnologischer Feldforschung, Berlin: Dietrich Reimer Verlag, pp. 119–142.

Schönhuth, M. (2005). Glossar Kultur und Entwicklung. Ein Vademecum durch den Kultur-Dschungel, GTZ, DEZA, Universität Trier: Trierer Materialien zur Ethnologie, Ausgabe 4.

Schütze, F. (1983). Biographieforschung und narratives Interview, In: Neue Praxis 13, pp. 283-293, retrieved from http://nbn-resolving.de/urn:nbn:de:0168-ssoar-53147 [20.10.18].

Scott, J. C. (1998). Seeing like a State: How certain schemes to improve the human condition have failed, London: Yale University Press.

Selassie, H.I.H. Prince Ermias Sahle & Ras Sekou S. Tafari (2004). The Wise Mind of H.I.M. Emperor Haile Selassie I., Research Associates School Times Publications; Frontline Distribution International Inc., pp. 33-34.

Sen, A. (1999): Development as Freedom. Cambridge: Oxford University Press.

Sen, A. (2007). Identity and Violence: The Illusion of Destiny. USA: Norton.

Sheller, M. & Urry, J. (2006). The New Mobilities Paradigm, In: Environment and Planning 38, pp. 207-226.

Sherlock, P. & Bennet, H. (1998). The Story of the Jamaican People. Kingston: Ian Randle Publishers.

Silverstone, R. (1994). Television and Everyday Life. London: Routledge.

Simon, S. (2006). Introduction: Moments of Translation in a Divided City, In: (Ed.) Translating Montreal: Episodes in the Life of a Divided City, pp. 3-27, Montreal: McGill-Queen's University Press, retrieved fromhttp://www.jstor.org/stable/j.ctt8oks1.5 [19.05.17].

Simmons, A. & Plaza, D. (2006). The Caribbean Community in Canada: Transnational Connections and Transformations, In: Satzewich, V. & Wong, L. (Eds.).

Transnational Identities and Practices in Canada, Vancouver: University of British Columbia Press, pp. 130-149.

Simmons, A. (2010). Immigration in Canada: Global and Transnational Perspectives, Toronto: Canadian Scholars Press.

Smith, R. T. (1988). Kinship and Class in the West Indies. Cambridge: Cambridge University Press.

Sobo, E. J. (1996). The Jamaican body's role in emotional experience and sense perception: Feelings, hearts, minds, and nerves, In: Culture, Medicine and Psychiatry, Volume 20, Issue 3, pp. 313-342

Soto, I. M. (1987). West Indian Child Fostering: It's Role in Migrant Exchanges, In: Sutton, C. and Chaney, E. (Eds.). Caribbean Life in New York City, pp. 131-149, New York: Centre for Migration Studies.

Spittler, G. (2001). Teilnehmende Beobachtung als Dichte Teilnahme, In: Zeitschrift für Ethnologie 126 (2001), pp. 1-25.

Spivak, G. C. (1985): The Rani of Simur, In: Francis Barker et al. (eds.): Europe and its Others, Vol. 1, Colchester: University of Sussex.

Spülbeck, S. (1997). Die Bedeutung der ethnologischen Begegnung für die Entstehung von Biographien, In: Biographie-Forschung in der Ethnologie. Berlin u.a.: LIT-Verlag.

Stanley-Niaah, S. (2004). Kingston's Dancehall: A Story of Space and Celebration, In: Space and Culture, 7 (1), pp. 102-118.

Stanley-Niaah, S. (2010). DanceHall: From Slave Ship to Ghetto. Ottawa: University of Ottawa Press, retrieved from www.jstor.org/stable/j.ctt1ckpdgg [12.02.20].

Statistics Canada (2017). Montréal [Population centre], Quebec and Ontario [Province] (table). Census Profile 2016 Census, Statistics Canada Catalogue, retrieved from https://www12.statcan.gc.ca/census-recensement/2016/dp-pd/pr of/index.cfm?Lang=E [24.01.20]

Statistics Canada (2019). Diversity of the Black Population in Canada: An Overview, retrieved from https://www150.statcan.gc.ca/n1/en/pub/89-657-x/89-657-x201 9002-eng.pdf?st=e3s6U8Hr [12.11.20].

Statistical Institute of Jamaica (2019). Unemployment Rate by Age Group as of July 2019 (7.8%), retrieved from https://statinja.gov.jm/LabourForce/NewLFS.aspx [14.12.20].

Stefansson, A. H. (2004). Homecomings to the Future: From Diasporic Mythographies to Social Projects of Return, In: F. Markowitz & A. H. Stefansson (Eds.). Homecomings: Unsettling Paths of Return, Lanham, MD: Lexington Books, pp. 2-20.

Stevenson, N. (2007). Cultural Citizenship, In: Ritzer, G. (Ed.) The Blackwell Encyclopaedia of Sociology, Vol. 9, Massachusetts: Blackwell.

Stolzoff, N. C. (2002). Wake the Town and Tell the People: Dancehall Culture in Jamaica, In: Journal of Popular Music Studies 14 (2), pp. 166-167.

Tator, C., Henry, F., Smith, C., & Brown, M. (2006). Racial Profiling in Canada: Challenging the Myth of 'a Few Bad Apples'. University of Toronto Press, retrieved from www.jstor.org/stable/10.3138/9781442678972 [12.02.20].

The Gleaner (2014). "Quebec Needs Nurses", Jamaica Gleaner online, retrieved from http://jamaica-gleaner.com/gleaner/20140408/news/news3.html [10.11.16].

The Gleaner (2018). "More Canadian Women Migrating to Canada, Statistics reveal", Jamaica Gleaner online, retrieved from http://old.jamaica-gleaner.com/extra/article.php?id=4840 [10.11.16].

The World Bank (2015). Country Profile: Jamaica, http://www.worldbank.org/en/country/jamaica/overview [25.01.17].

Thomas, K. J.A. (2012). A Demographic Profile of Black Caribbean Immigrants in the United States. Washington, DC: Migration Policy Institute, pp. 1-21.

Thomas-Hope, E. (1988). Caribbean skilled international migration and the transnational household, In: Geoforum 19 (4): pp. 423-432.

Thomas-Hope, E. (2002). Caribbean Migration. Kingston: University of the West Indies Press.

Thomas-Hope, E. (2010). Globalization and the development of a Caribbean migration culture. Perspectives on the Caribbean: A Reader in Culture, History and Representation, pp. 247-255.

Thomas-Hope, E.; Knight, P. & Noel, C. (2018). Migration in Jamaica. A Country Profile; International Organization for Migration (IOM), Geneva, retrieved from http://www.migration-eu- lac.eu/documents/keydocs/EN/Migration_Profile_Jamaica_2010.pdf [20.12.16].

Toney, J. G. (2010). Locating Diaspora: Afro-Caribbean Narratives of Migration and Settlement in Toronto, 1914–1929. In: Urban History Review, 38 (2), pp. 75-87.

Treiber, M. (2013). Leaving Eritrea, Entering the World – Migrants in the Making. In: Mekonnen, Daniel R. & Tesfagiorgis, Mussie (eds.): The Horn of Africa at the Brink of the 21st Century: Coping with Fragmentation, Isolation and Marginalization in a Globalizing Environment. Edition Eins, Bd. 2. Felsberg: edition eins, pp. 127-137.

Tremblay, S. (2011). La négociation des frontières ethniques dans l'espace scolaire: un regard québécois. Revue européenne des migrations internationales, vol. 27 (2), pp. 117-138., retrieved from https://www.cairn.info/revue-europeenne-des-migrations-internationales-2011-2-page-117.html [23.02.19].

Troper, H. (2018). Immigration in Canada. The Canadian Encyclopaedia, Historical Canada, n.p., retrieved from https://www.thecanadianencyclopedia.ca/en/article/immigration. [15.01.19].

Tsing, A. L. (2011). Friction: An Ethnography of Global Connection. Princeton: Princeton University Press.

Tsuda, T. (2009). Introduction: Ethnic Return Migration a Global Phenomenon, In: (ed.) Diasporic Homecomings. Ethnic Return Migration in Comparative Perspective. Redwood City: Stanford University Press.

Turner, V. (1969). Liminality and Communitas. In: The Ritual Process: Structure and Anti-Structure, Chicago: Aldine Publishing, pp. 94-113.

UN Women Training Centre (2017). Gender Equality Glossary, Letter G (Gender), retrieved from https://trainingcentre.unwomen.org/mod/glossary/view.php?id=36&mode=letter&hook=G&sortkey=&sortorder= [02.02.20].

Vallières, P. (1968). Nègres Blancs de Amériques: Autobiographie précoce d'un "terroriste" Québécois, Montréal: Edition Typo 1994 (1968), original Édition Parti pris 1968.

Vertovec, S. (1997). Three Meanings of "Diaspora" Exemplified among South Asian Religions, In: Diaspora: A Journal of Transnational Studies 6.3, pp. 277-299.

Vertovec, S. (2009). Cosmopolitanism in attitude, practice and competence, Max-Planck-Institute, MMG Working Papers 09-08, pp. 6-11, retrieved from https://www.mmg.mpg.de/58492/WP_09-08_Vertovec_Cosmopolitanism.pdf [07.08.19].

Vickerman, M. (1999). Crosscurrents: West Indians and Race in America. New York: Oxford University Press.

Vickerman, M. (2001). Jamaicans balancing Race and Ethnicity, In: New Immigrants in New York, (ed.) Foner, N., pp. 201-228. New York: Columbia University Press.

Walcott, R. (2003). Black like Who? Writing Black Canada. Second Edition, Toronto: Insomniac Press.

Walcott, R (2011). Disgraceful: Intellectual Dishonesty, white Anxieties, and multicultural Critique thirty-six years later, In: Chazan, M.; Helps, L. & Stanley, A. (eds.). Home and Native Land: Unsettling Multiculturalism in Canada. Toronto: Between the Lines Publishers, pp. 15–30.

Waldinger, R. (2017). A Cross-Border Perspective on Migration: Beyond the assimilation/transnationalism debate, In: Journal of Ethnic and Migration Studies, 43(1), pp. 3-17.

Walker, J. (2013). Black Canadians. The Canadian Encyclopaedia, retrieved from http://www.thecanadianencyclopedia.ca/en/article/black-canadians/#top [05.12.16].

Wang, H., & Liu, Y. (2016). Entrepreneurship and Talent Management from a Global Perspective: Global returnees. Cheltenham: Edward Elgar Publishing.

Watts, L., & Urry, J. (2008). Moving Methods, Travelling Times, In: Environment and Planning D: Society and Space, 26 (5), pp. 860–874.

Weis, R. S. (1994). Learning from Strangers: The Art and Method of Qualitative Interview Studies, New York: The Free Press.

Welsch, W. (1999). Transculturality – the Puzzling Form of Cultures Today, In: Spaces of Culture: City, Nation, World, (eds.) Mike Featherstone & Scott Lash, London: Sage, pp. 194-213.

Wieczoreck, A. X. (2018). Migration and (Im)Mobility. Biographical Experiences of Polish Migrants in Germany and Canada, Bielefeld: Transcript.

Winks, R. W. (1997). The Blacks in Canada: A History, Second Edition, Montreal: McGill-Queen's University Press.

Williams, C. W. (2018). Women's Health Survey 2016 – Jamaica, UN Women Caribbean, Co-Publication of the Statistical Institute of Jamaica, Inter-American Development Bank and the United Nations Entity for Gender Equality and the Empowerment of Women, retrieved from https://www2.unw omen.org/-/media/field%20office%20caribbean/attachments/publications/201 8/af%2020180618%20jamaica%20health%20report%20for%20web.pdf?la=en&v s=5614 [29.11.19].

Williams, D. (1997). The Road to Now: A History of Blacks in Montreal, Dossier Quebec: Vehicule Press.

Wilson, T. D. (1998). Weak Ties, Strong Ties: Network Principles in Mexican Migration, In: Human Organization, pp. 394-403.

Wimmer, A. (2002). Gleichschaltung ohne Grenzen? Isomorphisierung und Heteromorphisierung in einer verflochtenen Welt, In: Hauser-Schäublin, B. & Braukämper, U. (Eds.). Ethnologie der Globalisierung. Perspektiven kultureller Verflechtungen. Berlin: Dietrich Reimer Verlag, pp. 77-94.

Wimmer, A., & Glick Schiller, N. (2003). Methodological Nationalism, the Social Sciences, and the Study of Migration: An Essay in Historical Epistemology, In: The International Migration Review, 37(3), pp. 576-610.

Wortley, S. & Marshall, L. (2005). Race and Police Stops in Kingston, Ontario: Results of a Pilot Project. Kingston, ON: Kingston Police Services Board.

Wortley, S. & Owosu-Bempah, A. (2011). The Usual Suspects: Police Stop and Search Practices in Canada, In: Policing and Society 21 (4), pp. 395-407.

Zips, W. (2003). Afrikanische Diaspora. Out of Africa into New Worlds, (ed.). Afrika und ihre Diaspora Band 1, Münster: LIT Verlag, pp. 19-52.

Zips, W. (2011). Schwarze Rebellen, Maroon-Widerstand in Jamaica, (ed.) Afrika und ihre Diaspora Band 5, Münster: LIT Verlag.

Cultural Studies

Gabriele Klein
Pina Bausch's Dance Theater
Company, Artistic Practices and Reception

2020, 440 p., pb., col. ill.
29,99 € (DE), 978-3-8376-5055-6
E-Book:
PDF: 29,99 € (DE), ISBN 978-3-8394-5055-0

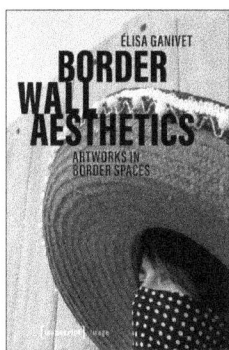

Elisa Ganivet
Border Wall Aesthetics
Artworks in Border Spaces

2019, 250 p., hardcover, ill.
79,99 € (DE), 978-3-8376-4777-8
E-Book:
PDF: 79,99 € (DE), ISBN 978-3-8394-4777-2

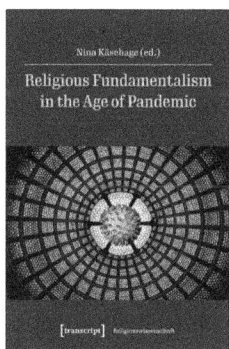

Nina Käsehage (ed.)
**Religious Fundamentalism
in the Age of Pandemic**

April 2021, 278 p., pb., col. ill.
37,00 € (DE), 978-3-8376-5485-1
E-Book: available as free open access publication
PDF: ISBN 978-3-8394-5485-5

Cultural Studies

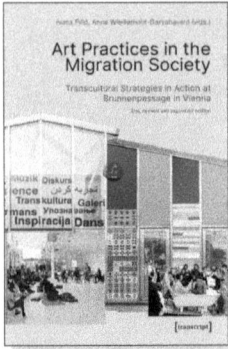

Ivana Pilic, Anne Wiederhold-Daryanavard (eds.)
Art Practices in the Migration Society
Transcultural Strategies in Action
at Brunnenpassage in Vienna

March 2021, 244 p., pb.
29,00 € (DE), 978-3-8376-5620-6
E-Book:
PDF: 25,99 € (DE), ISBN 978-3-8394-5620-0

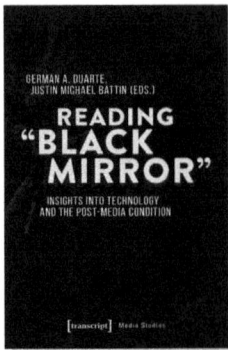

German A. Duarte, Justin Michael Battin (eds.)
Reading »Black Mirror«
Insights into Technology and the Post-Media Condition

January 2021, 334 p., pb.
32,00 € (DE), 978-3-8376-5232-1
E-Book:
PDF: 31,99 € (DE), ISBN 978-3-8394-5232-5

Cindy Kohtala, Yana Boeva, Peter Troxler (eds.)
Digital Culture & Society (DCS)
Vol. 6, Issue 1/2020 –
Alternative Histories in DIY Cultures and Maker Utopias

February 2021, 214 p., pb., ill.
29,99 € (DE), 978-3-8376-4955-0
E-Book:
PDF: 29,99 € (DE), ISBN 978-3-8394-4955-4

**All print, e-book and open access versions of the titles in our list
are available in our online shop www.transcript-publishing.com**

GPSR Authorized Representative: Easy Access System Europe, Mustamäe tee 50, 10621 Tallinn, Estonia, gpsr.requests@easproject.com